Chile, the C
the Cold War

Series Editors: Richard J. Aldrich, Rory Cormac, Michael S. Goodman and Hugh Wilford

This series explores the full spectrum of spying and secret warfare in a globalised world

Intelligence has changed. Secret service is no longer just about spying or passively watching a target. Espionage chiefs now command secret armies and legions of cyber warriors who can quietly shape international relations itself. Intelligence actively supports diplomacy, peacekeeping and warfare: the entire spectrum of security activities. As traditional inter-state wars become more costly, covert action, black propaganda and other forms of secret interventionism become more important. This ranges from proxy warfare to covert action; from targeted killing to disruption activity. Meanwhile, surveillance permeates communications to the point where many feel there is little privacy. Intelligence, and the accelerating technology that surrounds it, have never been more important for the citizen and the state.

Titles in the *Intelligence, Surveillance and Secret Warfare* series include:

Published:

The Arab World and Western Intelligence: Analysing the Middle East, 1956–1981
Dina Rezk

The Twilight of the British Empire: British Intelligence and Counter-Subversion in the Middle East, 1948–63
Chikara Hashimoto

Chile, the CIA and the Cold War: A Transatlantic Perspective
James Lockhart

Forthcoming:

Outsourcing US Intelligence: Private Contractors and Government Accountability
Damien Van Puyvelde

The Snowden Era on Screen: Signals Intelligence and Digital Surveillance
James Smith

The Clandestine Lives of Colonel David Smiley: Code Name 'Grin'
Clive Jones

The Problem of Secret Intelligence
Kjetil Anders Hatlebrekke

The CIA and the Pursuit of Security: History, Documents and Contexts
Hew Dylan

http://edinburghuniversitypress.com/series-intelligence-surveillance-and-secret-warfare.html

Chile, the CIA and the Cold War

A Transatlantic Perspective

James Lockhart

EDINBURGH
University Press

Edinburgh University Press is one of the leading
university presses in the UK. We publish academic
books and journals in our selected subject areas across
the humanities and social sciences, combining cutting-
edge scholarship with high editorial and production
values to produce academic works of lasting
importance. For more information visit our website:
edinburghuniversitypress.com

First published in hardback by Edinburgh University Press 2019

Edinburgh University Press Ltd
The Tun – Holyrood Road
12(2f) Jackson's Entry
Edinburgh EH8 8PJ

Typeset in 11/13 Adobe Sabon by
IDSUK (Dataconnection) Ltd

A CIP record for this book is available from the
British Library

ISBN 978 1 4744 3561 1 (hardback)
ISBN 978 1 4744 8182 3 (paperback)
ISBN 978 1 4744 3562 8 (webready PDF)
ISBN 978 1 4744 3563 5 (epub)

Contents

Introduction

At 8:15 on Thursday morning, 22 October 1970, Gen. René Schneider, chief of staff of the Chilean army, left his residence in Las Condes for the Ministry of Defense in downtown Santiago. At 8:17, five to eight assailants in four cars crashed into the general's official Mercedes. They dashed to Schneider's position with small arms and sledgehammers, intending to abduct him. When the general reached for his sidearm to fight back, they panicked, shooting him in his neck, chest, and arm. Then they fled in confusion. Schneider's stunned driver rushed him to the military hospital in Providencia, where he died on the operating table three days later.[1]

A Chilean military court named retired Brig. Gen. Roberto Viaux responsible for the attack, sentencing him to twenty years in prison and exile. Viaux's movement included a handful of high-ranking Christian Democratic Party (PDC) officials in the outgoing Frei administration (1964–70) and several of the most senior officers within the armed forces and the *Carabineros*, the national police. Members of an anticommunist organization called *El Movimiento Cívico Patria y Libertad* were almost certainly working with Viaux, although their precise relationship remains, as an American ambassador characterized it, "fuzzy."[2]

Viaux had intended the kidnapping to serve as a pretext to preempt the Chilean congress's anticipated election of Salvador Allende (1970–3) as president. As the retired general explained, because Allende's coalition included the Chilean Communist Party (PCCh), which had long cultivated close relations with the Soviet Union (USSR), and because he saw President Eduardo Frei as an indecisive "Chilean Kerensky," he believed that Chile was in imminent danger and felt compelled to act. He would never

I

accept "that my Chile should become dependent on a foreign power and that my people become slaves . . . to international communism."[3]

Viaux had been in contact with the Nixon administration (1969–74) through National Security Advisor Henry Kissinger and the Central Intelligence Agency's (CIA) Santiago Station for several weeks. Kissinger and the Agency knew some of his plans. Indeed, they had encouraged him while offering financial support to *Patria y Libertad*.

Viaux called an emergency meeting with his CIA liaison after the assault against Schneider. He asked the chief of station to get the ambassador to tell Frei that the attack had represented a Soviet move against Chile. Members of his movement in the cabinet and armed services would follow this up by advising the president to declare a state of emergency, which would allow them to assume control first of the capital and then the government. The chief of station refused to do this, Frei remained silent, and Allende was inaugurated shortly thereafter.[4]

For these and other reasons, historians have tended to focus on the Nixon administration and the Agency when reconstructing Chile's Cold War experience, particularly the coup that overthrew the Allende government on 11 September 1973. Indeed, questions concerning the nature, extent, and effectiveness of American involvement in this coup still influence the production of historical knowledge. Journalists, historians and political scientists, lawyers, senators, congressmen, and courts have often assumed that the United States' intelligence community played the decisive part. Some claim that US officials directed the Chilean armed forces, even their tactical communications. Others think that American pilots flew the Hawker Hunters that struck the presidential palace. Still others hold Kissinger and intelligence officers responsible for Allende's death, a suicide that they approach as an assassination, execution, or some other malicious act. Chileans even asked President Barack Obama (2009–17) to accept responsibility and apologize for this coup when he visited Santiago in March 2011. Thus, historians and other writers have pored over the declassified record seeking confirmation of these and other allegations since the 1970s.[5]

Critics have characterized the literature that this produced as "axe-grinding in nature" and "a narrow historiography of blame." As historian Kenneth Maxwell, while reviewing the National Security Archive's Peter Kornbluh's *The Pinochet File: A Declassified Dossier on Atrocity and Accountability*, wrote,

> what is lacking in the forensic approach (and is a weakness of much writing on U.S. diplomatic history) is location in time and space. We see only the U.S. side of a story that is at least two-sided, if not multifaceted . . . Very little of the complex political and social history of Chile in the 1970s enters here; nor do we see the roles of many actors beyond the Chilean military, U.S. clandestine operatives, and their political masters.[6]

Kornbluh and the others' shortcomings notwithstanding, they have revealed much of the American role in the coup. They showed how United States intervention exacerbated the human suffering that followed – which included more than 3,000 documented executions, and a much larger number of disappeared, imprisoned, tortured, and exiled people. Today, no one denies that this intervention contributed to, and worsened, Chile's Cold War history.[7]

Meanwhile, some historians and political scientists have acknowledged Maxwell's points and responded constructively. They remain attentive to American intervention, but they have also begun to decenter the narrative while exploring Chilean politics and history in an increasingly international context. This has enabled them to start to reframe and rebalance Chile's Cold War experience. They began in an inter-American context and then gradually moved into a transatlantic one. The literature from the inter-American framework tends to start with Fidel Castro, Ernesto Che Guevara, and the Cuban Revolution in 1959. Castro and Guevara's subsequent calls for radical change in Latin America inspired a wave of guerrilla warfare, reform, and reaction that consumed the region in the 1960s and 1970s.[8]

The Kennedy (1961–3) and Johnson administrations (1963–9), working closely with Latin American anticommunists, attempted to preempt these revolutionary movements through ambitious reform strategies, including development, modernization, and counterinsurgency programs under the Alliance for Progress. These efforts failed, however. Military dictatorships – including Gen. Augusto Pinochet's (1973–90) in Chile – seized power, beginning with Brazil. This violence abated somewhat in the 1980s. But it did not end until Pinochet's Chile and Sandinista Nicaragua (1979–90) submitted to democratic elections and their leaders withdrew from power in the late 1980s and early 1990s.[9]

Historian Tanya Harmer continued to research this inter-American context in *Allende's Chile and the Inter-American Cold War*, calling attention to the importance of intra-Latin American relations, particularly Brazilian and Cuban intervention. Harmer argued that "it was Chilean military leaders who launched the coup with the help of sympathetic Brazilian friends, not the United States. And our effort to understand why they did inevitably leads us back to Cuban involvement in Chile and Latin America." As she revealed, many within the Brazilian dictatorship (1964–85) feared that the Nixon administration was failing to counter the threat Allende posed. This motivated Brazilians to take the initiative. Harmer's research helps to explain why Chief of Naval Operations Adm. José Toribio Merino praised Brazil's ambassador to Chile – Antonio Castro da Câmara Canto – for having braved the streets of Santiago in order to support him, Pinochet, and the other service commanders during the fighting and its aftermath on 11 September.[10]

Although the Cuban Revolution represents a watershed in modern Latin American history, and intra-regional relations remain central to appreciating the complexity of Chile's Cold War experience, Chilean Communists and anticommunists had already become belligerents in the Cold War by 1959. And they had never confined their politics to the western hemisphere, either. Some have appreciated this and started to fold Chile's Cold War history into a larger, transatlantic framework. For example, historian Kirsten Weld, attracted to Pinochet's comment that "It is a long term struggle we are a part of. It is a further stage of the same conflict which erupted into the Spanish Civil War," found that

> the Civil War – or at least one interpretation of it, in which the military had expunged Communist vice and disorder from Spain in a

kind of Christian reconquest – was an important component of the paradigm that anti-Allende revanchists used to understand their world.[11]

Yet, as Pinochet implied, this transatlantic context went back even further than the Spanish Civil War. Indeed, late nineteenth-century industrialization and globalization set the stage for the long-term struggle that evolved into the Cold War. This unleashed far-reaching processes that destabilized and transformed politics, societies, and economies at every level over the following hundred years, as "one set of conflicts was repeated over and over again," as historian Odd Arne Westad has recently phrased it. These conflicts happened in Europe, the United States, the Soviet Union, Latin America, Asia, and Africa, and peaked between 1945 and 1991.[12]

As both communists and anticommunists remarked in the late 1940s, these conflicts had divided much of the planet into two hostile camps. In one camp, Moscow and Marxist-Leninists all over Eastern Europe, East Asia, and the decolonizing, developing world, or the Global South, dreamed of leading a sweeping proletarian revolution, establishing a collective and socially just world order, and inaugurating a new era free from industrial capitalism's inequities. Thus, Allende, one such idealist, spoke of "the transcendence of a historical period" while voicing his administration's politics. By this, he and other Marxist-Leninists understood that they were on the cutting edge of global history, leading humanity from bourgeois industrial capitalism and imperialism into communist theorist Karl Marx's utopian future.[13]

In the other camp, conservative, liberal, and social-democratic anticommunists and other noncommunist leftists in the United States, Western Europe, and the developing world fought for an international order that protected individual rights, including private property, freedom of speech, and a capitalist, free-market socioeconomic system against communism. They, too, perceived a global-historical struggle. As Merino and his colleagues on the *junta* explained, they feared that the only two alternatives remained either the communist or the liberal one, which Chilean conservatives and anticommunists – being influenced by *Generalísimo* Francisco Franco's (1936–75) rhetoric – often referred to as Christian or Western civilization. The *junta* chose the latter, proclaiming that "our Fatherland has decided to directly confront international communism and the Marxist ideology that sustains it, inflicting it with the most serious defeat it has suffered over the last thirty years" – yet another reference to the Spanish Civil War and transatlantic history. Both camps were terrified of the possibility that the other side might prevail. To them, all means to stop this were justified. Thus, they resorted to brutal forms of violence to survive – as exemplified by the *junta*'s vigorous suppression of the Chilean left in the 1970s.[14]

This book represents my contribution to historians' efforts to reframe and rebalance Chile's Cold War experience. I remain interested in American intervention, particularly the Agency's operations in the 1960s and 1970s, and indeed the narrative climax of the book occurs between 1968 and 1973, but I do not center this history on these operations. Rather, I integrate Chilean politics and history into inter-American and transatlantic contexts that include US and other governments' involvement from the late nineteenth century to the late twentieth. I rely on Westad's concept of the essence of the long Cold War. His remains the most comprehensive, big-picture treatment of the conflict that historians have offered. I use a transatlantic perspective because, as historian Joaquín Fermandois has recognized, "it not only explain[s] other dimensions of the nexus between [the Americas] and Europe, but also clarif[ies] aspects of inter-American relations, which should not be seen in isolation." These interpretive choices permit us to begin to reimagine Chile's Cold War history, allowing us to better comprehend and discuss the nature, extent, and effectiveness of United States intervention and the role that American- and other foreign-directed intelligence, surveillance, and secret warfare played in southern South America.[15]

Arguments

I offer three, interrelated arguments. First, Chileans made their own history during the Cold War – even if they did not make it as all of them would have liked. This backs Harmer's finding that

"Chileans were the key determiners of their country's foreign relations and its future rather than being passive bystanders viewing – and being affected by – the actions of outsiders."[16]

Second, Chileans consciously did this as internationalists who defined themselves, explained their politics and behavior, and tried – and often succeeded – to influence local, national, inter-American, and transatlantic affairs as such. Just as inter-American and transatlantic events shaped and conditioned Chilean politics and history, so Chileans swayed inter-American and transatlantic affairs during the Cold War. This supports others – for example, historian Steve Stern and the late political scientist Robert Pastor – who have long urged researchers to take Latin Americans seriously as world-historical actors.[17]

Third, Chile and the rest of Latin America's Cold War experience featured foreign and domestic intelligence operations, surveillance, and secret warfare. This pervaded the region's guerrilla and revolutionary movements, counterinsurgency campaigns, *coups d'état*, dirty wars, death squads, covert activities like the Condor alliance, the Falklands War, and more. The foreign elements of these operations, however, did not decide this history. Ground conditions in Chile and other Latin American nations were far more influential, and any explanation that fails to appreciate this will remain incomplete and potentially misleading.

To be more specific with respect to the CIA, the Agency's operations in Chile were most effective when they were aligned with preexisting local or national trends that would likely have succeeded even without CIA intervention – such as Frei's conservative-backed election in 1964. They were least effective when they went against such trends or attempted to impose outcomes that key Chilean institutions, groups, and individuals were not prepared to accept or implement. President Richard Nixon, Kissinger, and Ambassador Edward Korry, much to the National Security Council (NSC) staff and the Agency's frustration, learned this the hard way in September and October 1970.

This does not let Nixon, Kissinger, Korry, or the CIA off the hook. Neither does it go so far as novelist John le Carré, who has suggested that "Spies did not win the Cold War. They made absolutely no difference in the long run." But it does back historian

Kristian Gustafson and others' opinions that much of the literature has exaggerated the United States' influence. Even Soviet officials such as the Ministry of External Relations' Yuri Pavlov privately acknowledged that, although the Agency had much to do with the coup, it was "not the main reason." "Coups and revolutions," the Committee for State Security's (KGB) Lt. Gen. Nikolai Leonov elaborated, "occur for internal reasons. Documents and words from other countries cannot stop anything. They count for very little in these matters." The following nine chapters further articulate these three arguments.[18]

Structure and Organization

The first chapter, "The England of South America," advances the first and second arguments, above. The next eight chapters develop all three. Chile burst into the inter-American and transatlantic communities as the England of South America, as Chileans have often referred to their nation since independence in the early nineteenth century. It became politically, militarily, and economically important by the 1880s, and it helped to construct and institutionalize the inter-American system from the late nineteenth century to the mid-twentieth, when Chileans and the rest of the inter-American community, reflecting broad consensus and partnership, created the Organization of American States (OAS).

The second chapter, "Chilean Anticommunism," recreates the initial moments of Chile's Cold War history through the appearance of the labor movement and the PCCh, and the emergence of an anticommunist response from the late nineteenth century to the mid-twentieth. The Chilean Communist Party had an international orientation from the time it enlisted in the Comintern, declared itself the organization's Chilean section, and pledged to fight for its cause. This placed Chilean Communists in conflict with the conservative Chilean establishment and other noncommunists, including the Chilean Socialist Party (PS), which was fundamentally Marxist-Leninist in orientation but averse to Soviet control, after the 1930s. Although these anticommunists and noncommunists were not united, they nevertheless tended to jointly oppose the PCCh and communist internationalism.

This chapter also explains the rise of Chile's Prussian-trained officer corps, which led to Chile's first anticommunist dictatorship in 1927. Gen. Carlos Ibáñez (1927–31 and 1952–8) believed that he was waging a wider war against the USSR and communist internationalism, and that Chile was merely one battleground. He treated Chilean Communists accordingly. He forced the PCCh underground and nearly eradicated it before losing power in 1931.

Chilean anticommunists failed to enlist American support during these years, particularly after Chilean politics collapsed into anarchy in the aftermath of the Great Depression. They failed because the Hoover administration (1929–33) did not share their perceptions with respect to Soviet capabilities and intentions in Chile and the rest of Latin America. Washington interpreted Chile's problems as precisely that: Chilean problems. Further, as Department of State officials explained, the United States lacked any anticommunist expertise to share, in any case. This chapter shows how Chilean Communists, anticommunists, and noncommunists were fighting the Cold War decades before the Second World War and the Cuban Revolution. It also suggests that people in the northern and southern hemispheres sometimes saw and experienced the Cold War differently.

The third and fourth chapters, "Gabriel González Videla and the Transatlantic Origins of the Cold War" and "*La Ley Maldita*: The Law for the Permanent Defense of Democracy," connect the continuing struggles of Chilean Communists and anticommunists to the crises that engulfed the inter-American and transatlantic communities in the late 1940s. Although the PCCh had cooperated with others in Popular Front coalitions, partly responsive to Soviet instructions deriving from lessons learned from the Spanish Civil War, backed pro-Alliance governments against Nazi Germany, and even helped González (1946–52) win the presidency, these tactically expedient measures glossed over irreconcilably different views and objectives that soon returned to the surface. This became clear after PCCh leaders demanded, among other things, that González disassociate his government from the Truman doctrine, the Marshall Plan, and the Rio Pact while cultivating closer ties with the Soviet Union in 1947 and 1948. Consequently, the president and the party fell out with each other.

González declared a state of emergency, militarized his cabinet, and banned communism in response. This represented the second time that a Chilean president, citing an international context and acting with the support of conservatives and the armed forces, went after the PCCh and its sympathizers. This confrontation paralleled the difficulties of Americans and Soviets – and it paralleled the concomitant problems of European Communists, anticommunists, and noncommunists in Belgium, France, Italy, Czechoslovakia, and many Eastern European nations at the same time. This was because they were all caught up in the same transatlantic event.

González and Chilean Communists were acutely conscious of this at the time. They pressed the inter-American and transatlantic communities to align with them and back them against each other. They continued to fail to attract the international support they wanted, however.

As already mentioned, the Cuban Revolution quickened Latin America and indeed the Global South's Cold War history after 1959. The United States became more important to and more involved in the story that was unfolding. The fifth chapter, "The Frei Administration," explores Frei's response to the forces Castro unleashed while clarifying his relationship with the US and the Alliance for Progress. Frei represented a continuation of centrally planned developmental strategies that Chileans had started experimenting with thirty years earlier. These strategies were more technologically ambitious and transatlantic in scope than the Alliance, which tended to focus on low-technology problems in the region like agricultural modernization, land reform, and urban housing programs. For example, Frei's agenda included backing Chilean nuclear scientists' growing participation in the United Nations' (UN) Vienna-based International Atomic Energy Agency's (IAEA) global endeavors, while the Johnson administration's attention to this level of technology came only later. Meanwhile, Frei attracted British and French investment, which he skillfully used to diversify his government's dependence on foreign aid.

Johnson officials encouraged this while continuing to support Frei. This notwithstanding, Frei lost the initiative as Chilean politics started to polarize in the mid- to late 1960s. His coalition and even his own party splintered during these turbulent years. Viaux and his followers undermined Chile's traditional civilian-dominated civil–military relations, which contributed to the mistrust that was dividing Chileans. The sixth chapter, "The Viaux Movement," reconstructs this to the *Tacnazo*, a *pronunciamiento*, a politically motivated move against the Frei administration by Viaux and many sympathetic units within the army that fizzled out before it could become a coup in October 1969.

Viaux's undeterred movement continued to gain traction into the early 1970s. It partly represented the officer corps' response to the Frei and Allende administrations' foreign and defense policies, which alienated many in the lower ranks. It also represented a resurgence of Chilean anticommunists' fears of the PCCh and, behind it, communist internationalism. Viaux and his followers worried that Chilean Communists would "divide the country and tear it apart to achieve power, and then deliver it into the arms of Soviet imperialism" if left unchecked.[19]

The CIA, although well informed, was not involved in the *Tacnazo*. But the Agency had become deeply invested in Chilean politics by the early 1970s. The seventh chapter, "*Plan Alfa*," clears up much of the confusion that still lingers about the CIA's relationship with the Viaux movement, particularly in September and October 1970. It shows how Viaux's group remained the sole movement that the Agency backed during these four to six weeks. The CIA and others, including the United States Senate's Church Committee staff, erroneously thought that the Agency was dealing with two loosely connected but nevertheless separate groups – Viaux's, on the one hand, and Brig. Gen. Camilo Valenzuela's, on the other. Chilean sources, supplemented by declassified American documents, reveal what Viaux, Valenzuela, and their coconspirators called *Plan Alfa*, which remained an expression of one overarching movement with a single agenda, even if it was a somewhat disorganized and, in the CIA's view, unprofessional one.

The eighth chapter, "Cool and Correct," clarifies the Nixon administration's response to the Allende government. Allende remained a Marxist-Leninist and an internationalist who believed that he could reorient Chile's position in world affairs away from the liberal, anticommunist order, which he called imperialism, and toward the Soviet- and Cuban-associated communist one without resorting to violence. Nixon, in turn, remained committed to ensuring that Allende failed, or at least that he did not influence others who might have been inclined to follow his example in Europe and Latin America.

The ninth chapter, "*Jefe de la Plaza*: The Rise of Augusto Pinochet," shows how Allende's politics and leadership style cultivated a broad opposition against his government in Chile. The president particularly alienated the professional officer corps at the field-grade and company level. His idea to use Soviet military aid – and the training and spare parts relationships it entailed, not to mention the political influence that came with them – to reorient the Chilean armed forces to buttress his larger effort was one of his worst miscalculations.

This chapter describes Pinochet's rise from *jefe de la plaza*, a command position responsible for the security of the capital region during states or emergency or siege, in early 1971, to chief of staff in late August 1973. The general became a coup plotter, something he was never enthusiastic about, very late – indeed, just days before the coup. Others, primarily Merino and the officers and marines under his command in Valparaíso's *Primera Zona Naval* (PRIZONA), planned and initiated Allende's overthrow. Pinochet warily went along with them at first. Then he exploited the situation and consolidated what became a personalist dictatorship that ruled Chile through the end of the Cold War.

Sources and Acknowledgments

I reviewed declassified documents from the Truman, Kennedy, Johnson, and Nixon administrations; the American embassy's cables from Santiago; the CIA Records Search Tool (CREST); the Chile Declassification Project (CDP); and the Department of State's *Foreign Relations of the United States* (FRUS) series. I also read the British Foreign Office's files and the British embassy's reporting from Santiago. I conducted research in Chile's National Library and the Archive of the Ministry of Foreign Relations (AMRREE). I reviewed information in the Chilean Nuclear Energy Commission's (CChEN) *Centro Nacional de Estudios Nucleares*, La Reina (CNEN). I relied on underutilized memoirs and other published sources in English and Spanish, including newspapers. Historian Olga Ulianova's Russian-to-Spanish translations of the Soviet Union and Comintern's papers on the PCCh proved invaluable. And I visited the *Museo de la Memoria y los Derechos Humanos*, which contained important oral and video information pertaining to the coup, human rights violations, and the plebiscite that voted the Pinochet dictatorship out of power in 1988.

I thank historian Mark Stout, who recorded a podcast interview with me about my research and thinking while offering comments at an early stage at Johns Hopkins. I also thank historian Alejandro San Francisco for his collegiality and helpful suggestions while I was in Santiago. And I thank Fredrick Nunn, a peerless historian of Chilean military affairs, for his feedback and views, and for introducing me to San Francisco while I was still planning my dissertation at the University of Arizona.

I received generous support from the Harry Truman, John Kennedy, and Lyndon Johnson presidential libraries; the George Marshall Foundation; the Social and Behavioral Sciences Research Institute at the University of Arizona; and the Department of History at the University of Arizona. Historians Thomas Wright and Thomas Davies, and political scientist Brian Loveman taught me Chilean and southern South American history, and I remain grateful that they shared their research and experience with me as a student. I thank my dissertation committee, historians Michael Schaller, Elizabeth Cobbs, Jadwiger Pieper Mooney, and Fabio Lanza. Schaller, Cobbs, and political scientist David Gibbs trained me in the history of American foreign relations and foreign policy analysis. I also appreciate series editors Richard Aldrich and Hugh Wilford, the anonymous reviewers, and the editors and staff at Edinburgh University Press for their encouragement, suggestions, and impeccable professionalism. My conclusions, findings, and interpretations remain my own. Any residual errors that may have persisted through review and publication remain my responsibility as well.

Notes

1. Carlos Prats, *Memorias: testimonio de un soldado* (Santiago de Chile: Pehuén Editores, 1985), 184, 187; United States Senate, *Alleged Assassination Plots Involving Foreign Leaders* (Washington, DC: Government Printing Office, 1975), 225–54; Florencia Varas, *Conversaciones con Viaux* (Santiago de Chile: Impresiones EIRE, 1972), 123–201; CIA, "Report on CIA Chilean Task Force Activities, 15 September to 3 November 1970," 18 November 1970. Chile Declassification Project (CDP), at <http://www.state.gov>; and "Chile Quiet on Eve of Crucial Vote," *Washington Post*, 23 October 1970. Chileans called their service commanders, in the army, navy, and air force, *comandante en jefe*, the second highest office of the Chilean army being *jefe del estado mayor*. I have translated these positions as chief of staff and deputy chief of staff with respect to the army, chief of naval operations for the navy, and commander of the air force.

2. José Díaz Nieva, *Patria y Libertad: el nacionalismo frente a la Unidad Popular* (Santiago de Chile: Ediciones Centro de Estudios Bicentenario, 2015), 19–70; Mario Valdés Urrutia and Danny Monsálvez Araneda, "Recogiendo los pasos: los movimientos deliberativos al interior de las filas del Ejército (1969–1973)," *Notas Históricas y Geográficas* 13–14 (2002–3), 202–8; Nathaniel Davis to Department of State, "Patria y Libertad," 23 December 1971. CDP; and Edward Korry to Henry Kissinger and U. Alexis Johnson, 9 October 1970. Department of State, *Foreign Relations of the United States, 1969–1976* XXI: *Chile, 1969–1973* (Washington, DC: Government Printing Office, 2014), document 144.

3. Varas, *Conversaciones con Viaux*, 127, 147.

4. CIA, Briefing notes, "Recent Developments – Track II," 12 August 1975. Department of State, *FRUS, 1969–1976* XXI: *Chile, 1969–1973*, document 168; and Santiago Station to CIA, 24 October 1970. CDP. I use CIA and the Agency interchangeably.

5. For example, Stephen Rabe, *The Killing Zone: The United States Wages Cold War in Latin America* [2012], 2nd edn (New York: Oxford University Press, 2016), 127–47; Peter Kornbluh, *The Pinochet File: A Declassified Dossier on Atrocity and Accountability* [2003], 2nd edn (New York: The New Press, 2013); Carlos Basso Prieto, *La CIA en Chile, 1970–1973* (Santiago de Chile: Aguilar Chilena de Ediciones, 2013); Lubna Qureshi, *Nixon, Kissinger, and Allende: U.S. Involvement in the 1973 Coup in Chile* [2009]

(Lanham: Lexington, 2010); Mark Atwood Lawrence, "History from Below: The United States and Latin America in the Nixon Years." Fredrik Logevall and Andrew Preston, eds., *Nixon and the World: American Foreign Relations, 1969–1977* (New York: Oxford University Press, 2008), 269–88; Jonathan Haslam, *The Nixon Administration and the Death of Allende's Chile: A Case of Assisted Suicide* (London: Verso, 2005); Patricia Verdugo, *Allende: cómo la Casa Blanca provocó su muerte* (Santiago de Chile: Catalonia, 2003); Christopher Hitchens, *The Trial of Henry Kissinger* (London: Verso, 2001); CIA, "CIA Activities in Chile," 18 September 2000, at <https://cia.gov>; Seymour Hersh, *The Price of Power: Kissinger in the Nixon White House* (New York: Summit Books, 1983); Konstantinos Gavras [Costa Gavras], *Missing* (Hollywood: Universal Pictures, 1982); Thomas Hauser, *The Execution of Charles Horman: An American Sacrifice* (New York: Harcourt Brace Jovanovich, 1978); Róbinson Rojas Sandford, *The Murder of Allende and the End of the Chilean Way to Socialism* (New York: Harper & Row, 1976); United States Senate, *Alleged Assassination Plots Involving Foreign Leaders*; United States Senate, *Covert Action in Chile, 1963–1973* (Washington, DC: Government Printing Office, 1975); Armando Uribe, *The Black Book of American Intervention in Chile* [1974], trans. Jonathan Casart (Boston: Beacon, 1975); and Gabriel García Márquez, "The Death of Salvador Allende," trans. Gregory Rabassa, *Harper's* (March 1974): 46–53. For Chileans' request for an apology, see "Chile President [Sebastián Piñera] to Ask Obama for Pinochet Files," BBC, 23 March 2011, at <http://www.bbc.com>.

6. Kenneth Maxwell, "The Other 9/11: The United States and Chile, 1973," *Foreign Affairs* 82 (Nov.–Dec. 2003), 151. For "narrow historiography of blame," Tanya Harmer, *Allende's Chile and the Inter-American Cold War* (Chapel Hill: University of North Carolina Press, 2011), 7. For "axe-grinding in nature," Simon Collier and William Sater, *A History of Chile, 1808–2002* [1996], 2nd edn (Cambridge: Cambridge University Press, 2004), 426.

7. For example, see Rabe, *Killing Zone*; Thomas Wright, *State Terrorism in Latin America: Chile, Argentina, and International Human Rights* (Lanham: Rowman & Littlefield, 2007); and John Dinges, *The Condor Years: How Pinochet and His Allies Brought Terrorism to Three Continents* [2004] (New York: The New Press, 2005).

8. For the Cuban Revolution and international affairs, see Thomas Wright, *Latin America in the Era of the Cuban Revolution and*

Beyond [1991], 3rd edn (Santa Barbara: DBC-CLIO/Praeger, 2018); Jonathan Brown, *Cuba's Revolutionary World* (Cambridge, MA: Harvard University Press, 2017); and Hal Brands, *Latin America's Cold War* (Cambridge, MA: Harvard University Press, 2010).

9. For Chilean politics and history within this inter-American context, see Margaret Power, *Right-Wing Women in Chile: Feminine Power and the Struggle against Allende, 1964–1973* (University Park: Pennsylvania State University Press, 2002); Wright, *Latin America in the Era of the Cuban Revolution*; and Paul Sigmund, *The Overthrow of Allende and the Politics of Chile, 1964–1976* (Pittsburgh: University of Pittsburgh Press, 1977).

10. Harmer, *Allende's Chile*, 17; and José Toribio Merino, *Bitácora de un almirante: memorias* (Santiago de Chile: Editorial Andrés Bello, 1998), 255. For Brazilian involvement in Chile, also see Tanya Harmer, "Brazil's Cold War in the Southern Cone, 1970–1975," *Cold War History* 12 (2012): 659–81. For Cuban intervention in Chile, elsewhere in Latin America, and in sub-Saharan Africa, also see Brown, *Cuba's Revolutionary World*; Kristian Gustafson and Christopher Andrew, "The Other Hidden Hand: Soviet and Cuban Intelligence in Allende's Chile," *Intelligence and National Security* 33 (2017), published online on 1 December 2017, at <http://www.tandfonline.com>; Piero Gleijeses, *Visions of Freedom: Havana, Washington, Pretoria, and the Struggle for Southern Africa, 1976–1991* (Chapel Hill: University of North Carolina Press, 2013); Piero Gleijeses, *Conflicting Missions: Havana, Washington, and Africa, 1959–1976* (Chapel Hill: University of North Carolina Press, 2002); and Cristián Pérez, "Salvador Allende, Apuntes sobre su dispositivo de seguridad: el grupo de amigos personales (GAP)," *Estudios Públicos* 79 (2000): 31–81.

11. Kirsten Weld, "The Spanish Civil War and the Construction of a Reactionary Historical Consciousness in Augusto Pinochet's Chile," *Hispanic American Historical Review* 98 (2018), 79; and William Rogers, "U.S.–Chilean Relations," 8 June 1976. Department of State, *Foreign Relations of the United States, 1969–1976* E-11 II: *Documents on South America, 1973–1976* (Washington, DC: Government Printing Office, 2015), document 228. Weld also found that the civil war had shaped, conditioned, and helped to frame Chilean leftists' consciousness as historical actors, but her research focused on anticommunists, who remain less studied. For Chile and the Spanish Civil War, also see José Díaz Nieva, *Chile: de la Falange Nacional a la Democracia Cristiana* (Madrid: Universidad Nacional de Educación y

Distancia, 2000); Cristián Garay Vera, *Relaciones tempestuosas: Chile y España, 1936–1940* (Santiago de Chile: Instituto de Estudios Avanzados (IDEA), Universidad de Santiago, 2000); and Cristían Garay and Cristían Medina, *Chile y la guerra civil española, 1936– 1939: relaciones diplomáticas y paradigmas políticos* (Santiago de Chile: Fundación Mario Góngora, 1994).

12. Odd Arne Westad, *The Cold War: A World History* (New York: Basic Books, 2017), 5.

13. Salvador Allende, "First Annual Message to the National Congress," 21 May 1971. James Cockcroft, ed., *Salvador Allende Reader: Chile's Voice of Democracy* (Melbourne and New York: Ocean Press, 2000), 196.

14. Junta Militar de Gobierno, "Chile en el contexto mundial: base para una definición," 11 September 1973. Merino, *Bitácora de un almirante*, 476. For the United States' commitment to the liberal international order, or global or international society, see Frank Ninkovich, *The Global Republic: America's Inadvertent Rise to World Power* (Chicago: University of Chicago Press, 2014). For an introduction to the Cold War as a conflict between those backing an empire of justice versus an empire of liberty, see Odd Arne Westad, *The Global Cold War: Third World Interventions and the Making of Our Times* [2005] (Cambridge: Cambridge University Press, 2007). For the end of the Cold War as the triumph of liberalism, see Francis Fukuyama, "The End of History?" *The National Interest* 16 (Summer 1989): 3–18. For the same discussion but with an emphasis on the more subtle victory of the spread of mass consumerism, see Emily Rosenberg, "Consumer Capitalism and the End of the Cold War." Melvyn Leffler and Odd Arne Westad, eds., *The Cambridge History of the Cold War* III: *Endings* [2010] (Cambridge: Cambridge University Press, 2011), 489–512.

15. Joaquín Fermandois, "The Hero on the Latin American Scene." Christian Nuenlist, Anna Locher, and Garret Martin, eds., *Globalizing de Gaulle: International Perspectives on French Foreign Policies, 1958–1969* [2010] (Lanham: Rowman & Littlefield, 2011), 271.

16. Harmer, *Allende's Chile*, 6. This remains an old argument with respect to Chile's Cold War experience. See, for example, the exchange between historian Kenneth Maxwell and Nixon administration official William Rogers in *Foreign Affairs*. Maxwell, "The Other 9/11"; and William Rogers and Kenneth Maxwell, "Fleeing the Chilean Coup: The Debate over U.S. Complicity," *Foreign Affairs* 83 (2004): 160–5. For one Chilean historian's frustration with this tendency

to reduce the Chilean past to American intervention, see Joaquín Fermandois, "La persistencia del mito: Chile en el huracán de la Guerra Fría," *Estudios Públicos* 92 (2003): 287–312.

17. For example, Robert Pastor, <u>Not</u> *Condemned to Repetition: The United States and Nicaragua* [1987], rev. edn (Boulder: Westview Press, 2002); Robert Pastor, *Exiting the Whirlpool: U.S. Foreign Policy toward Latin America and the Caribbean* [1992], rev. edn (Boulder: Westview Press, 2001); and Steve Stern and Immanuel Wallerstein, "Feudalism, Capitalism, and the World-System in the Perspective of Latin America and the Caribbean," *American Historical Review* 93 (1988): 829–97.

18. Sarah Lyall, "Spies Like Us: A Conversation with John le Carré and Ben Macintyre," *New York Times*, 25 August 2017, at <http://www.nytimes.com>; Kristian Gustafson, *Hostile Intent: U.S. Covert Operations in Chile, 1964–1974* (Washington, DC: Potomac Books, 2007); Nikolai Leonov, Eugenia Fediakova, Joaquín Fermandois, et al., "El General Nikolai Leonov en el CEP," *Estudios Públicos* 73 (1999), 74; and Interview with Yuri Pavlov, Roll 10842, n.d. CNN, *Cold War* (1998). Transcript courtesy of the National Security Archive, at <http://www.nsarchive.gwu.edu>. For a comparison of Soviet officials and propagandists' public and private responses to the coup, see Olga Ulianova, "La Unidad Popular y el golpe militar en Chile: percepciones y análisis soviéticos," *Estudios Públicos* 79 (2000), 114–35.

19. Varas, *Conversaciones con Viaux*, 119.

1 The England of South America

Chile appeared in modern history as a young nation within the Atlantic world after declaring independence from Spain in the early nineteenth century. Chilean elites believed that theirs was an exceptional, model republic – the England of South America, as many still proudly call their country today. They actively helped to build the inter-American system that began to take shape in the late nineteenth century, and they were influential members of the larger, transatlantic community as well. This positioned them, for better and for worse, to experience the effects of industrialization, globalization, and the onset of the Cold War as liberals aligned with likeminded liberals in Latin America, the United States, and Europe.[1]

To the War of the Pacific

Chileans came into sustained contact with their southern South American neighbors, the United States, and Europe in the mid- to late nineteenth century. They had embraced autocracy by that time, after a merchant named Diego Portales settled their relatively brief post-independence civil wars. Portales inaugurated an authoritarian but pragmatic, pro-business, and socially conservative political order that lasted from the 1830s to the 1890s, although Portales's constitution endured until the mid-1920s.

Portales's system concentrated power in the executive branch. Presidents appointed provincial governors and other regional officials to serve them. These officials functioned as presidential agents while controlling the country's electoral machinery. Presidents thus selected their own successors and ensured the legislative branch's compliance.

Presidents used these powers to silence dissent and suppress disorder, particularly during the civil wars that erupted in 1851 and 1859, and the much more serious conflict that happened in 1891. Unless Congress was in regular session, which only occurred three months each year, presidents could declare states of emergency whenever they deemed it necessary. This permitted them to suspend the constitution and civil liberties within the affected zones, where they subjected those accused of subversion to military courts-martial. They used *relegación*, or internal exile, to deal with some of those convicted. They constructed internment centers in such locations as Más Afuera in the Juan Fernández Islands, Punta Arenas in the Magellan Straits, and later, Pisagua in the Atacama Desert.

Portales wanted practical, disciplined government and strict law and order, not liberal democracy. According to him, Chileans were not ready for it. "Democracy, which self-deceived men proclaim so often," he wrote, "remains absurd in the Americas, filled as it is with vices, where citizens lack the virtues required to establish true republics." He feared that civil liberties invited unrest and weakened good government. They remained, consequently, expendable. As he reiterated, "this lady called Constitution must be violated when the circumstances are extreme."[2]

Portales subordinated the army to the presidency and civilian rule when he declared the armed forces obedient and nondeliberative. He also created a militia, which outnumbered the army, as a counterforce. Portales's achievements and the civilian-dominated civil–military relations that followed were indeed exceptional in Latin America at the time. But he was no liberal democrat, and there were no democratic traditions in the Chilean armed services in the nineteenth century.

Instead, Portales's constitution laid the legal foundations for, and established the tradition of, repression. Portales's philosophy of government often reappeared during the crises that occurred in the nineteenth and twentieth centuries. As some have recognized, the armed forces' coup against the Allende administration (1970–3) and the particular form the Pinochet dictatorship (1973–90) took partly represented an expression of Portalian politics, in that the dictatorship was responding to what many in the professional officer corps regarded as the kind of irresponsible civilian government and social instability that Portales despised. Gen. Augusto Pinochet, seeking to legitimize his rule, partly through selective use of the Chilean past, acknowledged this often. "In a word," he once explained, "Portales wanted a strong central government whose men were models of prudence, dignity, and firmness – uncompromising men who repressed abuse and disorder."[3]

Meanwhile, Chileans confronted the basic problem that complicated all inter-American relations in the nineteenth century: security, particularly with respect to the new nations' borders, from Mexico to the Tierra del Fuego, which the collapse of Spain's imperial system had left poorly defined. Brazil and the United Provinces of Buenos Aires continued Portugal and Spain's older rivalries in Uruguay and in Misiones province. Mexico City and Lima, once Spain's two most powerful viceroyalties, lost control over the vast areas they had administered since the sixteenth century. The United States swept into what became the American Southwest as Central America broke away from Mexico City and then disintegrated into five smaller, independent countries. Gran Colombia's history followed a similar, disintegrative trajectory, leaving the republics of Ecuador, Colombia, and Venezuela in its aftermath. Panama declared independence from Colombia later.

Chileans, too, left their status as a captaincy general that had reported to the viceroy in Lima behind. They started projecting their own commercial, political, and naval strength along South America's Pacific coast in the mid-1830s. This soon led to armed conflict with Bolivia and Peru.

Bolivian Gen. Andrés Santa Cruz seized Peru in 1836, intending to restore Lima's preeminence by forging a Peruvian–Bolivian confederation while eyeing Chile's Pacific coast trade. He supported a group of Chilean exiles – dissidents opposed to Portales's constitution – who planned to overthrow Chilean President Joaquín Prieto (1831–41). Some of these exiles defected, however, and passed documents to Chilean authorities that partly revealed Santa Cruz's thinking.

The Prieto administration had already decided that it could not tolerate Santa Cruz's confederation, fearing that it would eventually threaten Chile's independence. Thus, Santiago dispatched an envoy to Peru who carried an ultimatum backed by five warships. "We do not care whether General Santa Cruz rules in Bolivia or in Peru," the government instructed the envoy; "what we do care about is the separation of the two nations . . . If Austria or France seized Spain or Italy . . . to form a single political body . . . would the other nations be indifferent?"[4]

The administration's first expedition to Lima failed, but the second one, which Gen. Manuel Bulnes Prieto commanded, succeeded. Bulnes defeated Santa Cruz's armies, forced the general into exile, and restored Peruvian independence. Chilean confidence soared after this. In the eminent Venezuelan–Chilean jurist Andrés Bello's estimation, this victory conferred "the title of champions of the American equilibrium and of the rights of peoples" onto his fellow citizens. Thus, Chileans became interested in using reason or force, as their national motto proclaimed, to preserve a balance of power that favored their growing hegemony in southern South America.[5]

Chile remained a small country, confined to the central valley surrounding Santiago, in the 1830s. Its territory extended no further north than Copiapó and no further south than the Rio Bío Bío, which demarcated Chile's Indian frontier. This changed as Chilean agricultural production surged – partly responding to temporary increases in demand in California and Australia, which were experiencing gold rushes, and partly serving industrializing European markets – in the 1840s. Chilean wheat and flour exports to California alone rose from 6,000 quintals in 1848 to 500,000 in 1850. This booming export economy soon included silver, copper, iron, and nitrate mining from the north, and coal from the south.[6]

These agricultural and mining activities induced further expansion into the southern Indian lands Chileans called Araucania. Chileans justified themselves in ways that historians well versed in the literature on American expansion will recognize – starting with their rationale for enlarging their navy, which they articulated decades before Rear Adm. Alfred Thayer Mahan (USN) published

The Influence of Sea Power upon History (1890). In the 1840s, the chief of naval operations told congressmen that

> if you cast a glance over the rest of the world and observe that the two most free and industrious nations are precisely those that possess the greatest naval forces, you will be tempted perhaps to study the intimate relationship between war and merchant fleets, and between merchant fleets and the greatness of a people.[7]

President Manuel Bulnes (1841–51) concurred, and Chileans began projecting sea power that decade. They seized positions in the Magellan Straits, at Punta Arenas and Fort Bulnes. These positions protected their access to transatlantic trade routes. The Chilean navy became the most significant in Pacific South America in the years that followed, and Chilean leaders were quite conscious of this, even to the point of overconfidence. As one Chilean senator would inform President Franklin Roosevelt (1933–45) a century later, "Mr. President, the Pacific Ocean, up to Panama, is ours."[8]

Chileans also conquered Araucania between the 1840s and 1880s. The Mapuche Indians there had resisted Incan and Spanish rule for centuries, but they were no match for the Chilean army, which possessed modern weaponry and had much shorter lines of communication and supply than Incas and Spaniards had had. This opened new tracts of land to settlement. Bello and his contemporaries considered this region "either completely deserted or transiently occupied by savage tribes." President Manuel Montt (1851–61) appointed Vicente Pérez Rosales colonization agent in Valdivia and Llanquihue in the 1850s. Then he named him consul in Hamburg, where he recruited German and other European immigrants to cross the Atlantic and populate the area. Modest numbers of Germans started moving into what became the Chilean south.[9]

Chile's southern expansion did not stop in Araucania. It spilled over the Andes to the southeast, into today's Argentine Patagonia. Argentines, whose country remained in disarray, objected to this, to no avail. Thus, when Pérez described Chile's political geography to European readers, he ignored these objections, arguing that his nation encompassed both cisandine and transandine lands. He also referred to his country's *acción civilizadora* – its civilizing mission – when justifying this:

> The Republic's maritime boundaries extend no further east than its Patagonian coast, from the mouth of the Río Negro to the Magellan Straits, and to the Pacific Ocean in the west, from Cape Horn to Mejillones . . . Our Constitution has contributed to the erroneous belief that Chile remains confined to the [South] American continent west of the Andes, between the Atacama and Cape Horn. This delineation, made during the independence war, certainly did not mean that Chile had renounced all the territory that had belonged to the Captaincy General of Chile. The Republic was limited to that which it could realistically defend against Spanish forces at the time, but this did not alienate Chile from lands that rightfully belonged to it. Thus, when peaceful conditions returned, and when Chile's population, power, and wealth permitted it to extend its civilizing mission into Patagonia, it founded a colony in the Magellan Straits as its principal base of operations there.[10]

Back in Santiago, Chileans contemplated the surviving Mapuches' future with less patience every day. Some advised treating these Indians quite harshly. For example, one newspaper's editors disdained them as "savages . . . this stupid race . . . odious and prejudicial guests in Chile," and called for "prompt and extreme measures" to deal with them. The Indian wars that followed were remarkably similar to the ones Americans and Argentines waged in support of their own western expansions at roughly the same time. Thus, Chileans settled Araucania from Valdivia to Puerto Montt during the closing decades of the nineteenth century.[11]

Meanwhile, Chilean mining operations continued to push north into the Atacama, all the way into Peru's Tarapacá province. Chileans had invested approximately 20 million pesos and imported over 10,000 miners – Chilean peasants from the central valley who sought higher wages and a better life in the mines – into this desert by the 1870s. Chileans, Bolivians, and Peruvians had only recognized the area's importance after they discovered large deposits of *guano* – mountains of bird droppings that had accumulated for centuries – there. American and European agricultural producers prized this *guano* as high-grade fertilizer. This created new conflicts as all three governments maneuvered to secure this commodity.[12]

Chileans and Bolivians began clashing over this as early as the 1860s. President José Joaquín Perez (1861–71) negotiated an agreement with the Bolivian government that fixed the two nations' border at the 24th parallel in 1866. Santiago and La Paz would jointly administer and tax "the minerals extracted" from the territory between the 23rd and 25th parallels thereafter.[13]

This treaty clearly favored Chilean interests. Although Bolivian authorities would operate the customs office at Mejillones, Chilean officials would have a presence there to ensure that their imports passed through duty free and that their exports left without hassle. Bolivians still regarded this coastal area as a peripheral wasteland, so they did not object to what amounted to shared sovereignty on their coast. This soon changed.

Chilean prospector José Díaz Gana discovered the Caracoles silver mine in this region in 1870. Caracoles yielded approximately 1,000 metric tons of silver over the next decade. Bolivians now worried that Chileans were becoming too comfortable, exploiting too many resources, which now included nitrates, in what suddenly became a disputed area, and they moved, belatedly, to reassert their sovereign rights there. They argued that the existing treaty limited Chilean mining activities to *guano*. Chileans, intending to consolidate their expanding interests in what was rapidly becoming their *de facto* colony, retorted that the treaty broadly included *any* minerals from there.[14]

Santiago and La Paz resolved this by revising their agreement in 1874. They reaffirmed that the Chilean–Bolivian border remained at the 24th parallel. Chileans renounced their claims to condominium between the 23rd and 25th parallels in exchange for Bolivians' pledge to continue sharing half the *guano* revenues and not to raise taxes on whatever other minerals Chileans extracted for the next twenty-five years. Bolivians, in turn, would allow Chileans to continue enjoying duty-free imports into the area. The two governments also agreed to submit any new dispute that might arise to arbitration.[15]

The underlying issues remained unresolved, however, and both countries prepared to settle them through war. The Bolivian government signed a secret pact with Peru to act jointly against further Chilean encroachments, while the Chilean navy bought two state-of-the-art, ironclad warships from Britain. These tensions reached their breaking point when Bolivian Gen. Hilarión Daza Groselle (1876–9), determined to restore Bolivian sovereignty in the Atacama, seized power.[16]

Outbreak of War

Daza's efforts to impose a solution, particularly his harassment of the Antofagasta Nitrate and Railroad Company (*Compañía de Salitres y Ferrocarril de Antofagasta*), a Chilean corporation operating within the disputed area, triggered the War of the Pacific (1879–83). In December 1878, Daza raised the company's taxes and instructed it to pay this higher rate retroactively, covering the preceding year. Chilean President Aníbal Pinto (1876–81) argued that this violated the two nations' agreement. The president asked Daza to submit the issue to arbitration. The general ignored this, seizing the company's assets to recover the taxes he said it owed his government. Pinto dispatched Chilean warships and ground forces to occupy the area in February 1879. Daza declared war against Chile that March. Then Pinto asked the Peruvian government to abrogate its secret pact with Bolivia – it had been an open secret. Lima refused. Santiago declared war against both countries that April.[17]

Chileans promptly defeated their adversaries, stating terms during an American-sponsored conference the USS *Lackawanna* hosted at Arica in October 1880: The Peruvian and Bolivian governments must acknowledge responsibility for the war. Peru must cede all of Tarapacá to Chile while paying the Chilean government 20 million pesos in reparations, recognizing Chilean administrative rights in Tacna and Arica until it had paid this in full. Bolivia must cede its entire coast. These terms shocked both the Peruvian and Bolivian delegations, who rejected them.[18]

Chileans continued to prosecute the war, occupying Lima in January 1881. The Peruvian government withdrew from the capital. An insurgency arose in the surrounding countryside. The

Chilean army waged a counterinsurgency campaign there over the next two years.

Meanwhile, Chileans turned to Argentina. Argentines had unified their nation and established internal order by the 1860s, emerging on the winning side of a war against an expansionist Paraguay in 1870. Then they embarked upon their own, northwestern expansion. The Argentine government had contemplated joining Peru and Bolivia as part of an international effort to contain Chilean expansion before the outbreak of the War of the Pacific, but having witnessed Chile's easy victory over Peru and Bolivia, Buenos Aires now preferred to settle its differences with Santiago peacefully. The Chilean government, with most of its forces deployed far from the Argentine border, was similarly inclined.

President Domingo Santa María (1881–6) and his Argentine counterpart agreed that the Andes, "running from the highest summits that divide the waters and passing between the slopes that fall to one side or the other," would mark the Chilean–Argentine border to the 52nd parallel, just north of the Magellan Straits, which they neutralized, in July 1881. They drew a straight, north–south line from Cabo del Espíritu Santo, at the Atlantic entrance to the straits, to the Beagle Channel, specifying that Chilean territory fell to the west of this line, and Argentine to the east. Chile would possess "all islands south of the channel to Cape Horn and all to the west of Tierra del Fuego." Both governments would appoint a mixed commission to mark this border and submit any disputes that might arise to arbitration.[19]

Having reduced Chilean–Argentine tensions, at least for the moment, Chileans returned to Peru to negotiate an end to the war. In the Treaty of Ancón, Lima ceded Tarapacá to Chile unconditionally and in perpetuity. The agreement further stipulated that Chileans would administer Peru's Tacna and Arica provinces for the next ten years, until 1894. When this expired, the two governments would supervise a plebiscite that would allow the residents there to decide their own future.[20]

Chileans would also occupy Lima and Las Islas de Lobos until the Peruvian government ratified the treaty. Peruvians would cede 50 percent of the islands' *guano* revenues to Chile and pay 300,000 pesos to offset the Chilean army's costs each month. The

Tacna–Arica issue, however, like the Chilean–Bolivian war and the Chilean–Argentine border conflict, would plague inter-American relations for decades.

Enter the United States

The *Lackawanna* conference reflected an emerging preference for negotiation and persuasion over older patterns of coercion and force in international relations, particularly within the inter-American and transatlantic communities. For example, the United States and the United Kingdom had already agreed to arbitrate American claims arising from Britain's providing commerce raiders to the Confederacy during the US Civil War (1861–5). Simón Bolívar and other Latin Americans had long expressed their interest in this. For example, Bolívar invited representatives from Mexico, Guatemala, Colombia, Argentina, Chile, and Brazil to a regional conference in 1826, "to serve as advisors in moments of great conflict, as facilitators of communication in the face of common dangers, as faithful interpreters in public negotiations in difficult times, and lastly as mediators of our differences."[21]

Latin Americans' growing mistrust and security problems prevented them from working together at the time, however, and Bolívar's efforts collapsed. But Bello, perhaps the leading Spanish-American international jurist of his generation, among others, continued to argue the merits of such an inter-American gathering into the 1840s. He wrote:

> A congress of plenipotentiaries does the same thing that ten or twelve men do who have contemplated businesses in which their interests conflict: they sign a contract to prevent, as far as prudence reaches, occasions for dispute . . . and, with anticipation, to establish rules for settling them in what appears the fairest manner.[22]

Some also desired to organize a common defense. Peruvian, Chilean, and several other nations' representatives wanted to create a regional military alliance directed against Spain at the Congress of Lima in 1865. Chileans attempted to make it operational after Spanish Adm. José Manuel Pareja attacked the Peruvian and Chilean coasts. But Brazilians, Argentines, and Uruguayans were fighting Paraguay, and Peruvians, Chileans, and Bolivians were becoming increasingly suspicious of each other as well.[23]

Latin Americans nevertheless kept this conversation going into the early 1880s, when the Colombian government proposed a regional arbitration agreement "with the aim of eliminating international wars forever." The moment was still not right, however, and Bogotá's efforts failed. With so many unresolved territorial disputes, many Latin American countries remained, as Bello once phrased it, "less disposed to listen to the advice of reason and justice."[24]

Following *Lackawanna*, the Garfield administration's (1881) Secretary of State James Blaine, too, learned that immovable obstacles still stood in the way of an inter-American system of arbitration. Blaine, fearing European intervention in the War of the Pacific, attempted to revive a now United States-led, Pan-American conference. He hoped to host a meeting in Washington, to mediate the war while also discussing broader issues of legal and commercial cooperation. He encountered stiff resistance, however, and President James Garfield's assassination led to Blaine's resignation before he could overcome it.[25]

Garfield and Blaine's successors, President Chester Arthur (1881–5) and Secretary of State Frederick Frelinghuysen, read the writing on the wall and canceled the conference. In the Arthur administration's estimation, "[the] peaceful condition of the South American Republics, which was contemplated as essential to a profitable and harmonious assembling of the Congress, does not exist." Frelinghuysen still offered to help arbitrate the war through "the consistent policy of equal and unprejudiced friendship towards [the] three sovereign republican states."[26]

Blaine's efforts and Frelinghuysen's offers alarmed Santiago. Chileans viewed these endeavors as unsolicited meddling between victors and vanquished. And they were not willing to risk losing any of their gains through a mediation process they might not be able to control.[27]

US–Chilean relations reached their nadir the following decade, during Chile's civil war in 1891, when Congress, Capt.

Jorge Montt Álvarez, and much of the navy formed the *Junta Revolucionaria de Iquique* and revolted against President José Manuel Balmaceda (1886–91). The *junta* sailed north to Iquique that January, securing its nitrate fields as its base of operations. Balmaceda remained in Santiago and retained most of the army's loyalty in a war that pitted Congress and the navy against the president and the army.[28]

As Ambassador Patrick Egan, who openly sympathized with the Balmaceda administration, reported to Washington, this dispute represented an executive–legislative struggle over the specific balance the Chilean government should strike between presidential and congressional power. Egan highlighted

> the contention on the part of the President for a popular representative status similar to that occupied by the President of the United States, with the additional power to appoint and remove his ministers at pleasure, which right is given him under the constitution, while the opposition battles for a strictly parliamentary system and the removal of ministers whenever they cease to have the support of a majority in Congress.[29]

The *junta* won the war, and Adm. Montt returned to Santiago as interim president. Balmaceda's suicide that September marked the end of Portales's autocratic republic, although the constitution itself would linger into the 1920s.[30]

Montt's provisional government persecuted the late president's surviving supporters, intending to imprison and even execute some of them. Several had sought asylum in the American embassy in Santiago and onboard USS *Baltimore* in Valparaíso. The government started harassing both the embassy and the warship through aggressive surveillance in response.[31]

These tensions exploded after Chileans clashed with approximately 120 American sailors on liberty from *Baltimore* that October. One sailor died from gunshot wounds, five suffered injuries, and one of these died from his injuries later. More than thirty went to jail. Since this involved a United States warship, it brought Washington and Santiago into open confrontation.[32]

The Harrison administration (1889–93), which had reinstated Secretary of State Blaine, sympathized with the Balmaceda government, refused to sell the *junta*'s purchasing agents arms, and declined to recognize the *junta* during the war. *Baltimore* had not only sheltered some of the surviving *balmacedistas* but also transported them to Peru, where many of them lived in exile. Thus, President Benjamin Harrison interpreted the incident as retaliatory. Blaine pressed Montt to submit the matter to arbitration. According to the Department of State, "our sailors were unarmed and gave no provocation . . . the assaults upon them were by armed men, greatly superior in numbers, and as we must conclude, animated in their bloody work by hostility to these men as sailors of the United States." Further, "the public police, or some of them, took part in the attack." Montt's acting foreign minister, Manuel Antonio Matta, brushed off the incident as "a fight between some drunken sailors" and dismissed Harrison's position as "erroneous and deliberately incorrect."[33]

Meanwhile, Chileans formally elected Montt to the presidency, reestablishing constitutional government that December. The Montt administration (1891–6) promptly withdrew the surveillance from the United States embassy. Montt also consented to the remaining refugees' departure from the country. But the *Baltimore* affair remained unresolved, and Matta's words still hung in the air.[34]

Blaine responded the following month. Chileans had attacked "the uniform of the U.S. Navy, having its origin and motive in a feeling of hostility to this Government, and not in any act of the sailors," and "the public authorities . . . flagrantly failed their duty to protect our men, and . . . some of the police and of the Chilean soldiers and sailors were themselves guilty of unprovoked assaults upon our sailors before and after arrest." "No self-respecting government," he continued, "can consent that persons in its service, whether civil or military, shall be beaten and killed in a foreign territory in resentment of acts done by or imputed to their government without exacting reparation." The Harrison administration would "terminate diplomatic relations with the Government of Chile" unless it offered "a suitable apology" and "some adequate reparation."[35]

The Montt administration's new foreign minister, Luis Pereira, expressed his government's regret over the *Baltimore* affair seventy-two hours later. Pereira suggested that the US Supreme Court should hear the matter. The American and Chilean governments promptly resumed normal relations, and Santiago eventually paid compensation to the families of the dead and injured. This notwithstanding, US–Chilean relations remained cool into the 1920s.[36]

The Rise of the Inter-American System

Chilean attitudes toward the outside world changed after their civil war. This marked Chile's transition from autocratic to parliamentary republic. Chileans stopped expanding, and they adopted a defensiveness that has informed their strategic and security posture ever since. Most historians have connected this "slackening of Chilean power," as Burr put it, to the civil war's outcome, where previously dynamic presidents lost the initiative to govern and an aristocratic and more provincial Congress dominated the country's politics for the next thirty years or so. Thus, Chilean expansion – into the Atacama in the north, to the Andes in the east, and to the Magellan Straits in the south – reached its limits in the late nineteenth century.[37]

Chileans began the lengthy process of settling the War of the Pacific's outstanding issues thereafter. These problems, particularly the Tacna–Arica question, would "hang like a dark cloud over the inter-American movement" for the next several decades, as historians have recognized. Thus, while Chilean delegates attended the first two Pan-American conferences – in Washington (1889–90) and Mexico City (1901–2) – they did so with misgivings. As historian Frederick Pike explained, Chileans took "an extremely jaundiced view" of them.[38]

The compulsory, retroactive arbitration agreements that the Argentine, Peruvian, and Bolivian representatives were proposing at Mexico City aroused Chileans' suspicions. They worried that these agreements might deprive them of both Tacna and Arica, and that they would limit their options concerning their pending settlement with Bolivia as well. This led to Chilean officials' threatening to walk out of Mexico City several times. They understood that obstructing or preventing a consensus in these talks remained their most effective leverage. So, it served their interests to stay in these conferences, where they worked to weaken these agreements.[39]

Still, Chileans recognized that the Mexican and United States governments were attempting to construct an equitable regional arbitration system patterned after the Permanent Court of Arbitration at The Hague, and that they were not using this as a pretext to support one group of nations against others, as they believed some were doing. As Ambassador Juan José Fernández elaborated,

> On one side were Argentina, Bolivia, and Peru, favoring the broadest possible compulsory and retroactive arbitration agreement. Paraguay and Uruguay supported them, as did Guatemala and the Dominican Republic, which had ongoing conflicts with Mexico and Haiti. On the other side, Chile and Ecuador pressed the conference to adhere to The Hague's voluntary arbitration convention (1899). Mexico and the United States shared a position similar to the Chilean one, but the others were urging them to find a compromise formula that might save the Congress.[40]

American representatives confirmed this when they assured their Chilean counterparts that the United States would not offer to mediate the Tacna–Arica dispute unless both Peruvians and Chileans requested it.[41]

This freed Chileans to deal with Bolivia as they pleased. Successive Bolivian governments had been resisting any peace treaty that would permanently deprive them of sovereign access to the sea, which, in Chileans' view, was unrealistic and needlessly prolonging negotiations. Santiago lost patience with this in August 1900. Chilean Ambassador Abraham König gave the Bolivian foreign minister the cold, hard facts that month.

König reminded Bolivians that the Chilean government was demanding that they cede their whole coast to Chile. Santiago, as a matter of courtesy, would assume La Paz's debts while offering use of ports there, and it would construct a railroad from one or more of these ports into Bolivia, as Chileans deemed necessary, as well. Santiago understood that La Paz considered this territory far more valuable than that which Chileans were paying. König waved all of this aside. Chileans were not negotiating any of these points. "This coast," he continued, "is rich and worth many millions. We already knew this, and we are keeping it because of this. If it were not valuable, no one would be interested in it."[42]

Bolivians, König continued, wrongly assumed that this was a discussion between equal partners when, in fact, they were not any better positioned to make demands than France against Imperial Germany or Spain against the US:

> Chile has occupied the coast and taken possession of it by the same right that Germany annexed Alsace-Lorraine, and by the same right that the United States has taken Puerto Rico. Our rights are born of victory, the supreme law among nations.[43]

Even if Chileans were inclined to grant Bolivians sovereign control of a port, König told them, they did not need it and, further, they could not hope to defend it. If Santiago and La Paz fought another war, "Chilean forces would seize this port with the same ease that they occupied the entire Bolivian coast in 1879. This is no idle boast. As everyone knows, my country's offensive power has increased a hundredfold over the last twenty years." Bolivians, who had just learned that Argentines were not going to intervene in these negotiations, finally signed the treaty that officially terminated the war that October.[44]

Meanwhile, Chileans continued to occupy Tacna and Arica. They knew that the residents there – their sustained public-relations efforts to win them over notwithstanding – continued to self-identify as Peruvians and would vote accordingly in any plebiscite. Further complicating matters, Chileans now regarded this territory as strategically important. "In wartime," Fernández explained, these provinces became "strategic points in the defense of Tarapacá." Consequently, Santiago disregarded the Treaty of Ancón's required plebiscite after the deadline passed in 1894. Peruvians rejected all Chilean offers to purchase the territory, creating an impasse into the 1910s.[45]

A break occurred in the 1920s. President Arturo Alessandri's (1920–4, 1925, and 1932–8) election signaled the end of the parliamentary regime. Alessandri was the son of an Italian immigrant.

He came from outside the entrenched, anti-Balmaceda aristocracy that had ruled the country since the civil war. He did not share these elites' bitter history with Washington. Thus unencumbered, he sought a rapprochement with the United States while requesting American assistance to resolve the Tacna–Arica dispute.

Late nineteenth-century industrialization and globalization made much of this possible. As Fernández appreciated, Alessandri was interested in "a policy based on international law and hemispheric cooperation." The president saw the United States, the emerging inter-American system, and the larger international community's still nascent institutions in a friendly light, and he wished to cultivate close relations with Washington and others abroad.[46]

Chileans discovered that Americans, too, were changing in the 1920s. They had found President Woodrow Wilson's (1913–21) foreign policy too idealistic and utopian for their tastes. President Warren Harding (1921–3) and his Republican successors offered a more practical, businesslike relationship that they could better understand. Spanish-speaking American ambassadors charmed Santiago and further smoothed US–Chilean relations. These ambassadors and their Chilean counterparts indeed started exchanging views in confidence. As Fernández phrased it, "Mutual economic and trade interests did the rest." Thus, US–Chilean relations grew closer in the 1920s. These trends continued to 1970.[47]

This closeness notwithstanding, Americans found that they had little or no influence with respect to Tacna and Arica, which, like United States interventions in Central America and the Caribbean, remained a thorn in the inter-American community's side. The Peruvian and Chilean governments invited Harding to arbitrate the question in January 1922, submitting their respective positions to President Calvin Coolidge (1923–9) the following year. Coolidge ruled that Lima and Santiago should hold the plebiscite that the Treaty of Ancón had prescribed. Now, however, after over forty years of Chilean control, where Chileans had swayed residents' views in their favor, Peruvians feared they would be the ones who lost these provinces. So, it was they who refused to consent to the plebiscite this time.

Coolidge and then the Hoover administration (1929–33) continued proposing solutions, however. Coolidge recommended that both Peru and Chile cede Tacna and Arica to Bolivia. Lima and Santiago flatly rejected this. Then President Herbert Hoover suggested that Tacna go to Peru and Arica to Chile, and that Santiago pay Lima 6 million dollars for the territory. They accepted this the following month. This settlement, combined with the incoming Roosevelt administration's Good Neighbor policy, reduced longstanding tensions in the hemisphere enough to open the way for a functional inter-American system to arise, starting with the multilateral agreements to arbitrate international disputes and to collaborate in hemispheric defense that the inter-American community put into practice during the Second World War (1939–45). This culminated in the birth of the Bretton Woods system and the creation of several new multilateral institutions, including the United Nations (UN) and Organization of American States (OAS) that helped restructure the inter-American, transatlantic, and larger global communities in the late 1940s.[48]

Chileans actively contributed to these outcomes. They defined their own interests and vigorously pursued them within local, national, inter-American, and transatlantic contexts. This did not mean that all Chileans agreed and marched together in the same direction. Many of the outcomes this chapter has described unleashed a wave of political, social, and economic problems that divided Chileans in the late nineteenth and early twentieth centuries. These problems and Chileans' responses to them indeed helped set the stage for Chile's Cold War experience.

Notes

1. For Chilean elites' beliefs, see Alejandro San Francisco, "'La excepción honrosa de paz y estabilidad, de orden y libertad': la autoimagen política de Chile en el siglo XIX." Gabriel Cid and Alejandro San Francisco, eds., *Nación y nacionalismo en Chile*, Vol. 1: *Siglo XIX* (Santiago de Chile: Ediciones Centro de Estudios Bicentenario, 2009), 55–84.
2. Ibid., 63; and Brian Loveman, *The Constitution of Tyranny: Regimes of Exception in Spanish America* (Pittsburgh: University of Pittsburgh Press, 1993), 335.

3. Bernardino Bravo, *De Portales a Pinochet: gobierno y régimen de gobierno en Chile* (Santiago de Chile: Editorial Jurídica de Chile/ Editorial Andrés Bello, 1985), 101–2. Also see Carlos Huneeus, *El régimen de Pinochet* [2001], rev. edn (Santiago de Chile: Penguin Random House Grupo Editorial, 2016), 225–35. On describing the autocratic republic as Portales's achievement, I do understand that thirty-six prominent Chileans, including attorney Mariano Egaña, but not Portales himself, who remained in the background, met throughout 1831 and 1832, ostensibly to revise the decentralized, liberal constitution of 1828, but actually to write a new, centralized and conservative one. Portales's low profile notwithstanding, Chilean historians and politicians have long recognized him as the indispensable man who provided the political philosophy that the delegates put down on paper. For example, Alberto Edwards Vives and Eduardo Frei Montalva, *Historia de los partidos políticos chilenos* (Santiago de Chile: Editorial del Pacífico, 1949), 32.

4. Robert Burr, *By Reason or Force: Chile and the Balancing of Power in South America, 1830–1905* [1965] (Berkeley and Los Angeles: University of California Press, 1974), 40.

5. Ibid., 55. For more on what Chileans call their second war of independence, see San Francisco, "La excepción honrosa"; Harold Eugene Davis, John Finan, and F. Taylor Peck, *Latin American Diplomatic History* (Baton Rouge: Louisiana State University Press, 1977), 91–2; and Frederick Nunn, *The Military in Chilean History: Essays on Civil–Military Relations, 1810–1973* (Albuquerque: University of New Mexico Press, 1976), 46–8.

6. Biblioteca Nacional de Chile, "Trabajadores y empresarios en la industria del carbón: Lota y Coronel (1854–1995)," at <http:// www.memoriachilena.cl>; Simon Collier and William Sater, *A History of Chile, 1808–2002* [1996], 2nd edn (Cambridge: Cambridge University Press, 2004), 73–103; Brian Loveman, *Chile: The Legacy of Hispanic Capitalism* [1979], 3rd edn (New York: Oxford University Press, 2001), 119–44; and Burr, *By Reason or Force*, 107–16.

7. Burr, *By Reason or Force*, 72.

8. Marta Cruz-Coke Madrid, *Eduardo Cruz-Coke: testimonios* (Santiago de Chile: Fundación Procultura, 2015), 291.

9. Andrés Bello, "An American Congress," *El Araucano*, November 1844. Robert Burr and Roland Hussey, eds., *Documents on Inter-American Cooperation* I: *1810–1881* (Philadelphia: University of Philadelphia Press, 1955), 85. Also see Vicente Pérez Rosales, *Times*

Gone By: Memoirs of a Man of Action, trans. John Polt (New York: Oxford University Press, 2003), xvii–xxxii, 295–396.

10. Vicente Pérez Rosales, *Ensayo sobre Chile* [1857] (Santiago de Chile: Ediciones de la Universidad de Chile, 1986), 47.

11. Loveman, *Chile*, 135.

12. Burr, *By Reason or Force*, 131–2.

13. "Tratado de límites entre Chile y Bolivia," 10 August 1866. A. Bascuñan Montes, *Recopilación de tratados y convenciones celebrados entre la República de Chile y las potencias extranjeras, edición autorizada por el supremo gobierno y revisada por el Ministerio de Relaciones Exteriores* II: *1863–1893* (Santiago de Chile: Imprenta Cervantes, 1894), 22–8. Also see Jorge Basadre, *Chile, Perú y Bolivia independientes* (Barcelona and Buenos Aires: Salvat Editores, 1948), 454.

14. Biblioteca Nacional de Chile, "Mineral de Caracoles," at <http://www.memoriachilena.cl>; Collier and Sater, *History of Chile*, 77.

15. "Tratado de límites entre Chile y Bolivia," 6 August 1874. Bascuñan, *Recopilación de tratados y convenciones* II, 101–7. Also see Basadre, *Chile, Perú y Bolivia independientes*, 457–58.

16. Juan José Fernández Valdés, *Chile y Perú: historia de sus relaciones diplomáticas entre 1879–1929* (Santiago de Chile: RIL Editores: Asociación de Funcionarios Diplomáticos de Carrera del Ministerio de Relaciones Exteriores, 2004), 22; Burr, *By Reason or Force*, 124; and Basadre, *Chile, Perú y Bolivia independientes*, 455–6.

17. Chileans tend to blame Bolivia's treaty violations, and Peru and Bolivia's secret pact when explaining the war's causes and origins; Peruvians and Bolivians cite Chilean expansion into their territories. See Fernández, *Chile y Perú*, 17–30; Collier and Sater, *History of Chile*, 125–31; Burr, *By Reason or Force*, 117–39; and Basadre, *Chile, Perú y Bolivia independientes*, 458. For the military course of the war from American, Chilean, and Peruvian perspectives, see Carlos Donoso and Gonzalo Serrano, eds., *Chile y la Guerra del Pacífico* (Santiago de Chile: Ediciones Centro de Estudios Bicentenario, 2011); William Sater, *Andean Tragedy: Fighting the War of the Pacific, 1879–1884* (Lincoln: University of Nebraska Press, 2007); and Basadre, *Chile, Perú y Bolivia independientes*, 458–98.

18. Fernández, *Chile y Perú*, 41–5; and Burr, *By Reason or Force*, 152–3.

19. "Tratado de límites chileno-argentino," 23 July 1881. Bascuñan, *Recopilación de tratados y convenciones* II, 120–5. Also see Burr, *By Reason or Force*, 124–35. This fell apart in the Beagle Channel in the

late 1970s and contributed to the Pinochet dictatorship's support for the British naval task force against Argentina during the Falklands War in 1982. Consult Daniel Upp, "Risky Invasions: Decisions Made by the Argentine Junta Regarding Disputed Islands, 1978–1982" (Monterrey: Naval Postgraduate School, unpublished master's thesis, 2011); Lawrence Freedman, *The Official History of the Falklands Campaign* II: *War and Diplomacy* [2005], rev. edn (London: Routledge, 2007); and Max Hastings and Simon Jenkins, *The Battle for the Falklands* (New York: W.W. Norton, 1983).

20. "Chile-Peru tratado de amistad," 20 October 1883. Bascuñan, *Recopilación de tratados y convenciones* II, 158–66. Also see Basadre, *Chile, Perú y Bolivia independientes*, 497–8.

21. Simón Bolívar, "Invitation to the Governments of Colombia, Mexico, Río de la Plata, Chile, and Guatemala to Hold a Congress in Panama [7 December 1824]." David Bushnell, ed., Frederick Fornoff, trans., *El Libertador: Writings of Simón Bolívar* (New York: Oxford University Press, 2003), 159. For the Panama conference, see Joseph Byrne Lockey, *Pan-Americanism: Its Beginnings* (New York: Macmillan, 1920).

22. Bello, "American Congress," 87.

23. Congress of Lima, "Treaty of Defensive Alliance and Union among Bolivia, Chile, Colombia, Ecuador, Peru, El Salvador, Venezuela," 23 January 1865. Burr and Hussey, *Documents on Inter-American Cooperation* I, 159–61. Also see Davis et al., *Latin American Diplomatic History*, 121–4; and Burr, *By Reason or Force*, 90–6.

24. Colombian Secretary of Foreign Relations Eustancio Santa María to Governments of Spanish America, 11 October 1880. Burr and Hussey, *Documents on Inter-American Cooperation* I, 168–70; and Bello, "American Congress," 87.

25. James Blaine to Diplomatic Representatives of the United States in the Capitals of Latin America, 29 November 1881. James Scott, ed., *The International Conferences of American States, 1889–1928* (New York: Oxford University Press, 1931), 447–8. Also see Davis et al., *Latin American Diplomatic History*, 166–72.

26. Frederick Frelinghuysen to Diplomatic Representatives of the United States in the Capitals of Latin America, 9 August 1882. Scott, *International Conferences of American States, 1889–1928*, 449. Frelinghuysen to Cornelius Logan, 30 July 1883. Department of State, *Papers Relating to the Foreign Relations of the United States, transmitted to Congress, with the annual message*

of the President, 4 December 1883 (Washington, DC: Government Printing Office, 1884), 118. Americans continued moving in other directions, however. For example, for the influence of European naval power and the War of the Pacific on the US Navy's modernization programs, particularly the creation of the Office of Naval Intelligence, see Jeffery Dorwat, *The Office of Naval Intelligence: The Birth of America's First Intelligence Agency, 1865–1918* (Annapolis: Naval Institute Press, 1979), 9–11.

27. Fernández, *Chile y Perú*, 51–112; and Frederick Pike, *Chile and the United States, 1880–1962: The Emergence of Chile's Social Crisis and the Challenge to United States Diplomacy* (Notre Dame: University of Notre Dame Press, 1963), 47–62.

28. For reports of the civil war's outbreak, see Patrick Egan to Blaine, 12 January 1891; Egan to Blaine, 12 January 1891; and Egan to Blaine, 17 January 1891. Department of State, *The executive documents of the House of Representatives for the first session of the fifty-second Congress, 1891–1892* (Washington, DC: Government Printing Office, 1892), 91–3. See Balmaceda's explanation, attached to Egan to Blaine, 19 January 1891. Ibid., 94–104. For the two Chilean factions' correspondence with the Department of State, see ibid., 313–24.

29. Egan to Blaine, 12 January 1891.

30. For Balmaceda's suicide, see Egan to Blaine, 21 September 1891, with Balmaceda's note enclosed. Department of State, *Executive documents for fifty-second Congress, 1891–1892*, 165–6. Leading historians of this conflict have tended to concur with Egan's assessment that it represented an executive–legislative power struggle while Marxists interpret it as an expression of imperialism. See Alejandro San Francisco, ed., *La guerra civil de 1891*, 2 vols. (Santiago de Chile: Ediciones Centro de Estudios Bicentenario, 2016); Harold Blakemore, *British Nitrates and Chilean Politics, 1886–1896: Balmaceda and North* (London: Athlone Press for the Institute of Latin American Studies, 1974); Harold Blakemore, "The Chilean Revolution of 1891 and Its Historiography," *Hispanic American Historical Review* 45 (1965): 393–421; and Hernán Ramírez Necochea, *Balmaceda y la contrarrevolución de 1891* (Santiago de Chile: Editorial Universitaria, 1958).

31. For example, Egan to Blaine, 7 September 1891; Egan to Blaine, 24 September 1891; Egan to Blaine, 29 September 1891; Egan to Blaine, 30 September 1891. Department of State, *Executive documents for fifty-second Congress, 1891–1892*, 161–2, 166, 168–71.

32. Egan to Blaine, 18 October 1891; Egan to Blaine, 19 October 1891, which includes the *Baltimore*'s commanding officer's protests to Chilean authorities; and William McCreery to Blaine, 8 November 1891. Ibid., 194–5, 220–1.

33. William Wharton to Egan, 23 October 1891. Ibid., 196–7. See the *Baltimore*'s reports and Egan and the *junta*'s foreign minister's exchange enclosed in Egan to Blaine, 28 October 1891. Ibid., 204–10. See Manuel Antonio Matta's response in Egan to Blaine, 3 November 1891. Ibid., 211–17. Also see Matta to Ambassador Pedro Montt, 11 December 1891, read into the Chilean Senate's record, published in Chilean newspapers, and distributed to the American press in Washington the following day, enclosed in Egan to Blaine, 12 December 1891. Ibid., 267–9.

34. Egan to Blaine, 12 January 1892. Ibid., 285.

35. Blaine to Egan, 21 January 1892. Ibid., 307–8.

36. See Egan to Blaine, 25 January 1892, with Pereira's apology enclosed. Ibid., 309–12; and see Blaine's correspondence with the Chilean ambassador in Washington on this subject. Ibid., 347–52. Also see Collier and Sater, *History of Chile*, 186–7; and Pike, *Chile and the United States*, 73–85.

37. Burr, *By Reason or Force*, 197–8.

38. Davis et al., *Latin American Diplomatic History*, 185; and Pike, *Chile and the United States*, 126.

39. See Washington and Mexico City's plans of arbitration, which some delegates signed, but no governments ratified. First International Conference of American States, "Plan of Arbitration," 24 April 1890. Scott, *International Conferences of American States, 1889–1928*, 40–4; and Second International Conference of American States, "Treaty on Compulsory Arbitration," 29 January 1902. Ibid., 100–4.

40. Fernández, *Chile y Perú*, 266–7.

41. Burr, *By Reason or Force*, 240–4. For background on the conference at The Hague, see Elizabeth Cobbs Hoffman, *American Umpire* (Cambridge, MA: Harvard University Press, 2013), 185–91. For a discussion of the larger trends this supported in the international community, see Daniel Gorman, *International Cooperation in the Early Twentieth Century* (London: Bloomsbury, 2017).

42. Abraham König to His Excellency the Minister of Foreign Relations of Bolivia Eliodoro Villazón, 13 August 1900. Abraham König, *Memorias íntimas, políticas y diplomáticas de Don Abraham König* (Santiago de Chile: Imprenta Cervantes, 1927), 83.

43. Ibid.

44. Ibid., 82; "Tratado de paz, Amistad y comercio celebrado entre Chile y Bolivia," 20 October 1904. Bernardino Toro C., *Recopilación de tratados, convenciones, protocolos y otros actos internacionales celebrados por la República de Chile* IV: *1902–1911*, Edición oficial (Santiago de Chile: Sociedad Imprenta y Litografía Universo, 1913), 147–67; and Basadre, *Chile, Perú y Bolivia independientes*, 600–2.
45. Fernández, *Chile y Perú*, 94.
46. Ibid., 355.
47. Ibid., 358.
48. On the negotiations leading to the Tacna–Arica settlement, see ibid., 355–616; Davis et al., *Latin American Diplomatic History*, 184–90; and Department of State, Bureau of Intelligence and Research, Office of the Geographer, "International Boundary Study No. 65: Chile–Peru Boundary," 28 February 1966, at <http://www.law.fsu.edu>.

2   Chilean Anticommunism

As historian Odd Arne Westad has argued, the Cold War "was born from global transformations of the late nineteenth century." Different responses to these transformations – including the appearance of communist theorist Karl Marx and politically organized labor movements in Europe and elsewhere – remained responsible for the emergence of communists, anticommunists, and the noncommunist left in Chile. These groups fought the struggles that followed in the twentieth century.[1]

Communists never represented more than a minority. But they were a determined minority. Their uncompromising application of Marxism and their tendency to seize the initiative in the pursuit of overthrowing governments and systems conferred onto them a disproportionate influence that tended to shock established institutions and leaders everywhere. This led to a series of escalating actions and reactions, beginning in Europe and then spreading into the Atlantic world – through transatlantic and inter-American communications, trade, and immigration networks – to areas like southern South America.

In Chile, the working class, especially miners; the Chilean Communist Party (PCCh); the conservative establishment, or landowners and industrialists who controlled Congress; and the professional officer corps all combined to create a set of conflicts that raged from about the 1890s until Chileans found some stability in the aftermath of the Great Depression in the mid-1930s. By the end of this approximately forty-year period, an anticommunist movement had risen. Local, national, inter-American, and transatlantic trends and events had shaped and conditioned it. Although it appeared within the same global context as other articulations of anticommunism, such as those that occurred in the United States, it tended to express itself more forcefully and violently. This became clear as differences in the American and Chilean governments' perceptions emerged with respect to the Soviet Union (USSR) and the threat it seemed to pose in Latin America.

The Chilean Communist Party

Chile's conservative establishment derived much profit from the War of the Pacific (1879–83). This and Congress's victory over President José Manuel Balmaceda (1886–91) in the civil war of 1891, the revised interpretation of Chile's political system that legislators imposed afterward, and the accelerating pace of industrialization and globalization created a working class in Chile by the 1890s. This, in turn, prepared the ground for the appearance of politically organized labor and the PCCh.

Much of this started in the northern mining communities. Chilean and British investors jointly exploited the nitrate fields in the Atacama, creating what became an export enclave there. The Chilean government had inherited state control of Peru's nitrate works after Lima nationalized them and then Santiago seized them in that condition. Public ownership, however, remained anathema to conservative Chileans' *laissez-faire* business philosophy at the time. Two legislative committees studied the issue before Congress privatized the mines in 1881. Both Chilean and British investors quickly bought them. Chilean presidents remained content to tax them thereafter. This was just as President Domingo Santa María (1881–6) and his successors wanted it: "Let the gringos work the nitrate freely," Santa María said. "I shall be waiting for them at the door."[2]

These same attitudes accounted for increasing foreign investment in Chilean copper. Chilean mine owners had exhausted the copper deposits most accessible to unskilled human labor by the 1880s. Since they lacked the expertise and equipment to dig deeper, copper production declined over the next twenty years. Then entrepreneur William Braden, founder of the Braden Copper Company, improved these mines. Braden introduced the capital,

44

technology, and managerial know-how that enabled Chilean copper to prosper under private, American ownership well into the twentieth century.[3]

The Chilean government's income derived mostly from these mines. This revenue, which had not existed before the War of the Pacific, contributed to the civil war, where the two sides partly fought over how to spend this money. Balmaceda favored investment in infrastructure and public employment, including military and naval modernization, while Congress preferred small government and a strictly free-market approach to the economy.

Congress won the war and the argument. Its members, primarily landowners, dominated national politics during the so-called parliamentary era into the 1920s. They jealously controlled the government's budget and constantly removed cabinet members via interpellation, a procedure they learned from parliamentary politics in Europe. But they merely created "a shallow, grossly inefficient copy of the British parliamentary system," according to historian Frederick Nunn and other informed observers.[4]

Indeed, Senator Eduardo Frei characterized this period's politicians as "*inútiles*," or useless, in a history he coauthored in 1949. He blamed them for miring themselves in trivial debates that revolved around parliamentary procedure while mindlessly combating the executive branch and generally wasting their time. They accomplished little else.[5]

Parliamentary-era politicians constantly maneuvered for position in a fluid environment of rapidly shifting alliances and coalitions, backroom deals in the *Club de la Unión*, and rampant vote buying during elections. They ignored the social and economic conflicts that were engulfing the country. As President Ramón Barros Luco (1910–15), perhaps best known for the sandwich that still bears his name, phrased it, "There are two kinds of problems: those that solve themselves, and those that have no solution."[6]

Consequently, presidents and their cabinets remained immobilized. They could not have engaged Chile's worsening socioeconomic problems even if they had been inclined to do so. For example, by historian Frederick Pike's count, approximately 120 ministers of interior alone came and went during this period.[7]

Outside of Congress, Chilean landowners remained focused on their quest to become European-style aristocrats. They spent vast sums on luxury imports, including all the latest fashions from Paris, which they wore to the theater, to the races at *Club Hípico*, and to see and be seen while strolling down the *Alameda* in Santiago. They led charmed lives.

Meanwhile, increasing numbers of Chilean laborers worked the nitrate and copper mines in the north. The introduction of coal mining in the south brought them to Coronel and Lota as well. Chileans also built ports and laid train tracks. Chilean cities, from Iquique to Valparaíso and Concepción, boomed. This required constant infusions of labor to construct and service buildings, horse-drawn trolleys, and streets with electric lighting.[8]

Chileans did not import immigrant laborers from Europe or East Asia, as Americans did. They recruited peasants and Indians from their own central valley and southern regions. These workers found insecure, low-wage employment in the mines. Wealthy and middle-class Chileans employed some of these peasants and Indians in the informal domestic-services sector, mostly as housecleaners and babysitters in the cities. The rest, the majority, remained tied to *haciendas* as *inquilinos*, or tenants. Others, called *rotos*, drifted from *hacienda* to *hacienda* for seasonal work. They led less than charmed lives.

Nitrate miners served an unstable export market that often left them laid off or worse. They lived in poor, unsanitary housing, had no insurance or retirement benefits, and remained subject to company scrip, company stores, and company bars. Their earliest leaders demanded nothing more ambitious than that management might cover the open pits that processed caliche ores. Some had fallen into these scalding pits and burned to death. Those who survived were so badly disfigured that they would never work again or even leave the area. They struggled for subsistence, often resorting to begging in Iquique and other mining areas in what remained of their lives.[9]

Chile's labor movement emerged within and spread out from these nitrate mines. It started as a collection of loosely networked mutual-aid groups from Iquique to Punta Arenas. Workers, although initially responding to the immediate conditions they faced in Chile, soon came into contact with the Marxist, socialist, and anarchist literature that had been arriving from Europe since the 1850s. PCCh historian Hernán Ramírez listed Marx, Henri de Saint-Simon, and Pierre-Joseph Proudhon among the many authors whose works were popular in Chilean bookstores in the mid- to late nineteenth century. This literature helped the labor movement's leaders develop their worldviews and vocabulary, which they passed down to workers.[10]

Immigrants with Marxist politics crossed the Atlantic to Chile as well. In Ramírez's estimation, "many . . . had been militants in workers' organizations and adhered to socialist doctrines. So, for example, some 300 French nationals arrived in Punta Arenas in the 1870s. They had been exiled from their country for their participation in the Paris Commune." Chilean authorities distributed these immigrants throughout the nation. Thus, partly from transatlantic communication, trade, and immigration, the Chilean labor movement found its voice and matured within the still nascent international labor movement. Some Chilean workers came to believe that their problems derived from an oppressive political-economic system that was affecting the entire world, and not merely from their own, local troubles.[11]

Chile's labor movement doubled at the turn of the century. According to Ramírez, the working class increased from approximately 150,000 in 1890 to 300,000 in 1910. It also became more confrontational. Political scientist Brian Loveman counted ten strikes involving nearly 5,000 laborers in 1911. This rose to 105 shutdowns with some 50,000 workers by 1920.[12]

Marxist calls to action appeared in the labor-friendly press as well, as early as the 1890s. For example, a La Serena paper announced,

Chilean workers! Today is the day that the naked, hungry people energetically protest against the existing order, against bourgeois society . . . This cry of protest launched by those of the oppressed who work and have nothing is universal. It recognizes neither borders nor races, and wherever the exploited and exploiters, victims and their cruel oppressors, are found, the formidable struggle for economic equality against tyranny, the struggle for social liberty against the luxurious lives of the nobility, the struggle for brotherhood and the sovereignty of the people against the selfishness of the privileged classes, will be found. We do not want to be beasts of burden whipped by the overseer's lash ... Let our brothers in Europe and the Americas know that here, too ... we stand ready to defend our sovereignty and our natural rights. Let the exploited and oppressed stand up! Let all the hungry victims stand up![13]

Proclamations like these led to swift and violent reaction. Perhaps the worst case occurred in Iquique, in December 1907. Miners and sympathetic laborers had begun gathering there that January, protesting the hardships they were experiencing as the government's inflationary policies led to rising prices and a falling peso, a common practice that would plague the Chilean economy well into the twentieth century. They demanded pay raises to keep up with it, the introduction of new services that would compete with company stores inside their towns and camps, and iron bars to cover the pits. About 1,000 started marching in what coalesced into a larger strike. They pledged to maintain the walkout until employers met their demands.

Somewhere between 15,000 and 23,000 strikers had arrived in Iquique, when Minister of Interior Rafael Sotomayor declared a state of emergency, dispatched warships to the port, and ordered workers to leave the city. Some complied. Others defied the order and sought refuge with their families in a schoolhouse. Gen. Roberto Silva Renard's soldiers pinned them down and fired upon them, killing approximately 200 and wounding some 300. Ninety of these died from their wounds later.[14]

The PCCh's founders emerged within this combative environment. They filled a vacuum in an increasingly diverse political spectrum. Conservatives represented Chileans' centralized, authoritarian tendencies as manifested in the constitution of 1833. Liberals wanted to decentralize and reform this constitution to create a more secular order. These two parties, representing the conservative establishment, remained socially and economically indistinct apart from these mostly Church-related issues. For example, they were both *laissez-faire* with respect to the economy. The Radical Party, representing the rising middle class and more pronounced anticlerical interests, had broken away from Liberals in the 1860s. The Democratic Party represented the interests of artisans and skilled workers. Its members had splintered from Radicals in 1887.

One of these Democrats, Luis Emilio Recabarren, led a small, dissatisfied faction that joined the Second International, which advocated politics in line with European socialism and reform, in 1908. Recabarren convened a meeting of approximately twenty miners and shoemakers in Iquique on 6 June 1912. He asked them to break from the Democratic Party because it did not advocate the kind of change he believed necessary. Recabarren proposed they create the Socialist Workers' Party (POS), which would unify and educate laborers under one banner while working within the system to improve their lives, particularly their working conditions. This motion passed fifteen to five, and several sections arose from the Atacama to the Magellan Straits.[15]

Recabarren was an indefatigable internationalist. He created the first Chilean labor federation (FOCH) in 1916. Then he helped to organize what became the Argentine Communist Party.

Recabarren and his associates paid close attention to the First World War (1914–18) and the Russian Revolution (1917), where Vladimir Lenin's Bolsheviks seized power in what became the Soviet Union. When the Bolsheviks formed the Communist International (the Comintern) "to unite the efforts of all truly revolutionary parties of the world's proletariat, thus facilitating and hastening the victory of the communistic revolution throughout the world," around a year and a half later, in March 1919, Recabarren proposed that the POS join it. The party's leaders assembled in Valparaíso the following year, where they transformed the POS into "an authentic communist party, integrated in the international communist movement." They changed the POS's name to the PCCh, submitted to Moscow's twenty-one requirements for membership, and purged so-called counterrevolutionaries – that is, socialists, anarchists, and anyone whose political sympathies remained closer to the Second International than the Comintern – from its ranks.[16]

The PCCh's leadership forwarded these resolutions to its various sections for debate in 1921. These sections followed the reasoning that appeared in one Antofagasta paper that March: "There is no middle ground . . . There are only two paths to follow: Either we go with our Russian brothers and social revolution or not . . . Those who go against the Russian proletariat necessarily stand with capitalist society and with our oppressors." The party reconvened for its first congress in Rancagua in January 1922. There, it proclaimed that it "constitutes the Chilean Section of the Communist International, accepts its thesis and fights for its cause, the cause of the proletariat."[17]

Also that month, M. A. Komin-Alexandrovski, the Comintern's representative in Buenos Aires, reported favorably on the PCCh and its counterparts in Brazil, Uruguay, and Argentina. "In reality," he urged Moscow, "these South American republics are nothing more than British and American colonies. We must give them serious attention." As Soviet foreign service officer Yuri Pavlov elaborated later,

> it was Lenin's idea that what was later to be called Third World countries should be and will be the reservoir of revolutionary activities and support for the proletarians of Russia and other countries in Europe . . . he was thinking in terms of the millions and millions of masses and colonialist and semi-colonial countries . . . Latin America in that sense was termed as a semi-colonial area under the domination of the US, would join in the struggle against imperialism. So that was the general direction of the policy and the Comintern, acting for the local communist parties, was trying to foster revolutionary movements in Latin America.[18]

Recabarren traveled to the USSR in December 1922. He reported on Chilean conditions and the PCCh's organization and strength. He requested Soviet financial aid several months later. Moscow was interested in Latin America, but it could not send any money to Chilean Communists because it was concentrating its resources in Germany. For the moment, the Comintern advised Recabarren to develop relationships with other communists in the region and it trained him in subversion and tradecraft.[19]

The Soviet Union announced its strategy for Latin America in 1924. Ideally, this strategy would throw established governments and institutions on the defensive throughout the region while uniting workers and peasants behind the Comintern:

In those Latin American countries where sections of our party exist, these sections' oral and written propaganda should demonstrate the advance of imperialism . . . The Argentine, Uruguayan, and Chilean parties should denounce all manifestations of imperialism in neighboring countries such as Bolivia, Peru, Paraguay, and even Ecuador and Colombia, to influence worker and peasant opinion there.[20]

Moscow created the Comintern's South American Bureau, headquartered in Buenos Aires, to better coordinate this, in February 1925.[21]

PCCh leaders zealously followed this line over the next several decades. The party advanced it in its analyses, propaganda, and slogans with such stridency and so often that the Soviet Politburo and the PCCh's leadership became virtually indistinguishable to Chilean anticommunists and noncommunists. This was a voluntary friendship. Their views naturally coincided. The USSR was not pulling Chilean Communists' strings. Rather, Chilean Communists, down to the grassroots level, tended to adore and submit to the Soviet Union – "the older sister of Recabarren's people," as one wrote in *El Siglo*, the party's newspaper – of their own free will.[22]

Moscow regarded the PCCh very favorably in turn, as a trusted "brother party," forming what historian Olga Ulianova characterized as "a privileged relationship." Indeed, Soviets frequently invited Chilean Communists to attend important events in the USSR, and Politburo members and other ranking Soviets often traveled to Chile to attend significant PCCh meetings as well. As historian María Soledad Gómez reconfirmed, this rapport accounted for the party's changing structure and evolving strategies and tactics, both internationally and nationally, thereafter.[23]

The Professional Officer Corps

Meanwhile, back in the late nineteenth century, the Santa María and Balmaceda administrations invested in military modernization. This created a new class of professional army officers with its own sense of identity and mission. These officers perceived their institution as representing the nation's highest interests while operating at a level above politics and partisanship. Their antipolitics was not so neutral, however. They became explicitly anticommunist by the 1920s.[24]

Santa María contracted Capt. Emil Körner to command a Prussian military mission in Chile in the mid-1880s. Körner's group established the *Academia de Guerra*, the Chilean army's War College, in September 1886. The War College offered a two- to three-year postgraduate course that trained select, early-career officers in military professionalism. These courses included seminars in European military history; geography; war games, strategies, and tactics; weapons and ballistics; fortifications; and physics and inorganic chemistry. Cavalry and infantry officers learned Western history and German while engineers and artillerymen studied advanced mathematics. Those who remained for a third year specialized in Chilean military history, with attention to the country's ongoing territorial disputes and an introduction to command and staff planning based on these problems. They also completed some coursework in diplomacy and international law.[25]

As historian Enrique Brahm García has explained, no other foreign influence would imprint the Chilean army as profoundly as this Prussian mission did. Körner deeply transformed Chile's professional officer corps well beyond the technical training, uniforms, and arms his group offered. He fostered an esprit de corps that taught Chilean officers to see themselves as their fatherland's last line of defense, the ultimate guardians of national security, not only against foreign threats, but against domestic ones as well, including civilian politicians, whom they viewed as inevitably corrupt. While Peruvians, Argentines, and Brazilians contracted European military missions, too, "Nowhere," in Loveman's estimation, "did European military missions more thoroughly penetrate a Latin American army than Chile, and nowhere did a supposedly apolitical professional army become more imbued with doctrine that made its officers contemptuous of civilian politics and politicians."[26]

These officers became the parliamentary regime's strikebreakers. This immersed them in national politics, exposing them to organized labor and the so-called social question. They began deliberating this question's various problems by the early 1920s. They did this because the regime had alienated them over the previous two decades and they lost confidence in their civilian leaders. Politicians' paralysis and pettiness, and the nation's instability – which many officers feared was empowering Bolshevism within their country – worsened this and contributed a sense of urgency.[27]

President Arturo Alessandri (1920–4, 1925, and 1932–8), "the Lion of Tarapacá," challenged the parliamentary regime and won the presidency in this environment. He promised to strengthen the executive branch while passing labor legislation and other badly needed reforms. He came from outside the establishment and approached politics through direct appeals to the masses. He commanded large-scale popular demonstrations and, through them, had the old regime on the run.[28]

But he encountered an obstructionist, business-as-usual Congress after his inauguration. Even senators and deputies from his own coalition failed to back him. Some even opposed him. As Collier and Sater explained, "The euphoria of 1920 gradually shifted into a mood of disappointment and frustration. The Parliamentary Republic had not, after all, been broken. Who would cut the Gordian knot?"[29]

Junior and field-grade army officers fingered their swords as the instrument to cut this knot. Approximately twenty to fifty of them attended Senate hearings on congressional salaries one day in September 1924. They were exasperated by Congress's ignoring the nation's problems and the armed forces' material needs while its members so nonchalantly granted themselves pay raises. These officers' presence represented its own message. They made a show of applauding those lawmakers who spoke against the salary bill for those who had not received that message.

Senators were outraged and demanded that the minister of war instruct these officers to leave when they reappeared the next day. The minister ran into defiance. They refused to go. He ordered a captain to record names, and the captain retorted that he was not a stenographer. The minister fell back on persuasion, the officers finally agreeing to retire to the *Club Militar*. They rattled their sabers on the way out.[30]

When the army's high command, which consisted of an older, pre-War College generation that remained connected to landowners and the rest of the establishment through kinship ties, declined to discipline the younger officers lest it lose control of them, it only emboldened the latter, who continued pressing forward. These younger officers formed the *Junta Militar y Naval* – the Army–Navy Committee – and rallied around Maj. Carlos Ibáñez del Campo, a cavalryman who emerged as their spokesman on Friday, 5 September. Ibáñez demanded that Congress reject the salary proposal, enact the labor code that Alessandri had been putting forward, pass an income-tax law, and improve army pay and conditions. The president received the major in *la Moneda*, the presidential palace, and forwarded the *junta*'s demands to Congress the same day. Lawmakers submitted within hours.[31]

Ibáñez followed this up by instructing Alessandri to dismiss the minister of war and two other cabinet ministers. The president declined, ordering the major to disband the *junta*. Ibáñez refused, creating a constitutional crisis. The three ministers resigned on their own to save the president further embarrassment. But the *junta* remained committed to the course it had chosen even after this, its members being in no mood to suffer what they perceived as civilian cronyism and ineptitude anymore. One officer's backhanded compliment of a cabinet officer illustrates their state of mind:

> Even though you, at this time and place, represent for us the most disgusting element in our country – politicians – that is, all that is corrupt, the dismal factional disputes, depravities and immoralities, in other words, the causes of our national degeneration, we recognize that you, despite the fact that you must defend sinecures, hand out public posts, and support avaricious ambitions, that you are one of the few honest politicians.[32]

Alessandri attempted to resolve this by dissolving Congress. Fearing that he and his family were in personal danger, he sought asylum with them in the American embassy in the middle of the night between Tuesday and Wednesday, 8–9 September 1924. He explained that he was moving to Rome, into exile.

Ambassador William Collier, who, at Alessandri's request, accompanied the president as far as Mendoza, reported that he had offered his resignation twice before the *junta* granted him six months' leave. Alessandri resigned a third time from Argentina, explaining to Collier that "he believes it to be inconsistent with his self-respect and dignity to remain in office when he is not permitted by the military junta to perform the duties of his office." Then he told the press that "there is no constitutional government in Chile." Two days later, on Friday, 11 September, a military government composed of Gen. Luis Altamirano, Gen. Juan Bennett, and Adm. Francisco Nef accepted his resignation and assumed power.[33]

Ibáñez's movement deposed Altamirano's military government, who, to its dismay, was simply continuing the parliamentary regime's politics, four months later. Its leaders deployed two regiments to seize and occupy *la Moneda*, declaring that they had wished to stimulate reform, not reaction. As Collier related to Washington, they detained Altamirano, Bennett, Nef, and some civilian members of the cabinet for several hours, "while young Army officer with loaded revolver walked up and down the room holding them virtual prisoners and lecturing them as to the purpose of military movement and as to its having been betrayed by late junta and its ministry."[34]

The Ibáñez Dictatorship

Ibáñez, now a lieutenant colonel and the minister of war, and the armed services' senior officers agreed to form a military cabinet days after the coup, in January 1925. This new cabinet acknowledged that Alessandri remained president by law, invited him to return to Chile, and then started drafting a new constitution. They acted purposefully, believing that time was running out. As Collier reported, "Country is seething with social unrest."[35]

The cabinet's constitutional committee completed its work and Chileans approved the new political system that August. It became effective the following month, in September. Chileans subsequently elected a new Congress. This constitution strengthened the presidency, separated Church and state, and created the multiparty, democratic system that governed Chile until 1973. Ibáñez remained in the cabinet. He would stay there until Chile's new political system functioned as intended. This renewed the tension in what became a bitter power struggle between Alessandri and Ibáñez – and it led to the president's resigning yet again in October 1925.

Emiliano Figeroa Larrain (1925–7) became president that month. Both he and Congress soon returned to parliamentary-era habits, much to Ibáñez's frustration. Ibáñez was promoted to full colonel as he assumed the office of minister of interior in February 1927. He removed judges and replaced them with those committed to the new order without consulting an increasingly powerless Figeroa, who soon resigned. This left Ibáñez as acting president. He called an election, won it, and thus formalized his term of office that May. So began the Ibáñez dictatorship (1927–31).[36]

President and Gen. Ibáñez purged Chilean politics over the next four years. Much fell within his sights, including most professional politicians. But he gave special attention to the Soviet Union and the PCCh, which he had signaled he would do as minister of interior months before:

> The times through which the Country now passes are not the times for words but for immediate and energetic action.
>
> The final hour – the hour for settling accounts – has arrived. The malevolent propaganda of a few professional politicians and the disunifying propaganda of an audacious few who oppose all authority is not acceptable. It is necessary to apply cauterization from top to bottom . . .
>
> I am certain that the overwhelming majority of citizens only wish peace and work. This majority cannot be trampled under foot by the actions of a minority which represents no positive values, and which, through its written and spoken word, is undermining our institutions and destroying the virtues of the race. We have reached deplorable extremes: a Chamber of Deputies that pays homage to the Communists who trample under foot the right to work and who incite the workers to the subversion of public order . . . The moment has come to break forcefully the red ties of Moscow.[37]

Ibáñez outlawed the PCCh and started persecuting Communists immediately. He relegated eighty-nine of them to an internment camp in Más Afuera. They remained defiant. Their first act upon arriving on this remote South Pacific island was to form the party's Más Afuera section. Others fled the country. Some were murdered.[38]

Like Ibáñez, the PCCh's surviving leadership interpreted these events within a larger, international framework. Thus, Chilean Communists borrowed some vocabulary from Italian politics when characterizing the general's "national-fascist government" as "an agent of Yankee imperialism." The president nearly destroyed the party over the next several years.[39]

Ibáñez directed an activist government with respect to the economy. He invested nearly 1 billion pesos in Chile's infrastructure. His was the first of several Chilean administrations to attempt to stimulate industrial development, particularly manufacturing. He also created the Chilean air force, transformed the *Carabinero* Regiment into the *Carabineros de Chile*, and enacted Chile's labor code, among many other accomplishments. This required constant spending, and Ibáñez borrowed heavily from foreign banks – primarily American, British, and Swiss – to pay for it. The Chilean government owed 62 million pounds to these banks by 1930.

Ibáñez relied on nitrate and other export revenues to maintain his government's relatively high credit rating while servicing the foreign debt. But Chilean nitrate production had slowed since the First World War, when German chemists created synthetic nitrates to compensate for their inability to import these and other Chilean products through Britain's blockade. The Great Depression destroyed what remained. Chilean nitrate production never recovered from these two blows. As nitrate exports collapsed, and as foreign loans fell from 682 million dollars in 1930 to 22 million dollars in 1932, the Ibáñez dictatorship came to an end.[40]

Ibáñez could neither maintain spending nor service the debt by 1930. So, he cut spending, suspended repayments, and raised taxes on imports – which made money scarce while raising prices – to compensate. This austerity program led to the dictator's laying off large numbers of public employees and reducing the salaries of those who remained in government service. This failed to halt the depression's calamitous effects. Massive public disapproval, including a wave of strikes against Ibáñez personally, forced him to resign on 26 July 1931. He fled to Buenos Aires the following day.

A provisional government appeared, announcing that it would hold elections soon.[41]

Chile's Battleship *Potemkin*

Chilean politics descended into anarchy after the dictatorship collapsed. This began on 1 September 1931, when, as Ambassador William Culbertson related to Washington, Chilean sailors in Coquimbo "locked officers in their rooms, and took command of all ships including the *Almirante Latorre*," the Chilean navy's flagship. Sailors in Valparaíso and Talcahuano joined them in a mutiny that soon spread throughout the fleet. The provisional government declared a state of emergency and granted Gen. Carlos Vergara authority to suppress the uprising. Foreign Minister Luis Izquierdo told Culbertson, "rebels in control of the sea and inspired by agitators who advocate an independent communistic republic." He asked how long it would take the United States to move warships into Chilean waters.[42]

Vergara expanded Izquierdo's request the following day. "Chile felt no shame over what had happened in its Navy," he explained to Culbertson. "[H]e believed it was a result of an international movement against social order ... The General, who has just returned from Europe where he had an opportunity to observe communistic activities, spoke of imminent danger of social war and describing Chile's problem as continental rather than local, stated that he desired support from the United States," particularly tear gas, munitions, and "the purchase and ... immediate delivery of two or more submarine boats." Chileans had lost contact with their own submarines, which they presumed were somewhere at sea. Vergara stressed that he wanted this as a show of American backing to bolster the provisional government's legitimacy while it restored law and order.[43]

The Hoover administration's (1929–33) acting Secretary of State James Rogers responded the next day. The US government had no tear gas in its possession and could send no munitions, either. Vergara should seek commercial suppliers. Neither could the administration sell or transfer submarines to Chile: "The sale or transfer of submarines owned by this Government is forbidden by Article 18 of the treaty on the limitation of Naval Armament."[44]

Vergara suppressed the mutiny without American support days later, when Chilean aircraft attacked the fleet. Only three warships, including *Almirante Latorre*, remained outside the provisional government's control after this, but Vergara was confident that he would subdue them. The sailors who occupied them indeed surrendered two days later. After this, Vergara thanked Culberston for forwarding his request to Washington, but he dropped it, since, as the ambassador reported, "the situation has changed fundamentally in favor of the Government."[45]

This did not represent the end of this dialog. Both Izquierdo and Vergara met Culberston again on 7 September, expressing "the intention of the Government to make a thorough investigation of the communistic activities which they believe resulted in the mutiny. They are arresting about four leaders. They wish to investigate not only the activities of these men in Chile but also their contacts and sources of money abroad." They solicited "technical assistance . . . they desire the service of a specialist in communistic propaganda and activities in order to assist in ferreting out the ramifications and origins of the movement in Chile."[46]

The Hoover administration neither shared Chileans' interpretation of the mutiny nor believed that a larger, Soviet threat explained it. Culbertson had certainly been reporting on sailors' "demands of a communistic nature." But he also advised his superiors that "Apparently movement has no organized political backing." As Nunn explained, "That Marxist thought, socialism, and extremist solutions should have found their way into the navy should not seem strange . . . crewmen were recruited from lower sectors of society, and they did not lose touch with the civilian lower classes." This mutiny, although communist-influenced, was spontaneous and not Soviet- or PCCh-directed. Chilean commanders' announcements to their crews that the government was further reducing public employees' salaries, including their own, and not party instructions, had incited it. This showed that some grassroots, working-class movements remained local, primarily Chilean eruptions. They were not necessarily expressions of the Comintern or PCCh's politics, even if Chilean anticommunists and noncommunists could not always tell the difference.[47]

Meanwhile, Secretary of State Henry Stimson asked the provisional government to produce specific information "with respect to the basis for statements frequently made that alleged communist activities in Latin American countries are directed and controlled from Moscow." Even if the Hoover administration were inclined to intervene, "there is no Federal agency . . . charged with responsibility for investigating and studying communist activities in the United States . . . there is not available in Government service a specialist whose services it could offer . . . it is not in a position to suggest the name of a specialist in private life to undertake the work in question." The secretary could give the Chilean ambassador a copy of a congressional report on communism in the United States. But the administration had nothing else to offer. Izquierdo and Vergara did not press this, and, in any case, the provisional government was in no condition to launch such an inquiry.[48]

Chileans' descent into anarchy quickened after this mutiny. The PCCh had gradually reconstituted itself and reemerged in Chilean politics after Ibáñez's fall, but more at the grassroots than the national level at first. As historian Jody Pavilack described it, "the advance of the Communist Party took place through conversations and small actions, not only in the mines but also on the beaches and soccer fields and in neighborhood bars of the coal mining region." When Communist militants attacked an army barracks in Copiapó and got into a firefight with the *Carabineros* in October 1931, they were probably acting as an independent local cell following its own orders. But it nevertheless worsened the disorder that was overtaking Chile. The *Carabineros* dynamited Communist headquarters there. Then they snatched several Communists from their homes and shot them dead in retaliation.[49]

Those few members of the PCCh's leadership who had survived Ibáñez's purges were fighting each other and not the provisional government. An internal struggle had been raging since Lenin died and Joseph Stalin (mid-1920s–1953) directed all Latin American communist parties "to Bolshevize" their organizations – that is, to submit to his authority, which accounted for the slowing down of many revolutionary movements in the late 1920s. Two tendencies emerged within the PCCh, each contesting how Chilean Communists should reconstruct the party and which Soviet leader, and line, it should follow. Elías Lafertte and Carlos Contreras Labarca led the Stalinists, or those who remained loyal to the Comintern's South American Bureau. Manuel Hidalgo led the Trotskyists – or so Lafertte and Contreras's faction, and behind them, the bureau, labeled them.[50]

The South American Bureau intervened in the PCCh's affairs in January 1933. As Ulianova noted, the bureau's criticism was "extremely harsh." The party was not acting as a communist party, but rather as a liberal, social-democratic one. It was obsessed with Santiago's politics and rumors, and consequently ignoring critical areas, such as the mining regions, where it followed, rather than led, events. There was no discernible chain of command connecting the party's leadership and its regional and local cells. Some of the latter – such as the group that had attacked the army barracks in Copiapó – were directing themselves. In short, "The [post-Ibáñez] Central Committee is two years old and it is not functioning. It does not comprehend the problem . . . Our Party has failed to understand that its task is to organize the revolution through mass struggle."[51]

The South American Bureau instructed the PCCh to convene a national congress to redress this problem. It did so that June. The bureau condemned Recabarren's continuing influence on the party, comparing this to German Communists' failure to transcend Rosa Luxemburg's leadership. It blamed Recabarren for Hidalgo and others' deviationism, and it ordered Lafertte and Contreras to denounce both of them.

This was standard Stalinist politics. "The Stalinist Comintern," Ulianova explained, "did not want leaders with their own personalities, capable of making their own decisions. It wanted unconditional loyalty. It was no accident that the historical founders of practically every Western communist party were expelled from the very organizations they had created." And so it went, posthumously, for Recabarren.[52]

Thus, Lafertte and Contreras distanced themselves from "*recabarrenismo*," stating:

> His democratic illusion, his faith in universal suffrage, his bourgeois patriotism, his conception of the party as a party of social reformism, with a structure and form as a federation of organizations with purely electoral ends, his ignorance and absolute lack of understanding of the worker-peasant revolution as a necessary stage imposed by development, his abstract idea of the "social revolution," and finally his collaboration with the bourgeoisie excused away as a "realistic policy" had prevented the party from getting on with its real task of making revolution.[53]

This was how the South American Bureau Bolshevized the PCCh in 1933, then. The party reappeared in Chilean politics that year, although it would remain excluded from the registrar's official rolls and, consequently underground, until 1947. It had become, as historian Carmelo Furci understood, "a strict Leninist party organization . . . based on Stalin's version of Leninism." But it was weaker than before. Several factors account for this, the most important being that the PCCh was no longer the only Marxist-Leninist party in Chile.[54]

The Socialist Republic

Gen. Alberto Puga, Col. Marmaduke Grove, and civilians Carlos Dávila and Eugenio Matte formed a *junta*, seized power, and proclaimed "the Socialist Republic of Chile" in early June 1932. The *junta* explained that it was taking "the entire public power" into its hands as it forced President Juan Esteban Montero (1932) to flee *la Moneda*. It dissolved Congress, nationalized banking, credit, and other important industries, and moved to reorganize the Chilean armed forces so that security personnel might protect it against the country's propertied, reactionary classes. The *junta* also planned to draft a new constitution. It would respect the existing constitution "insofar as it may be compatible with the new order of things."[55]

This frightened Chilean Communists, who took to the streets in opposition. This prompted Grove to warn them that the *junta* "would deal severely with Communists seeking to overthrow [it]." The army was already rising against Grove and his colleagues, however. As Culbertson explained to Washington, the situation was deteriorating fast:

> On the one had are the extremists, the Communists, under the leadership of Lafertte. They have burrowed into the Government and into the armed forces. The extent of their influence and power cannot be measured. They hold meetings in the main avenue and their orators demand arms for the masses and threaten to burn and kill . . . The city is covered with posters proclaiming communism.[56]

The army forced the *junta* to withdraw from *la Moneda* several days later, after which it relegated Grove to Easter Island while expressing its desire to return to the barracks and leave politics to Dávila and other civilian leaders – "under the condition that communism be outlawed." As the army's leadership explained, the institution had only acted because "it could not remain impassive in the face of the actions of a group of adventurers without a country who while exploiting the socialistic ideals outraged the flag and ignored right." The new *junta* deployed the army to protect the train service while massing about 6,000 *Carabineros* to restore law and order in Santiago in the following days.[57]

At this point Culbertson lost track of Chilean politics. "On the shifting scene of Chilean politics," he reported, "dominated by personalities who change and even traffic their loyalties overnight, it is frankly impossible to make any prophesies concerning political stability." None of the contending factions recognized any of the others' legitimacy. The conservative establishment remained immobilized, "nurs[ing] their respectability behind the barred doors of the Union Club. The hope of intervention by the United States is often expressed in their conversations."[58]

Stimson had asked Culbertson to assess Chilean stability because the *juntas* that were rapidly coming and going were pressing the United States to recognize them, at least while they lasted. The Hoover administration, like most of its predecessors, would recognize any government that effectively ruled its territory, did not face serious internal opposition or disorder, and respected its international obligations without either approving or disapproving of its leaderships' politics. None of these *juntas* met these conditions. As Culbertson explained, "Confusion and uncertainty continue. The show is not over. Even my southeasterly colleagues are beginning to think that Chile is overdoing political instability."[59]

Assistant Secretary of State for Latin American affairs Francis White received Ambassador Miguel Cruchaga in his offices that October. Yet another provisional government had united around Abraham Oyandel, an attorney whom one of the previous *juntas* had appointed to the Supreme Court and then named minister of interior, from which he had inherited the presidency when still another *junta* had fallen. Culbertson deemed Oyandel's legal status "a fiction," but he recognized that it had enabled all of the warring factions to return to Ibáñez's constitution and start planning national elections. As Cruchaga elaborated, "the people of the country are tired of revolutions and military movements . . . All want to get back to a civilian, constitutional Government."[60]

The Hoover administration accepted Culbertson's advice that it would be better for both American and Chilean governments if the United States withheld recognition until a properly elected Chilean president appeared. Thus, as White informed Cruchaga, Washington declined to recognize Oyandel's provisional government:

> I pointed out that from the time Montero was overthrown on June 4 to the taking over of the Government by the present regime on October 4, that is to say in a period of four months, there had been five Governments in Chile. This does not speak well for the stability of conditions in Chile . . . The Ambassador said that recent regimes in Chile had come in as a result of *coup d'état*. The first Dávila junta came in through a *coup d'état*; the Grove junta came in through a *coup d'état*; the second Dávila regime came in through a *coup d'état*, and the [Gen. Bartolomé] Blanche regime also came in through a *coup d'état*. I observed that the Blanche regime also went out by a *coup d'état* to which Señor Cruchaga at once assented. I said that if the Blanche regime went out by a *coup d'état* it seemed incontestable that the present regime came in by *coup d'état*. The Ambassador was somewhat taken back by this and after a moment's hesitation smiled and said yes, he supposed the present regime did come

in by a *coup d'état* but that it was necessary to throw out the usurping unconstitutional Government by a *coup d'état* in order to bring in a constitutional Government.[61]

White's decision to postpone recognition did not set back Chilean progress, however. Cruchaga's predictions proved accurate. Chileans discarded the Socialist Republic and its successor *juntas* and then reelected a more practical and less demagogic Alessandri in November 1932. They elected a new Congress as well, returning to civilian-led, constitutional government thereafter. Alessandri completed his six-year term in 1938. He stabilized Chilean politics, reconfirming that Chile was a liberal nation aligned with likeminded liberals in Latin America, the United States, and Europe, and approximately forty years of peaceful transitions of power and democratic expansion followed.

The Emergence of Multiparty Democracy in Chile

Alessandri presided over the emergence of multiparty democracy in Chile in the mid-1930s. This represented Chileans' flourishing spectrum of worldviews and interests from left to right. Chilean politics became increasingly inclusive and pluralistic. For example, Chileans would recognize women's suffrage in 1949 and expand the vote even further in the late 1950s and 1960s.

This flourishing spectrum of worldviews included the Chilean Socialist Party (PS), an independent Marxist-Leninist party that Grove, Dr. Salvador Allende, and others formed in 1933. Some of Hidalgo's "Trotskyists" joined it, as did others from the middle and working classes. Socialists remained an eclectic grouping of people who were committed to proletarian internationalism and revolution, but who rejected Stalin's control. As Allende later clarified,

> we analysed the situation in Chile, and we believed that there was a place for a Party which, while holding similar views [to the PCCh] in terms of philosophy and doctrine – a Marxist approach to the interpretation of history – would be a Party free of ties of an international nature. However, this did not mean that we would disavow proletarian internationalism.[62]

Socialists' worldviews and ultimate objectives still derived from Marxist political thought. When journalist Régis Debray asked Allende, decades later, to talk about when and why he had joined the revolution, he referred to the Marxist-Leninist literature that he had been avidly reading since his days as a college student:

> I think that when one has read Lenin, particularly Imperialism, the Highest Stage of Capitalism, one has a grasp of the theory. The issue of imperialism has a great deal of meaning in under-developed countries, particularly in Latin America. We Socialists have proclaimed that imperialism is our number one enemy, and we therefore gave and still give first priority to national liberation.[63]

Although Chilean Communists and Socialists may have shared similar views and acted alike in many ways, they nevertheless opposed each other, sometimes violently so, into the late 1950s. Socialists tended to denounce Communists as representing Stalinist tyranny, and Communists dismissed Socialists as infantile adventurers who lacked ideological grounding and discipline. Socialists had a broader base, participated in national elections, and did not alarm Chilean anticommunists as the PCCh, which remained stronger in mining and the rest of the labor movement, did.

Although the conservative establishment gradually lost influence after the 1930s – Radical-led coalitions, representing the center and center-left, would dominate the presidency from 1938 to 1952, then independents and Christian Democrats until 1970 – anticommunism would remain a potent force in Chilean politics for the rest of the twentieth century. This was an indigenous force, not an expression of imperialism from abroad. Chile's Red Scare arose as part of a broad spectrum of responses to industrialism and globalization, responses that included the appearance of an increasingly militant labor movement in the late nineteenth century and the PCCh in the early twentieth. Chilean Communists' enlisting in the Comintern and pledging to fight for its cause further alarmed anticommunists, who included the professional officer corps. Thus, the initial moments of Chile's Cold War experience occurred when Chileans, having different interpretations of and experiences with the political, social, and cultural transformations of the late nineteenth century, developed conflicting perceptions and made choices that placed them sharply at odds with each other.

Notes

1. Odd Arne Westad, *The Cold War: A World History* (New York: Basic Books, 2017), 5.
2. Simon Collier and William Sater, *A History of Chile, 1808–2002* [1996], 2nd edn (Cambridge: Cambridge University Press, 2004), 144.
3. Ibid., 160–1.
4. Frederick Nunn, *Chilean Politics, 1920–1931: The Honorable Mission of the Armed Forces* (Albuquerque: University of New Mexico Press, 1970), 10.
5. Alberto Edwards Vives and Eduardo Frei Montalva, *Historia de los partidos políticos chilenos* (Santiago de Chile: Editorial del Pacífico, 1949), 191.
6. Biblioteca Nacional de Chile, "Ramón Barros Luco (1835–1919)," at <http://www.memoriachilena.cl>.
7. Frederick Pike, *Chile and the United States, 1880–1962: The Emergence of Chile's Social Crisis and the Challenge to United States Diplomacy* (Notre Dame: University of Notre Dame Press, 1963), 86. Ministers of interior were the senior cabinet officers, serving in a position analogous to an empowered vice president in the United States. They became acting president in the chief executive's absence, charged to maintain the existing government until special elections were held.
8. On the introduction of coal mining, see Biblioteca Nacional de Chile, "Trabajadores y empresarios en la industria del carbón: Lota y Coronel (1854–1995)," at <http://www.memoriachilena.cl>; and Jody Pavilack, *Mining for the Nation: The Politics of Chile's Coal Communities from the Popular Front to the Cold War* (University Park: Pennsylvania State University Press, 2011), 29–66.
9. For these labor conditions, see Brian Loveman, *Chile: The Legacy of Hispanic Capitalism* [1979], 3rd edn (New York: Oxford University Press, 2001), 119–44, 162–95; Carmelo Furci, *The Chilean Communist Party and the Road to Socialism* (London: Zed Books, 1984), 8–27; Pike, *Chile and the United States*, 103–11; and Hernán Ramírez Necochea, *Origen y formación del Partido Comunista de Chile* (Santiago de Chile: Editora Austral, 1965), 19–62.

10. Ramírez, *Origen y formación del Partido Comunista*, 26–8.
11. Ibid., 28.
12. Loveman, *Chile*, Table 7.2, 171; and Ramírez, *Origen y formación del Partido Comunista*, 35.
13. *El Obrero*, La Serena, 29 April 1893. Ramírez, *Origen y formación del Partido Comunista*, 37–8.
14. Biblioteca Nacional de Chile, "Masacre de la Escuela Santa María de Iquique," at <http://www.memoriachilena.cl>; and Edwards and Frei, *Historia de los partidos políticos chilenos*, 153–5.
15. Julio Faúndez, *Marxism and Democracy in Chile: From 1932 to the Fall of Allende* (New Haven: Yale University Press, 1988), 20–3; Furci, *Chilean Communist Party*, 24–7; Ramírez, *Origen y formación del Partido Comunista*, 45–6, 51–62.
16. Leon Trotsky, "Manifesto of the Communist International to the Proletarians of the World," March 1919. Robert Daniels, ed., *A Documentary History of Communism and the World: From Revolution to Collapse* (Hanover: University Press of New England, 1994), 25; and Ramírez, *Origen y formación del Partido Comunista*, 123–7. For the Comintern's conditions, see Second Comintern Congress, "Conditions of Admission to the Communist International," August 1920. Daniels, *Documentary History of Communism*, 32–4.
17. *El Socialista*, Antofagasta, 21 March 1921. Ramírez, *Origen y formación del Partido Comunista*, 126; PCCh, "Declaración de principios," First Party Congress in Rancagua, January 1922. Ibid., 134–5.
18. Interview with Yuri Pavlov, Roll 10842. CNN, *Cold War* (1998). Transcript courtesy of the National Security Archive, at <http://www. nsarchive.gwu.edu>; and M. A. Komin-Alexandrovski to Comintern, 18 January 1922. Olga Ulianova and Alfredo Riquelme Segovia, eds., *Chile en los archivos soviéticos, 1922–1991* I: *Komintern y Chile, 1922–1931* (Santiago de Chile: Dirección de Bibliotecas, Archivos y Museos/LOM Ediciones, 2005), 111–12.
19. Luis Emilio Recabarren, "Chile 1922." Ulianova and Segovia, *Chile en los archivos soviéticos: Komintern y Chile*, 116–22; and Profintern to Recabarren, 20 November 1923. Ibid., 123–5.
20. Comintern to Mexican, Brazilian, Uruguayan, Argentine, and Chilean Communist Parties, September 1924. Ibid., 125–6.
21. Comintern to South American Communist Parties (Argentina, Brazil, Chile, Uruguay, Bolivia, Peru, Paraguay, and Colombia), 18 February 1925. Ibid., 130–1.

22. "Un saludo proletario a la Unión Soviética," *El Siglo*, 26 April 1946. Also see "Inmenso público escuchó ayer conferencia de Pablo Neruda," *El Siglo*, 27 November 1946, where Neruda promoted the Soviet Union's successes in science and technology while describing the happiness of its citizens under the leadership of José Stalin, as his Chilean admirers referred to him.

23. Olga Ulianova, "La Unidad Popular y el golpe militar en Chile: percepciones y análisis soviéticos," *Estudios Públicos* 79 (2000), 88; and María Soledad Gómez, "Factores nacionales e internacionales de la política interna del partido comunista de Chile (1922–1952)." Augusto Varas, ed., *El partido comunista en Chile: estudio multidisciplinario* (Santiago de Chile: Centro de Estudios Sociales/FLACSO, 1988), 65–139. Also see Nikolai Leonov, "La inteligencia soviética en América Latina durante la guerra fría." *Estudios Públicos* 73 (1999), 38–9.

24. For antipolitics, see Brian Loveman and Thomas Davies, eds., *The Politics of Antipolitics: The Military in Latin America* [1978], 3rd edn (Wilmington: Scholarly Resources, 1997).

25. Domingo Santa María and Carlos Antúnez, "Fundación de la Academia de Guerra," decree dated 9 September 1886. Alejandro San Francisco, ed., *La Academia de Guerra del Ejército de Chile, 1886–2006: ciento veinte años de historia* (Santiago de Chile: Ediciones Centro de Estudios Bicentenario, 2006), 211–19. For additional context, see Frederick Nunn, *Yesterday's Soldiers: European Military Professionalism in South America, 1890–1940* (Lincoln: University of Nebraska Press, 1983).

26. Enrique Brahm García, "La impronta prusiana de la Academia de Guerra del Ejército (1885–1914)." San Francisco, *Academia de Guerra*, 3–25; and Brian Loveman, *For la Patria: Politics and the Armed Forces in Latin America* (Wilmington: Scholarly Resources, 1999), 81. For an alternative interpretation, see William Sater and Holger Herwig, *The Grand Illusion: The Prussianization of the Chilean Army* (Lincoln: University of Nebraska Press, 1999).

27. For example, Frederick Nunn, *The Military in Chilean History: Essays on Civil–Military Relations, 1810–1973* (Albuquerque: University of New Mexico Press, 1976), 119–27; and Nunn, *Chilean Politics*, 10–12, 17–18, 50–2.

28. Collier and Sater, *History of Chile*, 202–9; Nunn, *Chilean Politics*, 19–27; and Edwards and Frei, *Historia de los partidos políticos chilenos*, 183–91.

29. Collier and Sater, *History of Chile*, 207.

30. Nunn, *Chilean Politics*, 55–6; and Edwards and Frei, *Historia de los partidos políticos chilenos*, 192–3.
31. Nunn, *Chilean Politics*, 47–66.
32. Loveman, *Chile*, 162.
33. William Collier to Department of State, 9 September 1924; and 10 September 1924. Department of State, *Foreign Relations of the United States, 1924* I (Washington, DC: Government Printing Office, 1939), 357, 358–9; and Charles Evan Hughes to Collier, 13 September 1924. Ibid., 359.
34. Collier to Department of State, 24 January 1925. Department of State, *Foreign Relations of the United States, 1925* I (Washington, DC: Government Printing Office, 1940), 581; and Collier to Department of State, 25 January 1925. Ibid., 581–2.
35. Collier to Department of State, 27 January 1925. Ibid., 585–6; and Collier to Department of State, 12 February 1925. Ibid., 586. Alessandri returned to the presidency on 20 March.
36. Ibáñez ran unopposed and won 98 percent of the vote. See Ricardo Cruz-Coke, *Historia electoral de Chile, 1925–1973* (Santiago de Chile: Editorial Jurídica de Chile, 1984), 94–7. Also see Nunn, *Chilean Politics*, 58–133.
37. Carlos Ibáñez's declaration, 9 February 1927. Nunn, *Chilean Politics*, 183–4.
38. "Informe de los camaradas comunistas que estuvieron en la Isla Más Afuera," December 1928. Ulianova and Riquelme, *Chile en los archivos soviéticos: Komintern y Chile*, 377–9.
39. South American Bureau to PCCh's Santiago Committee and all members of the PCCh, August 1929. Ibid., 405–9; and Provisional Central Committee of the PCCh to South American Bureau, "Informe al Secretariado Sudamericano de la Internacional Comunista," 15 November 1929. Ibid., 416–35.
40. Faúndez, *Marxism and Democracy*, 14–16.
41. On the fall of the Ibáñez dictatorship, see Collier and Sater, *History of Chile*, 214–21; Loveman, *Chile*, 183–8; Nunn, *Chilean Politics*, 117–59; William Culbertson to Department of State, 26 July 1931. Department of State, *Foreign Relations of the United States, 1931* I (Washington, DC: Government Printing Office, 1946), 905; and Culbertson to Department of State, 27 July 1931. Ibid., 907.
42. Culbertson to Department of State, 2 September 1931. Department of State, *FRUS, 1931* I, 909; and Culbertson to Department of State, 5 September 1931. Ibid., 911–12.
43. Culbertson to Department of State, 6 September 1931. Ibid., 912–13.

44. James Rogers to Culbertson, 6 September 1931. Ibid., 914–15. This referred to the Washington Naval Treaty of 1922.
45. Culbertson to Department of State, 7 September 1931. Ibid., 915.
46. Culbertson to Department of State, 7 September 1931. Ibid., 916.
47. Culbertson to Department of State, 2 September 1931; Nunn, *Military in Chilean History*, 199.
48. Henry Stimson to Culbertson, 12 September 1931. Department of State, *FRUS, 1931* I, 917.
49. Pavilack, *Mining for the Nation*, 64; and Collier and Sater, *History of Chile*, 223.
50. Gómez, "Factores nacionales e internacionales," 67–8; Furci, *Chilean Communist Party*, 28–32; Ramírez, *Origen y formación del Partido Comunista*, 187–205; and Executive Committee of the Communist International, "Theses on the Bolshevization of Communist Parties," April 1925. Daniels, *Documentary History of Communism*, 45–8.
51. Olga Ulianova, "República socialista y soviética en Chile: seguimiento y evaluacíon de una ocasión revolucionaria perdida." Olga Ulianova and Alfredo Riquelme Segovia, eds., *Chile en los archivos soviéticos, 1922–1991* II: *Komintern en Chile, 1931–1935: crisis e ilusión revolucionaria* (Santiago de Chile: Dirección de Bibliotecas, Archivos y Museos/LOM Ediciones, 2009), 173–206; South American Bureau meeting with PCCh, "Sesión del BP de Chile 1," 1 June 1933. Ibid., 288–94; and Paulino González Alberdi, South American Bureau, "Discusión de la situación chilena," March 1934. Ibid., 372–80. Also see Faúndez, *Marxism and Democracy*, 24–6.
52. Ulianova, "República socialista y soviética en Chile," 196; and Fritz Glaufbauf, also known as Diego, South American Bureau, "Discusión chilena," March 1934. Ibid., 358–72.
53. PCCh, Resolution of the National Congress, July 1933. Furci, *Chilean Communist Party*, 32. Also see Gómez, "Factores nacionales e internacionales," 68–75.
54. Furci, *Chilean Communist Party*, 32.
55. Culbertson to Department of State, 4 June 1932. Department of State, *Foreign Relations of the United States, 1932* V: *The American Republics* (Washington, DC: Government Printing Office, 1948), 430; Culbertson to Department of State, 4 June 1932. Ibid., 430–1; and Culbertson to Department of State, 5 June 1932. Ibid., 431–2. See the *junta*'s declarations, included in Culbertson to Department of State, 5 June 1932; and Culbertson to Department of State, 5 June 1932. Ibid., 432–3.

56. Culbertson to Department of State, 11 June 1932. Ibid., 440; and Culbertson to Department of State, 13 June 1932. Ibid., 440–1.
57. Culbertson to Department of State, 16 June 1932. Ibid., 449–50; Culbertson to Department of State, 17 June 1932. Ibid., 450–1; and Culbertson to Department of State, 18 June 1932. Ibid., 452.
58. Culbertson to Department of State, 14 July 1932. Ibid., 460–2; and Culbertson to Department of State, 13 June 1932.
59. Culbertson to Department of State, 2 October 1932. Ibid., 491–2.
60. Francis White to Culbertson, 12 October 1932. Ibid., 495–9.
61. Culbertson to Department of State, 6 October 1932. Ibid., 493; and White to Culbertson, 12 October 1932.
62. Régis Debray, *The Chilean Revolution: Conversations with Allende* (New York: Pantheon Books, 1971), 62. On the rise of the PS, also see Faúndez, *Marxism and Democracy*, 26–9.
63. Debray, *Conversations with Allende*, 69–70.

3 Gabriel González Videla and the Transatlantic Origins of the Cold War

The Chilean government broke relations with the Soviet Union (USSR), Czechoslovakia, and Yugoslavia in 1947. It banned the Chilean Communist Party (PCCh) the following year, in September 1948. Chilean President Gabriel González Videla (1946–52) attempted to convince others in the inter-American and transatlantic communities, including the United States, to follow his lead – for example, in Bogotá, where the Organization of American States (OAS) convened, and in New York City, where the United Nations (UN) was headquartered, as well.

The following two chapters reconstruct these events within the context of the period historians traditionally refer to as the origins of the Cold War, where the US and the USSR came into conflict over the future of postwar Europe and indeed the world in the late 1940s. This chapter covers the period from the Second World War to 1947; the next from 1947 into the 1950s. These chapters expand the discussion on the origins of the conflict, incorporating Chile and southern South America into it in order to illuminate the transatlantic nature of many of these problems. They also show how Chileans participated in it as internationalists, and far more actively than recognized in the literature.

González and the PCCh's clashes occurred within the framework of a larger struggle that industrialization and globalization had unleashed in the late nineteenth century and was continuing into the twentieth, and they were very well aware of all of this. For example, González compared Chilean, French, and Italian Communists' behavior and found that "the situations and events were so alike . . . it was as if they were being directed by the same baton." Communist Senator Pablo Neruda warned his comrades, "They want to do with you what they're doing to Greece."[1]

It remains worth noting at the outset that it might have disappointed González and Neruda to learn what we know today, that neither superpower intervened in Chile or southern South America in the late 1940s. Perhaps it was frustrating enough to both of them that they attempted to do their part as internationalists but failed to attract the external allies they so vigorously sought. The Truman administration (1945–53) remained focused on Eurasia – particularly Germany and Eastern Europe, Greece, Turkey, Iran, and China – and had little time for Latin American issues, which seemed far less pressing. In Britain, González's behavior puzzled some. London wanted better trade relations in southern South America but was mostly occupied with managing its withdrawal from empire in Asia and Africa. When an agitated González told Michael Stewart, a young Member of Parliament who was visiting Chile, to warn the prime minister to "Distrust the Communists," he thanked him and let it go. Soviets, too, seemed to want little more than to improve trade relations while waging a campaign of what we would now call public diplomacy in Chile and southern South America. Moscow found many of the incidents that occurred in Chile, including an armed attack against its embassy by a group calling itself *Acción Chilena Anticomunista* (ACHA), strange. It tried to stay out of them to no avail. González and the PCCh nevertheless influenced some events beyond Chile, in southern South America, Europe, and the Soviet Union, and thus helped to shape and condition the evolving Cold War.[2]

Southern South America and the Second World War

Latin Americans were much more involved in the Second World War than the first one. Although the three major countries in southern South America – Brazil, Argentina, and Chile – experienced it very differently, they and others in the western hemisphere emerged from the conflagration more committed to the success of the inter-American and transatlantic communities than before. The United States had expressed some interest in leading these communities since the 1890s, particularly the inter-American one. Washington rededicated itself to both while offering an active defense of what historian Frank Ninkovich has characterized as global or international society, in the 1940s.[3]

In the inter-American sphere, the Roosevelt administration (1933–45) began by organizing a hemispheric military strategy centered on the Caribbean and the Brazilian northeast, which represented the closest points of contact between the Americas, on the one hand, and Europe, and North Africa, where the war against Nazi Germany was raging, on the other. The administration feared that Berlin might eventually use North Africa to establish a beachhead in Brazil or another point in the western hemisphere. Its submarines were already ravaging transatlantic shipping by spring 1940.

The inter-American community gathered in Rio de Janeiro, the Brazilian capital and site of its foreign ministry, about a month after the Japanese navy attacked Pearl Harbor, in January 1942. All expressed gratification that President Franklin Roosevelt had incorporated principles of sovereignty, juridical equality, and non-intervention into the Atlantic Charter. Concerning the administration's hemispheric strategy, they also agreed to cooperate in security matters. They would regard an attack against any of them as an attack against all. But they were wary about Washington's request that they break relations with Germany and Japan. The Argentine, Chilean, and Peruvian delegations particularly objected to a resolution mandating this break, and they pressed Undersecretary of State Sumner Welles to accept their pledge to consider doing so, but with no promises one way or the other. Welles yielded to this.[4]

Brazilians backed the United States as an ally during the war. They hosted Allied air transport and supply bases at Natal and Recife that helped supply the Soviet Union, which Nazi Germany had invaded in June 1941. Rio supported the Anglo-American invasion of North Africa in late 1942, deploying an expeditionary force to fight with the US Fifth Army in Italy in July 1944.

Argentines retained strong trade connections to Britain, but they were more closely tied to Germany through immigration and ongoing trade and military missions. They did not want to burn any bridges with Berlin, who, they believed, would likely win the war. Further, they felt little sympathy for the United States.

Buenos Aires and Washington's relations had deteriorated since President Theodore Roosevelt (1901–9) and Argentine Foreign Minister Luis María Drago had disagreed over the Venezuelan debt crisis at the turn of the century, presaging two decades of uni-lateral American intervention in the Caribbean. Thus, Argentines very resentfully broke relations with the Axis in January 1944 – after the Department of State pressed them by threatening to reveal their involvement in the Bolivian coup that had occurred the previ-ous month.

Chileans broke relations with the Axis earlier, in January 1943, declaring war two years later, in February 1945. The Roosevelt administration understood that Chileans were hesitating because they feared Japanese reprisals from across the Pacific. These fears partly explained why Santiago had taken the lead in convening the meeting in Rio. As Brazil's representatives, who were functioning as helpful intermediaries, explained to their American friends, Chileans were "much worried over newspaper reports from [US] Pacific coast regarding blackouts and alleged plans for evacuation."[5]

There was more to these Chilean fears than panicky press reports from California. The Japanese government was bullying Santiago. Ambassador Claude Bowers informed Washington that "Chile's Minister in Tokyo is practically a prisoner and held incom-municado." Meanwhile, Japan's ambassador to Santiago, Keyoshi Yamagata, had sent his attaché, a junior lieutenant from the Japanese navy, to address the Chilean minister of defense and the command-ers of the armed forces. This arrogant young lieutenant "asserted that the United States Navy was now vastly inferior . . . He prom-ised destruction of the Panama Canal and sinking of all ships carry-ing contraband . . . He also stressed strategic importance of Easter Island." Yamagata later menacingly asked Foreign Minister Juan Rossetti how Chileans would respond if Japanese warships attacked Panama, sank Peruvian merchant ships, or seized Lima's Talara oil-fields, while claiming that Japanese submarines were already operat-ing off South America's Pacific coast.[6]

Washington was nevertheless impatient with the Chilean govern-ment. Welles instructed Bowers to tell Rossetti that "the statement that Japanese submarines are operating in Western Hemisphere waters south of the Panama Canal was an absolute falsehood. The assertions . . . are typically boastful Japanese allegations which I believe will be fully disproved in a relatively short time."[7]

The Roosevelt administration knew that German intelligence services were collecting information in southern South America and it wanted Chileans to help it shut their networks down. German assets included a small fishing fleet that was sailing Chilean waters and at least one clandestine radio set in the country. These networks were reporting to the German embassy in Buenos Aires, which was forwarding their information to German stations in the Caribbean. This information – mostly pertaining to the ships that were passing through Chilean ports – was reaching German submarine commanders, who were using it to devastate Anglo-American communication and supply lines in the North Atlantic. Chileans could put an end to this by breaking relations with the Axis and expelling German and Japanese diplomats from their nation.[8]

Bowers shared Washington's concerns about German intelligence, as did the Chilean government. But his superiors' impatience with Santiago frustrated him. He explained that Chile – unlike the Central American and Caribbean dictatorships that had declared war against the Axis hours after Pearl Harbor – remained a sovereign, democratic republic with its own institutions, laws, and public opinion. Just as the Roosevelt administration had had to tread carefully with respect to Germany and Japan until December 1941, so Chileans had to watch their step in 1942.[9]

The Chilean government, moreover, was dealing with an unexpected presidential succession. President Pedro Aguierre Cerda (1938–41) had died of tuberculosis in November 1941. Minister of Interior Gerónimo Méndez became acting president until new elections could be held. President Juan Antonio Ríos (1942–6) won these elections in February 1942, but he did not assume office until April. This left several months of transition and uncertainty in Santiago.

The Ríos administration duly gathered evidence against Germany's intelligence networks after assuming office. It made prompt arrests and seized radio transmitters. The administration, working with Congress, also resolved to break relations with the Axis that December, which it formally did the following month, in January 1943. Minister of Interior Raúl Morales traveled to Washington to tell Roosevelt, who responded that "he was very glad indeed to receive this information." The president, sensitive to Chileans' concerns about the Japanese navy, explained the reasoning behind the Allies' Germany-first strategy to them.[10]

Meanwhile, Santiago's break with the Axis qualified Chile for Lend-Lease assistance, which included aircraft, antiaircraft batteries, and ammunition. Chileans desperately needed this assistance. They had disclosed to Bowers that "the Army had ammunition for about 15 minutes of fighting and no planes or anti-aircraft guns" that same month.[11]

The Return of the Soviet Union

Southern South Americans reestablished relations with the Soviet Union during the war. They had broken relations with Moscow in the 1920s and 1930s, after regional anticommunists linked local communist parties and communist-influenced labor movements to the Comintern and its offices in Buenos Aires. This partly accounted for the rise of the Ibáñez dictatorship (1927–31) in Chile, and for President Getúlio Vargas's (1930–45) consolidating power in Brazil as well.

Although the Soviet Union would enter Eastern Europe in force during and after the war, Moscow returned to southern South America peacefully and through diplomatic channels. By this time, the USSR's views of Latin American communists had changed. For example, according to Soviet foreign service officer Yuri Pavlov, the Kremlin recognized that it lacked the resources it needed to back communists in the region. They remained too weak to lead revolutions, in any case. Thus, Soviets returned to the region primarily in search of trade.[12]

Uruguayans made the first overture. Their sympathy for the Soviet Union had increased following the German invasion of the USSR. The Uruguayan labor movement was particularly pressing Montevideo to recognize Moscow. The current, conservative government was concerned that leftist political parties might exploit this for "vote-catching motives," and it wished to get ahead of it.

So, the Uruguayan foreign minister asked the American ambassador whether the Roosevelt administration would be willing act as go-between.[13]

Washington responded favorably, emphasizing that it considered this issue one of far-reaching importance. If the Soviet Union could be brought into the international community, it might abandon "its former policies" and possibly even play an important part in postwar world affairs. Washington warned Montevideo to arrive at "a clearcut and explicit understanding with the Soviet Government regarding nonintervention," but said it would be pleased to act as intermediary.[14]

At the Department of State, Welles asked Ambassador Maxim Litvinov for his views on this several months later. Litvinov expressed interest, but he worried that the circumstances and tone of the Uruguayan government's earlier break with the USSR would complicate matters. Moscow nevertheless instructed him to proceed. Litvinov and his counterpart from Montevideo reestablished Soviet–Uruguayan relations in January 1943. Brazil, Argentina, and Chile followed suit over the next three years.[15]

González's Election

The Soviets who returned to Chile encountered González and the Radical Party, who dominated Chilean politics in 1946. Radicals were adept power seekers who represented a mix of more or less centrist, secular interests. Some of the party's members, like Ríos, leaned toward the right while others, such as González, sympathized with the left. Indeed, González won the presidency with Chilean Communists' support.

González's Radical–PCCh coalition had formed while Allied wartime cooperation was at its zenith. This was never more than temporary, however. Chilean Communists had never stopped advancing the Soviet Union's changing positions. They advocated the Popular Front strategy in the mid-1930s. They backed the Nazi–Soviet Pact in 1939, declaring that since "the War interests only the oligarchy and imperialism," Chile should remain neutral.

They joined the Allied cause after Germany invaded the Soviet Union. As Secretary General Carlos Contreras explained, "our country's highest priority remains to seek broad military, financial, and economic cooperation with the United States. It represents the only major, anti-Hitler power in the western hemisphere capable of providing such assistance."[16]

González had entered politics as a deputy during the Ibáñez dictatorship's final year in power. He later served as ambassador to France (1938–42) and Brazil (1942–6), then returned to Santiago in order to run for president after the war. Ríos had contracted cancer, retired from office, and then passed away in June 1946. This led to a new round of special elections, which presented an opening for González. His postings had introduced him to inter-American and transatlantic affairs, where he formed a close relationship with Fleet Adm. William Leahy (USN), who had represented the United States in Vichy France, among others.[17]

González closely worked with the PCCh while campaigning in 1946. Conservatives, Liberals, and Socialists each ran their own candidates. This Radical–PCCh collaboration was sincere and in good faith. As González explained to Leahy, "Chilean communism, like French communism, is following a democratic line and promoting national union internally and peaceful coexistence internationally." The PCCh, in turn, called González "a loyal brother," as Neruda phrased it in the poem he composed as the president's campaign manager.[18]

González's coalition agreed on an election program in July. Communists believed that González had committed himself to what would become a PCCh-led bourgeois revolution. The party's leaders planned to restructure political, social, and economic life in Chile, and their program went to the heart of the matter in the countryside, where they proposed land reform and the organization of rural labor.[19]

Landowners' political influence, however, still rested on their reliance on peasants as voting cattle. They continued to use this influence to block the labor code's full application. González's program, if successful, could have undermined the conservative establishment's remaining hold on power.

The PCCh also understood that González would nationalize industry. Further, the party's leaders were particularly excited about "defend[ing] the nation from imperialism, especially American," while expanding Chilean relations with the Soviet Union. They dreamed of establishing a direct steamship service connecting Vladivostok to Valparaíso across the Pacific.[20]

The PCCh regarded González's program as if it were divine commandments carved in stone. As Senator Elías Lafertte confirmed,

> You can be certain that we Communists will be the most combative force during the campaign. You should also know that we will be the most inflexible fighters when demanding – without vacillating, without relenting, without accepting setbacks – the completion of this program that the people have elaborated.[21]

The party mobilized the working-class vote, organizing massive rallies in the mining regions. Political scientists and historians have assigned much importance to this when explaining González's victory.[22]

Communists' support notwithstanding, González won the election by a narrow plurality, garnering approximately 40 percent of the vote that September. Senator Eduardo Cruz-Coke, the Conservative candidate, took nearly 30 percent; the Liberal candidate, over 25 percent; and the Socialist, just less than 3 percent. Cruz-Coke declined to concede González's victory. This referred the election, per constitutional procedure, to Congress, which would decide the matter in a run-off vote – where Liberal congressmen had sufficient influence to determine who would prevail.[23]

Differences between González, the power-seeking politician, and the PCCh, the devoted revolutionaries, appeared when González appealed to Liberals to back him. Although Liberals had more in common with Conservatives than González's coalition, they recognized that González, who had the strongest claim to the presidency, could serve their interests. They offered to support him if he appointed three cabinet members from their party to counter the three Communists he had already invited into the government.

They also required that he suspend his pledge to extend the labor code to the countryside. González, without consulting his partners, agreed to these terms. Thus, he won the run-off with 134 votes to Cruz-Coke's 46 that October.[24]

Unsurprisingly, González's first cabinet soon fell. As political scientist Carlos Huneeus observed, González may have possessed a good grasp of global affairs, but his political experience remained limited to his brief term in Congress and his campaign for president. He had never dealt with national politics from a position of responsibility or held even junior ministerial rank. Thus, he did not seem to understand that he had created a divided, fractious cabinet, where two-thirds of its members opposed each other.[25]

González and the PCCh's Falling Out

González began having second thoughts about the PCCh just after his inauguration. This occurred within the context of several intense months in Chile and abroad – particularly in Europe, where the wartime alliance against Nazi Germany was falling apart. The United States and the Soviet Union started to form dark interpretations of each other's motives and behavior. Joseph Stalin (mid-1920s–1953) had already brought some of this out into the open in February 1946.

Stalin examined recent international history in strictly Marxist-Leninist terms, calling the two global wars the inevitable products of the contradictions of monopoly capitalism. "It would be wrong to think that the Second World War was a casual occurrence," he said. Although fascism had been defeated in Germany and Italy, it still existed within the bourgeois democracies in North America and Western Europe, whose governments were continuing their earlier policies of hostile encirclement. Soviet citizens had to work harder than they ever had, enhancing military readiness to prepare for the inevitable resumption of fighting.[26]

Foreign service officer George Kennan was working in the embassy in Moscow that February. The Department of State invited him to interpret Stalin's speech. According to Kennan, Americans could not have constructive relations with the Soviet

Union. This would remain so into the foreseeable future for two reasons. First, Moscow remained fanatically devoted to Marxism-Leninism, which postulated an innate, class-based antagonism in global history. Second, the men in the Kremlin represented merely the latest in a long line of brutally paranoid Russian rulers with whom Washington would not be able to reason. As Kennan elaborated, Stalin had constructed a police state that relied on a nearly omnipotent security establishment that he used to crush his rivals both within his borders and internationally. He was using the boogeyman of capitalist encirclement to justify all of this. The United States government, Kennan implored, must recognize that the alliance had ended and take steps to counter Moscow.[27]

American officials perceived Soviet escalation in Southern Europe later that year. Yugoslav and Albanian partisans had fiercely resisted Nazi occupation during the war. They continued this into the postwar era, as they constructed a Yugoslav-led Balkan confederation. Their politics were uncompromisingly communist. Marshal Josip Tito (1945–80) had already expanded past his country's borders to claim Trieste. Now he was encouraging Italian and Greek communists to wage guerrilla wars against their allegedly fascist governments. The Greek Communist Party raised an army of approximately 15,000–20,000 that started fighting in September.[28]

Stalin was not behind these events, but his position was hardening. Ambassador Nikolai Novikov had reported to Moscow that a reactionary ruling class had consolidated power in the United States and was planning to dominate the globe through a muscular military, naval, and air capability buttressed by a far-flung empire of forward-deployed bases. Further, Americans were bringing German imperialism back to life to use against the Soviet Union in the near future.[29]

None of these speeches or reports directly touched on southern South American or Chilean affairs. But Chilean Communists and anticommunists nevertheless responded to them, beginning with the PCCh's decision to relieve Contreras and replace him with Ricardo Fonseca, who had risen through the ranks as a confrontational Marxist-Leninist. This change followed Moscow's increasingly hardline position – particularly Soviets' rejection of

Browderism, from which communist parties had been distancing themselves since 1945.

This was named after Earl Browder, Secretary General of the American Communist Party, who had proposed a conciliatory, class-collaborationist approach between bourgeois society and communist parties during the war that he hoped would guide their relations afterward. The French Communist Party's Jacques Duclos criticized this after the war, however. Duclos faulted Browder for his "false concept . . . that at Teheran [December 1943] capitalism and socialism had begun to find the means of peaceful co-existence and collaboration in the framework of one and the same world." Browder's proposal derived from "erroneous conclusions," and they would only lead to communist parties' dissolution and the working class's loss of independence. All communists who had advocated Browder's line, including Contreras, fell into disgrace after this.[30]

This signaled, as historian Robert Daniels understood, "the revival of militance throughout the international Communist movement." Indeed, the PCCh praised Fonseca for his ceaseless opposition to Browder's deviationism, and for "his unshakable faith in the forces of peace, democracy, and socialism that the Great Soviet Union leads." An alarmed González described him as "cryptic, ill-tempered, and stubborn," and recalled feeling "an intuitive mistrust" of him. "I saw that Fonseca's replacing Contreras was going to cause me problems from the moment we met."[31]

González particularly "found it impossible to change Communists' totalitarian mentality, to get them to stop persecuting those Socialists in the labor movement who refused to submit to their directives." This became evident when two Socialist leaders, Pedro Arbulú and Evaristo Ortiz, were shot dead in Lota in early December 1946. The PCCh denied having anything to do with it, but González was not the only one pointing his finger at them. Socialist Senator Salvador Allende also denounced this "violent aggression on behalf of elements of the Communist Party." This represented but one example of what González called the wave of terror that Chilean Communists unleashed within the labor movement upon taking office with him.[32]

These problems appeared within González's cabinet as well. PCCh Minister of Agriculture Miguel Concha pressed González's campaign pledges with respect to land reform and the organization of rural labor as if his post-election promises to Liberals had never occurred. Chilean Communists, hoping to preempt Socialist gains in the countryside, inspired hundreds of peasant complaints and confrontations. This concerned landowners, many of whom grumbled to their Liberal representatives who, in turn, pressed González to rein in the PCCh. Minister of Hacienda and Economy Roberto Wachholtz, the only independent in the cabinet, resigned in early January 1947, reflecting the administration's polarization.[33]

Chilean Communists, in turn, interpreted González's increasingly evident anticommunism as proof that Truman's moves against Moscow and communists in Europe, especially after he declared that "it must be the policy of the United States to back free peoples who are resisting attempted subjugation by armed minorities or by outside pressures" that March, had come to southern South America. Thus, Chilean Communists proclaimed that their problems with the González administration derived from Chilean reactionaries who were colluding with imperialism.[34]

The Marshall Plan and the Rio Pact in Chile

International tensions worsened the falling out of González and the PCCh in mid-1947. In the United States, Secretary of State George Marshall created the Policy Planning Staff (PPS) to introduce strategic thinking in American policymaking that year. He named Kennan its first director in May.

Kennan advised Truman and Marshall to contain the Soviet Union, "by the adroit and vigilant application of counter-force at a series of constantly shifting geographical and political points, corresponding to the shifts and manoeuvres of Soviet policy" until Moscow's ideological fervor mellowed and the Kremlin adopted more reasonable positions. He believed such mellowing inevitable. It might even occur within the next ten to fifteen years.[35]

Marshall, building on the Truman administration's commitment to support anticommunists, introduced the European Recovery Plan (the Marshall Plan) at Harvard University's commencement in June. The United States would contribute more than 12 billion dollars toward European reconstruction over the next five years. Americans and Western Europeans started meeting in London and Paris to plan how to proceed. Stalin's Foreign Minister Vyacheslav Molotov denounced all of this as an expression of imperialism, a cynical device to lure Eastern Europeans away from the Soviet Union, before walking out of these meetings.[36]

Meanwhile, the inter-American community continued to discuss political, military, and economic cooperation. Many in Latin America expected the United States to invest in their nations after the war. Marshall's talk of large-scale American spending in Europe disappointed them. Truman traveled to Rio to explain this that September.

Truman told Latin Americans that the United States did not have the resources to invest in the region at the time:

> We have been obliged to differentiate between the urgent need for rehabilitation of war-shattered areas and the problems of development elsewhere . . . Our own troubles – and we have many – are small in contrast with the struggle for life itself that engrosses the peoples of Europe.[37]

The president asked Latin Americans to back the Marshall Plan and to sign the Inter-American Treaty of Reciprocal Assistance (the Rio Pact). This meant postponing the discussion on regional economic development.[38]

Back in the Soviet Union and Eastern Europe, Stalin reassembled the Comintern, now renamed the Communist Information Bureau (Cominform) and headquartered in Belgrade, Yugoslavia that same September. The Cominform's purpose remained the same as its predecessor's: to subordinate European, Latin American, and other communist parties to Moscow's leadership, which would coordinate these parties' activities. One of Stalin's deputies, Andrei Zhdanov, best reflected the USSR's position at the time. He divided the world into two camps: The reactionary United States and its allies in Western Europe represented imperialism and the continuation of fascism, while the Soviet Union and Eastern Europe stood for democracy.[39]

Further complicating matters, French and Italian anticommunists and noncommunists had ejected communists from their governing coalitions four months earlier, in May. Stalin had wanted these and other Western European communists to remain within these coalitions, but this was no longer possible. These communists seem to have acted too aggressively, precipitating their expulsions. Zhdanov, and behind him, Stalin, now urged them to challenge their nations' bourgeois power structures. Communist-directed agitation and labor unrest ensued in France, Italy, and elsewhere.

Stalin, however, did attempt to reduce tensions in the Balkans, particularly in Greece, where a guerrilla war was raging. He feared this was needlessly antagonizing Britain and the United States, and sharp exchanges between Moscow and Belgrade followed. He eventually expelled Tito from the Cominform, in June 1948. But this was likely part of his purging all communist parties of those not demonstrably loyal to him as much as it was about policy differences in 1947 and 1948.[40]

In Chile, González addressed these and other current events at the Rotary Club in Santiago also in September 1947 – the same month that Truman spoke in Rio and Zhdanov inaugurated the Cominform. The president said the planet was dividing into two parts: Asiatic Russia, as he phrased it, was denying people's rights and liberties while Anglo-Saxons were protecting them. González remained determined that Chileans should align themselves with the latter. He lamented that although Chilean Communists had helped him win office, and that he had consequently felt honor-bound to invite them into his cabinet, the PCCh had chosen the Asiatic Russian side, and consequently he was finished with them.[41]

González had reached this decision between April and September. The PCCh had used its position in the government to reenter national politics for the first time since Gen. Carlos Ibáñez had prohibited the party from doing so in 1927. Chilean Communists, operating under fronts like "the National Democratic Party" and "the National Progressive Party," had already elected three senators, including Lafertte and Neruda, in congressional elections in March 1945. Now they persuaded the office of the registrar to permit them to run as members of the PCCh in the municipal elections of April 1947.[42]

The PCCh performed well in these elections. Party leaders believed that they might have done even better had they not refrained from running candidates in some regions out of respect for their Radical coalition partners, whom they dutifully supported. In any case, Chilean Communists interpreted these results very optimistically, as if they showed that Chileans had repudiated anticommunism, and they aggressively attempted to build on this.[43]

This was not all wishful thinking. According to the registrar's projections, the PCCh was now positioned to become a major national party, depending on whether it maintained its momentum in the congressional elections scheduled for March 1949. González's cabinet disintegrated upon hearing this news. Liberals, concerned that some of their constituents would abandon them and turn to Conservatives, informed the president that they could not risk losing their congressional seats through continuing affiliation with his government. Thus, they withdrew from it.[44]

Chilean Communists, believing this development favored them, resigned from the González administration as well. They pressed the president to appoint a Radical–PCCh cabinet forthwith. They would, of course, take the lead in governing Chile. According to González,

> They informed me that President Truman, with the complicity of the reactionary and Trotskyist parties, was directing this crisis. Truman and his allies intended not only to destroy the ministry but to overthrow me as president of the republic. The Communist Party was the only party sustaining my power.[45]

González never felt more vulnerable than he did at that moment, when Liberals left his administration. He attempted to salvage a broader coalition. He sent feelers to Conservatives, to Liberals again, and to other parties as well. But Conservatives would only enter his administration if he expelled Communists, not only from the cabinet, but from the entire public administration. And Liberals flatly refused to come back. González consulted his own party's leadership and decided to form a provisional, all-Radical government. It was too narrowly constructed. It functioned for approximately two months before collapsing.[46]

González and the PCCh's relations deteriorated further after Communists initiated and apparently enforced PCCh-led bus strikes in Santiago on 12 June. Someone stabbed a noncompliant, noncommunist driver in the back and violence ensued. *Carabineros* put this down quickly, but they had left four dead and twenty wounded. This infuriated González, who addressed the country two days later. He blamed the Communist Party, which had recently denounced the Truman doctrine and the Rio Pact to him, rejecting them as part of an American conspiracy to colonize Latin America. He was sure the stoppages were meant to press him to submit to the PCCh. "The Communist Party's leadership is wrong if it believes I will be its instrument." "*My patience and tolerance,*" he later wrote, "*had ended.*" He declared a state of emergency in the capital.[47]

The PCCh denied involvement in the strike and faulted the United States, González, and the Chilean armed forces for it. But, as Bowers reported to Washington, "All papers except Communist *El Siglo* fix responsibility on Communists." The Socialist-controlled Chilean Labor Confederation (CTCh) singled out the PCCh's René Frías, administrator of Santiago province. Socialists urged González to fire him while purging Communists from government service.[48]

González appointed his third cabinet just after this incident. It was essentially a military cabinet. Rear Adm. Inmanuel Holger became minister of interior, Germán Vergara Donoso, a professional foreign service officer, handled foreign relations, and the army's chief of staff, Gen. Guillermo Barrios Tirado, served as minister of defense. When the president explained why he had done this, he said that he remained charged with the responsibility to govern

Chile, and "I will do it backed by sane public opinion and with the unconditional support of the Armed Forces." He instructed the cabinet "to confront and defeat Communist subversion, directed from abroad," thereafter.[49]

Fonseca and his colleague, Cipriano Pontigo, confronted González at *la Moneda*, the presidential palace, following this. According to González, they asked him to reorient Chilean foreign policy toward the Soviet Union's position in the Cold War. They wanted him to explicitly reject the Truman doctrine, the Marshall Plan, and the Rio Pact, which, they reiterated, was an American plot to gain control of Latin America. This made him "red with ire and indignation":

> I told Fonseca in categorical terms that I was in absolute and total disagreement with such an international position. I believed it not only absurd, but it also threatened Chilean sovereignty and Chilean interests . . . Aligning ourselves with [the USSR] would leave us isolated and alone in [the Americas]. Although we presently remain surrounded by friends, this could change. Internal upheavals, which frequently occur, could dig up old, revanchist policies [for example, in Peru, Bolivia, or Argentina], which could jeopardize our territorial integrity.[50]

González pounded his fist on the table to emphasize his feelings while telling them that he was directing Vergara to vote for the Rio Pact at the inter-American conference in Brazil later that summer. The president would even support calls for creating a regional military force under a unified command. He hoped "this would help put an end to the arms race which has weighed heavily on progress and wellbeing" in Chile and elsewhere. Fonseca and Pontigo stormed out.[51]

According to the PCCh, González had betrayed the Radical–Communist program that got him elected. As Fonseca reminded the president that day, the Communist Party had given its unconditional loyalty "to the people, to the program we have sworn to complete," and not to him personally. "President González Videla did not want to fight the right, and he did not want to face either the landowning oligarchy or imperialism, either. He did not want to complete the program." He had sabotaged Communists' work. The PCCh's "only 'crime' had been its struggle to duly complete its program."[52]

The crises of 1946 and 1947 derived from González and the PCCh's irreconcilable differences with respect to the part Chile should play in the Cold War and from mutual misunderstandings about the nature of Chilean politics, particularly the president's election. González's leftist leanings notwithstanding, he remained a power seeker who kept his options open. He treated campaign promises as revisable and, if necessary, expendable. Thus, he bargained away key parts of the Radical–PCCh program without ever looking back because that was the price Liberals asked him to pay in exchange for the backing he required to win the presidency and to govern with their participation. This was standard behavior for Radicals and indeed explained much of national politics in mid-twentieth-century Chile.

Thus, González discarded his campaign promise to reform the countryside because Liberals, not the Truman administration or imperialism, had pressed him to do so. Chilean Communists misread this and the entire situation as well, and they overreached. The PCCh chose to interpret world affairs and Chilean politics through the lenses of Marxist-Leninism and Soviet foreign policy when they might have compromised and picked a more moderate, long-term course, possibly even finding a way to remain on working terms with González while staying in government, however distasteful this would have been.

Chilean Communists also failed to understand that the Truman administration, although interested in adapting its predecessor's hemispheric military strategy to the Cold War, barely noticed González and the PCCh in 1946 and 1947. When Washington did look at Chile, it did so in the spirit of encouraging, not pressing, González. Indeed, the first contact between Truman and González occurred when Truman sent Leahy as his emissary to González's inauguration. González brought up the issue of Communist participation in his cabinet to clear the air. When González finished explaining how he expected the PCCh to back his government just as the French Communist Party was supporting its government across the Atlantic, the admiral replied:

> President Truman asked me to represent him at your inauguration because he knows of our friendship, and he thought that it would be agreeable for you to hear directly from me his wishes for the success of your government and his sincere and disinterested offer to cooperate in the task in which you have engaged to achieve the prosperity of Chile.[53]

With respect to Chilean Communists, Leahy said nothing.

González and Leahy continued this conversation after the admiral returned to Washington. González wrote that he intended "to transform the semicolonial economy in which we were living into a highly industrialized one." Leahy responded that Truman found this "realistic and just."[54]

The Truman administration's foreign policy was certainly shaping up as an anti-Soviet and generally anticommunist one in 1946 and 1947 – first in the Mediterranean, then in Western Europe, and finally in East Asia. Washington was only starting to fight the Cold War, however, a conflict that seemed limited to Eurasia during these years. Truman did intervene in European politics, but only on a hasty, improvised basis, beginning in Italy in December 1947. He did not start systematically intervening in France, Italy, and Eastern Europe until after the Czechoslovakian coup in 1948, and even this remained small-scale until the Chinese Revolution, the Soviet test-detonation of a nuclear weapon, and the Korean War panicked Americans in 1949 and 1950. And still, as will become clear in the following chapter, the United States did not intervene in Chile. Neither did the Soviet Union, for that matter.

This should not seem surprising. Chile's Cold War experience was not driven by American or Soviet intervention. Rather, industrialization and globalization had set the stage for the struggle that evolved into the Cold War in southern South America and elsewhere in the world from the late nineteenth century into the twentieth. This unleashed far-reaching processes that destabilized and transformed politics, societies, and economies at every level as a particular set of conflicts repeated itself all over the planet.

Notes

1. Gabriel González Videla, *Memorias* (Santiago de Chile: Editora Nacional Gabriela Mistral, 1975) I: 700; and Pablo Neruda, "They Receive Orders against Chile." Pablo Neruda, *Canto general* [1950], trans. Jack Schmitt (Berkeley and Los Angeles: University of California Press, 2011), 332.
2. Michael Stewart, *Life and Labour* (London: Sidgwick & Jackson, 1980), 60; J. H. Leche to Foreign Office, ambassador's annual report on Chilean affairs for 1947, 26 January 1948, FO 371/68205C. British National Archives (BNA); "Parlamentarios británicos visitaron ayer la Cámera," *La Nación*, 3 September 1947; and "Parlamentarios británicos visitarán hoy la Cámara," *La Nación*, 2 September 1947. For an example of Soviet public diplomacy in Chile, see "Inmenso público escuchó ayer conferencia de Pablo Neruda," *El Siglo*, 27 November 1946.
3. Frank Ninkovich, *The Global Republic: America's Inadvertent Rise to World Power* (Chicago: University of Chicago Press, 2014).
4. Governments of the American Republics, "Final Act of the Third Meeting of the Ministers of Foreign Affairs of the American Republics," Rio de Janeiro, Brazil, 15–28 January 1942, at <http://www.oas.org>; and Sumner Welles to Department of State, 22 January 1942. Department of State, *Foreign Relations of the United States, Diplomatic Papers 1942* V: *The American Republics* (Washington, DC: Government Printing Office, 1962), 32–3.
5. Jefferson Caffery to Department of State, 5 January 1942. Department of State, *FRUS, Diplomatic Papers 1942* V: *The American Republics*, 15–16; Welles to Hull, 25 January 1942. Ibid., 39–40; and Hull to Welles, 26 January 1942. Ibid., 41–2.
6. Bowers to Department of State, 30 December 1941. Ibid., 7–8; Bowers to Department of State, 15 January 1942. Department of State, *Foreign Relations of the United States, Diplomatic Papers 1942* VI: *The American Republics* (Washington, DC: Government Printing Office, 1963), 1; Bowers to Department of State, 14 February 1942. Ibid., 14–15; and Claude Bowers, *Chile through Embassy Windows, 1939–1953* [1958] (Westport: Greenwood Press, 1977), 107.
7. Welles to Bowers, 15 February 1942. Department of State, *FRUS, Diplomatic Papers 1942* VI: *The American Republics*, 15.
8. For German intelligence in Chile, see Department of State, *FRUS, Diplomatic Papers 1942* V: *The American Republics*, 186–261; and Bowers, *Chile through Embassy Windows*, 97–116.

9. Bowers to Department of State, 21 January 1942. Department of State, *FRUS, Diplomatic Papers 1942* V: *The American Republics*, 32; Bowers to Department of State, 23 January 1942. Ibid., 34; Bowers to Welles, 4 February 1942. Ibid., 43–4; and Bowers, *Chile through Embassy Windows*, 97–130.

10. Sumner Welles, Memorandum of conversation, 17 December 1942. Department of State, *FRUS, Diplomatic Papers 1942* VI: *The American Republics*, 41–2.

11. Bowers to Department of State, 20 January 1942. Ibid., 1–2.

12. Interview with Yuri Pavlov, Roll 10842, n.d. CNN, *Cold War* (1998). Transcript courtesy of the National Security Archive, at <http://www.nsarchive.gwu.edu>.

13. William Dawson to Department of State, 23 June 1942. Department of State, *FRUS, Diplomatic Papers 1942* V: *The American Republics*, 262–4.

14. Welles to Dawson, 25 June 1942. Ibid., 264.

15. Sumner Welles, Memorandum of conversation, 26 October 1942. Ibid., 266–7.

16. Julio Faúndez, *Marxism and Democracy in Chile: From 1932 to the Fall of Allende* (New Haven: Yale University Press, 1988), 59–68; María Soledad Gómez, "Factores nacionales e internacionales de la política interna del partido comunista de Chile (1922–1952)." Augusto Varas, ed., *El partido comunista en Chile: estudio multidisciplinario* (Santiago de Chile: Centro de Estudios Sociales/FLACSO, 1988), 77; and Carmelo Furci, *The Chilean Communist Party and the Road to Socialism* (London: Zed Books, 1984), 35.

17. Carlos Huneeus, *La guerra fría chilena: Gabriel González Videla y la ley maldita* (Santiago de Chile: Random House Mondadori, 2008), 51–4; and González, *Memorias* I: 223–437.

18. González, *Memorias* I: 519; and Pablo Neruda, "El pueblo lo llama Gabriel." Ibid., 759.

19. "Este es el programa del futuro gobierno," *El Siglo*, 31 August 1946.

20. Huneeus, *Guerra fría chilena*, 73–6; Gómez, "Factores nacionales e internacionales," 97–8; González, *Memorias* I: 470; PCCh, *Ricardo Fonseca, combatiente ejemplar* (Santiago de Chile: Talleres Gráficos Lautaro, 1952), 164–6; and "Por unanimidad de los 302 convencionales, González Videla ungido candidato unico," *El Siglo*, 22 July 1946.

21. "González Videla ungido candidato unico," *El Siglo*, 22 July 1946.

22. Jody Pavilack, *Mining for the Nation: The Politics of Chile's Coal Communities from the Popular Front to the Cold War* (University

Park: Pennsylvania State University Press, 2011), 245–9; Huneeus, *Guerra fría chilena*, 77–80.

23. Marta Cruz-Coke Madrid, *Eduardo Cruz-Coke: testimonios* (Santiago de Chile: Fundación Procultura, 2015), 303–37; and Ricardo Cruz-Coke, *Historia electoral de Chile, 1925–1973* (Santiago de Chile: Editorial Jurídica de Chile, 1984), 101–3.

24. Huneeus, *Guerra fría chilena*, 86–91; Cruz-Coke, *Historia electoral*, 101–3; Faúndez, *Marxism and Democracy*, 72–3; and González, *Memorias* I: 482–504.

25. Huneeus, *Guerra fría chilena*, 51–4.

26. Joseph Stalin, 9 February 1946. Robert Daniels, ed., *A Documentary History of Communism and the World: From Revolution to Collapse* (Hanover: University Press of New England, 1994), 101–3. Also see George Kennan to Department of State, 12 February 1946. Department of State, *Foreign Relations of the United States, 1946* VI: *Eastern Europe; The Soviet Union* (Washington, DC: Government Printing Office, 1969), 694–6.

27. Kennan to Department of State, 22 February 1946. Department of State, *FRUS, 1946* VI: *Eastern Europe; The Soviet Union*, 696–709.

28. Svetozar Rajak, "The Cold War in the Balkans, 1945–1956." Melvyn Leffler and Odd Arne Westad, eds., *The Cambridge History of the Cold War* I: *Origins* [2010] (Cambridge: Cambridge University Press, 2011), 198–220; and Thanasis Sfikas, "The Greek Civil War." Melvyn Leffler and David Painter, eds., *Origins of the Cold War: An International History* [1994], 2nd edn (New York: Routledge, 2005), 134–52.

29. Nikolai Novikov to the Kremlin, 27 September 1946, at <http://www.digitalarchive.wilsoncenter.org>.

30. Jacques Duclos, "On the Dissolution of the Communist Party of the United States," *Daily Worker*, 24 May 1945. Daniels, *Documentary History of Communism*, 99–101. Also see Pavilack, *Mining for the Nation*, 186–7, 210, 250–21; Gómez, "Factores nacionales e internacionales," 87–90; and Furci, *Chilean Communist Party*, 39–40.

31. González, *Memorias* I: 524–5; and PCCh, *Ricardo Fonseca*, 11.

32. González, *Memorias* I: 521, 587–8, 592. Also see Huneeus, *Guerra fría chilena*, 97; Gómez, "Factores nacionales e internacionales," 91–2; and Leche to Foreign Office, 16 January 1947, FO 371/61230. BNA.

33. Huneeus, *Guerra fría chilena*, 101–8; Brian Loveman, *Struggle in the Countryside: Politics and Rural Labor in Chile, 1919–1973* (Bloomington: Indiana University Press, 1976), Table 4, 130; and González, *Memorias* I: 521–7.

34. González, *Memorias* I: 546; "Intromisión extranjera para entregar el poder a la reacción, denuncia el PC," *El Siglo*, 13 April 1947; and Harry Truman Address to Joint Session of Congress, "Recommendation for Assistance to Greece and Turkey," 12 March 1947, at <http://www.trumanlibrary.org>.
35. George Kennan, "The Sources of Soviet Conduct," *Foreign Affairs* 25 (1947), 576.
36. See "The Marshall Plan Speech," 5 June 1947, at <http://www.marshallfoundation.org>.
37. Harry Truman, "Address before the Rio de Janeiro Inter-American Conference for the Maintenance of Continental Peace and Security," 2 September 1947, at <http://www.trumanlibrary.org>.
38. "Inter-American Treaty of Reciprocal Assistance," 2 September 1947, at <http://www.oas.org>.
39. Andrei Zhdanov, "Report on the International Situation," September 1947. Daniels, *Documentary History of Communism*, 107–10.
40. Communist Information Bureau, "Concerning the Situation in the Communist Party of Yugoslavia," 28 June 1948. Daniels, *Documentary History of Communism*, 114–16; and the Central Committee of the Communist Party of Yugoslavia's reply, 29 June 1948. Ibid., 116–17. Also see Rajak, "Cold War in the Balkans."
41. Claude Bowers to Department of State, 17 September 1947. Department of State, *Foreign Relations of the United States, 1947* VIII: *The American Republics* (Washington, DC: Government Printing Office, 1972), 499–500.
42. Huneeus, *Guerra fría chilena*, 79–80; "Reconocido oficialmente el P.C.," *El Siglo*, 7 January 1947; and "La inscripción electoral del Partido Comunista," *El Siglo*, 18 December 1946.
43. Huneeus, *Guerra fría chilena*, 108–16; and Cruz-Coke, *Historia electoral*, 78–81; "Comunistas no aumentaron sus regidores a expensas de sus aliados radicales," *El Siglo*, 9 April 1947; and "Grandioso triunfo del PC constituye un franco repudio al anticommunismo," ibid.
44. Huneeus, *Guerra fría chilena*, 112–13; Leche to Foreign Office, 16 April 1947, FO 371/61230. BNA; and "Renunciaron ministros liberales," *La Nación*, 16 April 1947.
45. González, *Memorias* I: 541.
46. Huneeus, *Guerra fría chilena*, 115–16; González, *Memorias* I: 540–6; and Leche to Foreign Office, 22 April 1947, FO 371/61230. BNA.
47. Gabriel González Videla, press release, 15 June 1947. González, *Memorias* I: 573–7. González's emphasis. Also see Huneeus, *Guerra*

fría chilena, 121–4; Leche to Foreign Office, 23 June 1947; Leche to Foreign Office, 18 June 1947; Leche to Foreign Office, 12 June 1947, FO 371/61231. BNA; Bowers to Department of State, 13 June 1947. Department of State, *FRUS, 1947* VIII: *The American Republics*, 497–8; and "Santiago, zona de emergéncia," *La Nación*, 13 June 1947.

48. González, *Memorias* I: 573, 577–8; and Bowers to Department of State, 15 June 1947. Department of State, *FRUS, 1947* VIII: *The American Republics*, 498.
49. González, *Memorias* I: 601, 603.
50. Ibid., 604–5.
51. Ibid.
52. PCCh, *Ricardo Fonseca*, 151–3.
53. González, *Memorias* I: 519–20.
54. Ibid.

4 La Ley Maldita: The Law for the Permanent Defense of Democracy

President Gabriel González (1946–52) anticipated further PCCh-directed labor confrontations after putting down the bus strikes in June 1947. Chilean Communists commanded particularly strong positions in the coal mining regions – especially in Coronel, Lota, and Schwager, which local, Chilean entrepreneurs had discovered, developed, owned, and operated since the mid-nineteenth century. The president realized that the party could use these strategically important positions to paralyze the country's economy and thus threaten his government. He asked Congress for discretionary authority to deal with states of emergency and to ration coal. He sought American coal to replenish Chile's depleted reserves at the same time. The Truman administration (1945–53), however, paid little attention to González's requests until approximately 18,000 miners closed the mines that October.[1]

González and the PCCh's conflicts, including the stoppages in October 1947, were part of Chileans' continuing and contested involvement in the Cold War, an industrial-era global struggle whose roots dated to the late nineteenth century. These Communist-led strikes, which González interpreted as the PCCh's retaliation for his failure to disavow the Marshall Plan and because he had joined the Rio Pact, led to his decision to break relations with the Soviet Union, Czechoslovakia, and Yugoslavia that month. González also moved to suppress the PCCh. This chapter picks up where the previous one left off, explaining the so-called *ley maldita*, or the accursed law – officially, the Law for the Permanent Defense of Democracy – in its transatlantic context.

The Coal Strikes of October 1947

On 24 September 1947, about 9,000 miners in Lota and Schwager decided to strike. On 4 October, another 9,000 stood with them. The PCCh had been raising these workers' consciousness of their social and economic problems for several weeks. As the British ambassador pointed out, this stoppage rendered the Chilean Communist Party and those workers who followed its instructions vulnerable to González's emergency powers, which he promptly used.[2]

González and his cabinet remained convinced that the PCCh's internationalism rather than Chilean coal miners' grassroots grievances concerning pay and benefits explained these strikes. The party had already organized one demonstration against the president to respond to the emergency powers Congress had granted him, which it had rejected as *golpismo*. Thus, González, acutely aware of the PCCh's pro-Soviet ties and politics, characterized these stoppages as "part of a larger Soviet plan to be simultaneously applied in France, Czechoslovakia, and several Latin American nations."[3]

Secretary General Ricardo Fonseca called Communists in every neighborhood in Santiago to a series of meetings to clarify the PCCh's position. Fonseca spoke about the deteriorating situation in world affairs and explained how what was happening in Chile, including the strikes, was merely an expression of American intervention. The United States, he continued, was transforming the United Nations (UN) into an aggressive, anticommunist instrument – for example, in Greece. He said that Americans were doing the same thing to the inter-American community through the Rio Pact. Further, Washington was using González to achieve its ends in Chile at that very moment. He called for broader cooperation and unified opposition from the left.[4]

Other experiences and interpretations were at play. For example, historian Jody Pavilack has studied the stoppages not from the PCCh leadership's perspective but from the miners' points of view. Many of these workers remained more interested in their economic problems and their families than international and national politics. As Communist Councilwoman Eusebia Torres Cerna elaborated, they were propelled by a breakdown in labor relations that had been in the making for several weeks and, most immediately, from "pressing bread-and-butter issues, especially the high price of basic goods."[5]

González and the PCCh, however, remained focused on global and Chilean politics. The president believed that he resolved the complaints these strikes had raised when he imposed wage and benefits increases that exceeded miners' demands. When Communist leaders and workers ignored these increases and the stoppages continued, he reasoned that this proved their political nature while undermining the sincerity of their economic grievances. Ambassador Claude Bowers seconded González's read on this in his cables to Washington. "Issue raised in Chile by Communist coal strike," he reported, "is now on purely political ground and should be so considered."[6]

These competing interpretations exploded into angry exchanges in Congress the week after the stoppages started. The left, including not only Fonseca and Senators Carlos Contreras Labarca and Pablo Neruda, but Socialist Senator Marmaduke Grove, too, questioned González's motives while assailing the United States. Fonseca, who spoke for the PCCh in the Chamber of Deputies, fired the opening salvo:

> The cause of these attacks remains the brutal and ill-tempered expansive character of imperialist capital in the United States, which mocks the freedom of the press, which deprives more than ten million [African-American citizens in the US] of their rights, which shamelessly practices racial discrimination and lynch law, which organizes the slavery of the labor movement through the Taft-Hartley Act, which brutally exploits the colonial and semi-colonial countries, and which now, with an arms industry enriched through war, is seeking world domination and the subjugation of all countries to the needs of its industries, businesses, and banks ... It is unleashing a new world war.[7]

Grove, in the much calmer Senate, asked why González could not have settled the issue without resorting to force. Why, the senator asked, had he and his colleagues only just learned that the president had increased miners' salaries and benefits? Neruda concurred, lamenting that no one had known about any of this until it was too late.[8]

Conservative Senator Manuel Muñoz Cornejo rejected this as posturing. Further, he accepted González's explanations. He suggested that workers' rejection of their raises revealed the international communist movement's strength in Chile. Chilean Communists, like their French and Brazilian counterparts, were showing, once again, that whenever a conflict between Soviet foreign policy and their own national interests occurred, "they sided with Moscow." Contreras parried this: "The traitors, Mr. Senator – they who have sold the country's riches – are found in other parties," reminding him that "[Pierre] Laval was no Communist."[9]

These competing narratives and the strikes intensified the following week. González's expanding state of emergency had empowered his cabinet, led by Minister of Interior Rear Adm. Inmanuel Holger and Minister of Defense Gen. Guillermo Barrios Tirado. Holger and Barrios deployed warships and soldiers to Lota and Coronel. They used the army to recall all miners subject to the reserves to active duty, promptly ordering them to return to work or face court-martial. The army recruited Indians and peasants from the south to labor in the mines as well. All went according to plan until 2,000–3,000 workers on the night shift seized the mines at Lirquén and Schwager and barricaded themselves in, using explosive charges to repel all attempts to regain control, early in the morning on 21 October.

The army's commander at the mines sent a squad of soldiers to parley with the entrenched workers. This squad leader reported that approximately 200 armed Communists were keeping the others inside. He used tear gas to get them out while securing the mines. Thus, the army put down the PCCh's rearguard effort, but González, Holger, and Barrios had only just begun.[10]

González declared Iquique, a nitrate mining area in the north, under martial law as well. When the government alerted the army garrison there to prepare for action late in the evening on 23 October, a young officer named Capt. Augusto Pinochet was among those who responded. Pinochet's unit raided the nitrate towns around 3:00 a.m. the following morning. It arrested

Communists and suspected Communists, then transported them to Pisagua, the government's detention center in the Atacama.[11]

Next, González suppressed the PCCh all over the country. The president seized Communist leaders, starting with each central committee member inside the areas under martial law. He relegated hundreds of them to Pisagua and other detention centers. González insisted that he was not turning against Chilean workers, many of whom were not members of the PCCh. Rather, he was liberating them and the entire nation from the Soviet-controlled Communist Party's grip. As he told the residents of Lota that November, "The Chilean worker is deceived and is serving a foreign power. The Communists who work for this power will be treated as traitors to the fatherland. These Communists neither ask for nor will be given quarter."[12]

González versus the Soviet Union, Act I

González became obsessed with the Soviet Union, which he saw as the prime mover behind Chile's instability in October 1947. The president believed that he found confirmation of this when the stoppages began, when, almost without warning, he sent Yugoslavia's *Chargé d'affaires*, Andres Cunja, and several other Yugoslav officials to the Argentine border. He explained that these Yugoslavs, the Czechoslovakian *Chargé*, Strantise Cejka, and a Slavic cultural front called the *Comité Coordinador Intereslavo en Chile*, had directed the PCCh to launch the strikes as a test of the Cominform's strength in southern South America.[13]

Holger reported to Congress that the Cominform's South American Bureau, still in Buenos Aires, counted on approximately 140,000 Slavic immigrants throughout southern South America. This included "an appreciable minority of Polacks, Ukrainians, and Russian Jews" in Argentina alone. Analysts at the new Central Intelligence Agency (CIA) in the United States agreed that "the USSR has placed particular emphasis on winning over the persons of Slavic descent now resident in Latin America. The Slavic colony in the River Plate area is unusually large and has been the target of extensive organization under Soviet direction." But these analysts seemed to be thinking more along the lines of Soviet public diplomacy than the kind of subversive warfare González had in mind.[14]

González accused Dalibor Jakasa, a member of the Yugoslav delegation in Buenos Aires, of having instructed Cunja and the PCCh "to (a) intensify the campaign against the US and the western democracies, (b) to attack the policy of continental defense, (c) to carry out sabotage of production through slowing down production or through strikes." In response, the Yugoslav government severed relations with Chile on 11 October. In retaliation to this, Santiago expelled the Soviet and Czech diplomatic missions to Chile on 22 October, alleging that Moscow had intervened in Chilean politics and labor relations, Foreign Minister Germán Vergara Donoso charging that Prague was "no longer a silver bridge between occidental democracies and Soviet Russia."[15]

The Yugoslav government denied the Chilean government's accusations, alleging that Chileans had subjected its officials to "most fantastic abuses." According to the Yugoslav Communist Party, the United States was behind these problems. Ambassador Cavendish Wells Cannon commented from Belgrade that the Chilean government's charges supplemented a growing list of complaints the embassy was receiving about Yugoslavia's behavior from other missions, but he could not verify them.[16]

González sent Vergara to explain his administration's actions to Congress on 28 October. Vergara offered Chilean anticommunists' first comprehensive narrative of the Cold War, explaining how Chile's current problems fit within it. He started out with the Comintern, which had appeared as a challenge to the international community just after the Russian Revolution in 1917. Its primary objective remained to unify and lead the working class everywhere to further its global plan. It neither recognized nor respected national sovereignty. Although the Comintern had stopped assaulting the international community during the Popular Front period and the Second World War, this was misleading. The international communist movement's alliance with

Western democracies against Nazi Germany was never more than "a transitory collaboration," its differences with the international community remaining unresolved.[17]

Then he reviewed the most salient events that had signaled the international communist movement's resurgence after the war, from problems in Greece, Turkey, and Iran to the instability of the Balkans. The press of these events and the division of the world that had accompanied them remained more daunting than even "the great President [Franklin] Roosevelt [1933–45]" could have managed had he survived. Thus "two well defined groups" emerged after 1945: "Western democracies and international communism." These groups followed "different ideologies and opposing political tendencies," and they had "absolutely disparate ends in mind." This explained why the Soviet Union had created the Cominform and intervened in Chile.[18]

This intervention, he concluded, had obliged the González administration to choose sides. And González's cabinet had decided that "the Chilean government, following its traditions, its principles, its blood relations, and its geographic situation, sides with its sister republics in the Americas and the powers that represent Western civilization and Christianity." González would thus continue to back inter-American cooperation in hemispheric defense, as most recently articulated in the Rio Pact.[19]

González's anticommunist exertions in Chile and abroad – combined with the Brazilian government's decision to break relations with the Soviet Union later in October 1947 – exacerbated the problems then wracking Europe, particularly within Czechoslovakia. Ambassador Lawrence Steinhardt, writing from Prague, warned Washington not to underestimate the impact that González's break with Czechoslovakia would have on this fragile government. Prime Minister Klement Gottwald and Vice Minister of Foreign Affairs Vladimir Clementis, both Communists, "were stunned. They have made no effort to conceal their extreme anxiety lest Brazil and Argentina follow suit."[20]

At the same time, this energized Czechoslovakian anticommunists, including Foreign Minister Jan Masaryk. Steinhardt elaborated:

Communists in Cabinet are for the first time in many months on the defensive. At Cabinet meeting last night anti-Communist leaders made a severe attack on Communist leaders. They accused them of having sent only Communist diplomatic representatives to South America and insisted that rupture by Chile and what they described as "probable" rupture by Brazil and Argentina should be ascribed primarily to these appointments.[21]

Gottwald, Clementis, and other Czechoslovakian Communists regained the initiative and seized power with Soviet support less than four months later, in February 1948. As remains well known, Masaryk either jumped or was pushed from a window to his death. This worsened Soviet–American relations and hastened the Truman administration's decision to create a covert operations capability. It contributed to the growing sense of urgency that led to the North Atlantic Treaty Organization (NATO) as well.

This coup in Czechoslovakia, in turn, strengthened González's resolve in Chile. Not only had Czechoslovakian Communists chosen the Soviet Union over their own country, the president proclaimed, but the Czechoslovakian Communist Party, once it had consolidated its position, *declared itself the sole party – no others had the right to exist.* Masaryk was murdered and President [Edvard Beneš (1945–8)] overthrown by the acts of his own Marxist-Leninist ministers." In González's estimation, this reaffirmed Moscow's intention to use the PCCh and the Chilean labor movement to transform his nation into a southern South American Czechoslovakia, and it revalidated his mistrust of the Chilean Communist Party. He transmitted these very firm attitudes to his colleagues in the inter-American community via the delegates he sent to Bogotá, hoping to influence its position on the Cold War, the following year.[22]

Chilean Cicero: Neruda's Prelude to Bogotá

Chilean Communists, too, tried to exert influence abroad in 1947 and early 1948. Neruda, an acclaimed poet, published "an intimate letter to millions" in a newspaper in Caracas that November.

According to the senator, the Second World War's horrors were repeating themselves in Chile. He accused American imperialism, the Department of State, and – in an era before the CIA had become the Latin American left's preferred scapegoat – the Federal Bureau of Investigation (FBI) of having taken control of his country via González. Washington "saturated the country with new FBI agents, assigning them specifically to direct repressions against the mine workers." And this represented merely the first step in a larger plan that would eventually lead to "the brutal domination of our continent." The United States' Latin American quislings would reveal the full extent of this at the upcoming inter-American conference:[23]

> In Bogotá, these puppets will recount how they have carried out their respective assignments. They will draw the dark net of slavery more closely around our countries. And each of these dancing dolls will hold as his Bible the *Reader's Digest* and a police code of torture, imprisonment, and exile.[24]

González, Neruda continued, had surrendered "our military defense secrets . . . to the North American Military Staff." Then he had ordered the Chilean armed forces to occupy the nation on behalf of the United States. The army had imprisoned miners in "concentration camps" surrounded by "Nazi-style barbed wire" and was proceeding to perpetrate "genocide."[25]

González petitioned the Chilean Supreme Court to impeach Neruda for defaming the office of the president after he read the senator's letter. Neruda responded in Congress on 6 January 1948, offering a short history of tyrants and those who had opposed them in nineteenth-century France, Argentina, and Chile, citing Victor Hugo, Domingo Sarmiento, and Francisco Bilbao. Then he named González as a fascist and a traitor.[26]

Neruda sought exile after this. He lived clandestinely in Chile for a year and a half before crossing into Argentina, eventually making his way from there across the Atlantic to France. European friends, including the renowned Spanish artist Pablo Picasso, helped him put his affairs in order in Paris. After Neruda obtained a new Chilean passport, he spent the next several years traveling in the Soviet Union, the People's Republic of China, and India before returning to Europe. He reentered Chile in August 1952, where the president, now on his way out of office, pardoned him.[27]

From exile, Neruda published *Canto general*, a poetic history of Latin America from the pre-Columbian era to the mid-twentieth century that he had been writing since the 1930s. As one literary critic has observed, "The *Canto* does have a recognizable plot, which leads from the prehistoric to a finale that pays homage to the Soviet Union and the Communist party, which appear as the restorers of broken promises."[28]

The *Canto* also had its villains, those who had broken these promises in the first place. Neruda reserved a special place for González, the "Judas" and "miserable mixture of monkey and rat, whose tail is combed with a gold pomade on Wall Street":

> *Gabriel González Videla*. Here I leave your name,
> so that when time has erased
> ignominy, when my country cleans
> its face illuminated by wheat and snow,
> those who later seek here the heritage
> that I leave in these lines like a hot green coal
> will also find the name of the traitor who brought
> the glass of agony that my people refused.[29]

González, for his part, later claimed that he had allowed Neruda's flight into exile, instructing the police "to look for him, but do not find him." The president elaborated that he had not taken anything the senator had said or written personally. Although he respected him as an intellectual, he found him little more than a Soviet mouthpiece with respect to his politics. González cited two examples. First, Neruda adored Joseph Stalin (mid-1920s–1953) until Premier Nikita Khrushchev (1958–64) denounced him. Then he criticized him as "this cruel man who suppresses life and gives orders from atop his statues." Second, although Neruda initially praised novelist Boris Pasternak's *Dr. Zhivago* (1957), he dismissed it after Khrushchev and the Politburo expressed their unhappiness with it. Thus, González regarded Neruda's opinions on political and even some cultural matters as simply reflections of Moscow's official views at any given time.[30]

Bogotá

Meanwhile, an undeterred González continued his plans to bring his anticommunist agenda to the inter-American conference in Bogotá, the gathering that created the Organization of American States (OAS), in April 1948. This US-led inter-American community dated to the first Pan-American conference in 1889. It had met several times since then, creating a commercial bureau and forming many other relationships treating such issues as postal services, criminal extradition, and fishing rights. It remained a loose collection of individual resolutions and treaties codified through different combinations of signatories and ratifications, however. After the war, within the larger framework of the Atlantic Charter and the creation of the UN, the countries of the western hemisphere moved to construct a more formal regional organization while clarifying how it would relate with the international community.

Most Latin American governments attended this conference with some expectation that the United States would commit to or at least discuss an economic program to develop the region. President Harry Truman had already explained why Washington was not well positioned to do this while in Rio in September 1947. There, he spoke of the US commitment to Europe, particularly the Marshall Plan, to a sympathetic audience that nevertheless felt let down.[31]

This discussion on economics and development represented but one of several issues that Secretary of State George Marshall, who led the US delegation to Bogotá, studied before arriving. The others included the political organization of the inter-American system, or the establishment of the OAS, arbitration and finance agreements, and several sub-regional issues. These latter problems ranged from the status of the remaining European colonies in the Caribbean and South Atlantic to questions Guatemalans had posed about withholding recognition of dictatorial regimes.[32]

Marshall prioritized the OAS, and he was not alone in this. The charter that emerged was broadly backed. The question of development, as the secretary recognized, represented a major disagreement between the United States and Latin Americans over the former's preference for private over public investment and the latter's wish to have it the other way around. This would remain unresolved into the late 1950s. Arbitration, however, represented another widely supported proposal that had been gaining traction since the late nineteenth century. The remaining sub-regional problems, such as the status of British Honduras, the Falkland Islands, and Antarctica, mattered to some but not all and consequently did not attract as much attention.[33]

There was yet another issue. Marshall carefully considered how he should respond to González's anticommunist initiative. González wanted to align the inter-American community into a common front against communist threats, both internationally and domestically, in an effort in some ways comparable to the Condor alliance that emerged in southern South America in the 1970s. The Chilean delegation, led by the University of Chile's provost, Juvenal Hernández, as Ambassador Willard Beaulac reported from Bogotá, was already "taking lead for strong action" in private discussions by the time the conference had begun.[34]

Hernández reported to Santiago that the Cuban, Dominican, Panamanian, Brazilian, and Paraguayan delegations had backed González's proposal early, with the caveat that the governments of Mexico, Ecuador, Bolivia, and Argentina remained opposed. Further, the US delegation warned Hernández to soften his proposal's language if he hoped to create the unanimity he needed, advice Marshall personally reiterated in "an extraordinarily cordial" private meeting on 3 April.[35]

Marshall's cordiality notwithstanding, the secretary remained wary about this initiative. Director of the Policy Planning Staff (PPS) George Kennan had recommended he avoid reaching such agreements with Chilean or other Latin American delegations. Indeed, Kennan thought that he should oppose any arrangements these governments might make on their own. In Kennan's estimation, communism posed no more than "a potential danger" to Latin America in the late 1940s. This could change – for example, if communist parties gained power in France or Italy, it would embolden their counterparts in the region. But Latin American conservatives were using an exaggerated threat of communism as a pretext to suppress all opposition, and this was strengthening communist and leftist criticism about the reactionary nature of the region's governments, alienating some who might have joined an alternative, noncommunist left. Kennan hoped that a middle class and perhaps even a strong, noncommunist labor movement would eventually emerge and stabilize Latin America. For the time being, however, Marshall should decline to enter into any anticommunist agreement. The secretary concurred.[36]

Marshall nevertheless supported Hernández at the conference. He asked "whether present agenda permits discussion problems foreign-inspired subversive activities directed against institutions and peace and security American republics" at the preliminary session while explaining that "he was told that this was subject of considerable concern to countries represented." Thus, delegates approved putting the Chilean proposal on the agenda. The US, Brazilian, and Chilean delegations agreed to present it together, when the time was right. Meanwhile, Marshall continued to revise and moderate the proposal behind the scenes.[37]

On 9 April, however, before these behind-the-scenes negotiations could make much progress, a lone assassin murdered popular Colombian Liberal Jorge Eliécer Gaitán in Bogotá. Chaos ensued. People in the streets shouted, "*¡Mataron a Gaitán!*" (They have killed Gaitán – *they* apparently referring to Conservative President Mariano Ospina Pérez [1946–50]). Colombians rose in anger, killed the assassin, stripped his corpse, dragged it to the presidential palace, and hanged it there before anyone could arrest and interrogate him. Others seized Bogotá's radio stations and called for a larger uprising. Riots spread through the city that night. This incident, which Colombians called the *bogotazo*, derived from Conservatives and Liberals' older rivalries and not the Cold War. It inaugurated more than a decade of civil strife known as "*la violencia*," which claimed the lives of approximately 200,000.[38]

The Colombian army imposed martial law the evening the riots commenced. But the fighting swept through Bogotá like a hurricane. As Maj. Vernon Walters (USA), who was translating for Marshall, recalled, "The damage and vandalism in the city were beyond belief. Bogotá looked as if it had been through a major air raid." The delegates withdrew to Marco Antonio Batres's residence – he was the acting presiding officer.[39]

At the time, many agreed with Marshall, who interpreted the *bogotazo* as a Soviet move "to sabotage conference and affect ERP [the Marshall Plan] and Italian election." Rioters had seized all of Bogotá's radio stations too quickly for it to have been spontaneous, the secretary reasoned. The Department of State informed Marshall that congressional pressure was building that delegates should return home and "do something about it." Marshall and the others, including Hernández's mission, decided to remain in Bogotá.[40]

No one wanted to do something about "the Communist *putsch* in Bogotá" more than González. The president had already instructed Hernández's delegation "to reveal the PCCh's betrayal to the people of [the Americas]" at the conference. He was convinced that the Soviet Union – with whom the Colombian government now broke relations – had directed Colombian Communists to disrupt the gathering in order to prevent the passage of anticommunist measures in solidarity with Chile. This remained, in his view, the meeting's most important objective.[41]

As the dust settled, Marshall, Hernández, and the Brazilian delegation jointly proposed a moderately worded anticommunist resolution. On 23 April, the OAS adopted it, declaring communism "incompatible with the concept of American freedom, which rests upon . . . the dignity of man as an individual and the sovereignty of the nation as a state." Each government within the inter-American community pledged to pass measures, responsive to its own situation, if and when required. González celebrated this as a success even as he was already engaged in his next battle.[42]

González versus the Soviet Union, Act II

That same April, González challenged the Soviet Union over the Czechoslovakian coup, this time at the UN, in New York. The president personally identified with Beneš and Masaryk's fate. He called the Chilean representative at the UN to give him his instructions himself. When the Security Council agreed to vote on the Chilean motion that the UN should investigate the coup and, if warranted, censure Moscow, González characterized it as "the happiest day of my life." His euphoria faded, however, after the Soviet and Ukrainian representatives vetoed the motion that May.[43]

González centered his discourse while opening the new legislative session in Congress on Czechoslovakia and other global affairs that month. Chile remained committed to the liberal-democratic international community and opposed to the alternative, communist-led world order that the Soviet Union and its allies represented. He reaffirmed Chile's commitment to the OAS and the Rio Pact. He denounced the Soviet veto of his motion at the UN, explaining that he had taken up the Czechoslovakian case because it presented "similar characteristics to that which we have been dealing with in our own country" and he felt it important to stand against such subversion.[44]

González did not let Czechoslovakia go. He continued to press his case, again and again, before Truman, the US Senate, and in a speech at the Waldorf Astoria in New York while on an official visit to the United States in April and May 1950. The planet had divided into two irreconcilable groups: US-led Western democracies in the international community, on the one hand, and Soviet-led communism, on the other. Chile had experienced Soviet aggression but had also confronted it early enough to stop it. Other nations, from Poland to Bulgaria and Czechoslovakia, had not been able to do so. The task that remained before the international community was to reform the UN so that it might function properly.

Thus, González, speaking in New York on 25 April, proposed that the UN should eliminate permanent members of the Security Council's veto. The UN should also demand that the Soviet Union cease backing communist parties abroad, through the Comintern, the Cominform, or whatever organization might come next. If Moscow refused to comply with this, Western democracies and the international community ought to regard the UN as a failure, and they should replace it with a Democratic International, which would confront the USSR and its allies everywhere. Most of this passed with little or no response or even comment.

González was, however, far more effective in confronting communism at home.[45]

González's Law

González remains known not for his sweeping anticommunist and anti-Soviet proposals in the OAS, the UN, and the US, which only a few paid much attention to, but rather for passing the Law for the Permanent Defense of Democracy, which the PCCh denounced as *la ley maldita*, or the accursed law, in Chile. González moved quickly, as he explained, "to negate the Chilean section of international communism . . . to pry the sheep's clothing off 'the red wolf' and declaw it" after the coal strikes, Czechoslovakia, Bogotá, and the Soviet veto. He understood that he could not maintain a state of emergency indefinitely, so he proposed passing legislation that would ban communism once and for all. This became effective in September 1948 and remained on the books for the next ten years.[46]

This law excluded the PCCh's leaders, the party's rank-and-file members, and anyone who may have supported any of its candidates in the past from holding public office and from voting. It forced Chilean Communists out of representative and administrative positions within the labor movement, and it dismissed Communist, pro-Communist, or Communist-sympathizing teachers from schools. It denied foreigners who preached communist doctrines entry into Chile, and it authorized officials to deport those already there. It forced the PCCh underground again.

This law exceeded anything Truman, Marshall, or Kennan had contemplated with respect to the Cold War in Latin America. Indeed, Kennan expressed his concern that

> some of the measures proposed at the Bogotá Conference by other American Republics might be so drastic in nature that they would, if accepted by the United States, increase international tension, give dictatorial governments in other countries a means of attacking all opposition, and might even infringe constitutional civil liberties in the United States.[47]

Thus, this law belonged to González and those who voted for it in Congress – primarily Conservatives, Liberals, and Radicals.

This influenced Chile's Cold War experience into the 1970s. Political scientist Carlos Huneeus assigned González "an enormous responsibility in the failure of Chilean democracy in 1973." Huneeus found that González's anticommunism had particularly resonated within the professional officer corps. Pinochet, for example, had participated in the nighttime raid in Iquique, commanded the internment camp at Pisagua, and then served in the emergency zone in Coronel and Lota in October 1947. So did most of the officers, ranked colonel or above, who overthrew President Salvador Allende (1970–3) and then served the Pinochet dictatorship (1973–90). These officers had learned, as Pinochet phrased it, that the PCCh and Chile's other Marxist-Leninist parties were not merely political parties competing for votes, but internal enemies that threatened Chilean security.[48]

This chapter has supported the book's three primary arguments – that Chileans made their own history, that they did so as internationalists operating within inter-American and transatlantic contexts, and that foreign intervention, although present, did not define the story. It particularly backs Vergara's assertions that the González administration acted "in absolute independence" and Huneeus's findings that "Chilean politics and not US pressure" explained González's anticommunism. This challenges much of the era's propaganda and parts of some of the literature on Chile's Cold War history. The Soviet and Yugoslav governments, the PCCh, and more than a few historians and political scientists have accused Truman of controlling or at least pressing González to do all that he did before and after the coal strikes. For example, some have cited Bower's cables and a memorandum that recorded a representative from Braden Copper Company telling González that his employer would be pleased to help him request a shipment of coal from the United States if he would fight Chilean Communists in July 1947. Others have pointed out that the Truman administration sold more coal than it had originally planned to Chile that October and November. This coal must have made powerful leverage, they have reasoned.[49]

These papers, particularly Bowers's cables, however, do not reveal that Truman pressed González about the PCCh. Rather, González and Bowers pressed the Department of State, and the department yielded to them. This should hardly surprise historians familiar with the ambassador. He closely identified with the three Chilean administrations to which he was accredited for more than ten years. He had been defending and even advocating the Chilean government's positions, actions, and inactions, and expressing his own frustration with his superiors' responses to them, since as early as Secretary of State Cordell Hull and others showed their impatience with Santiago's reluctance to break relations with the Axis in January 1942.

González started asking Bowers for coal in June 1947, months after he and the PCCh had already fallen out. He escalated these requests, seeking 100,000 tons of coal each month from October 1947 through January 1948. Bowers's cables became urgent, even frantic, after this. He warned that if the United States failed "to supply as much coal as possible . . . [it] will inevitably create the impression here we are indifferent to struggle now in decisive state . . . [and] will have serious repercussions, discourage our friends and have bad effect on armed forces." He also forwarded Vergara's direct appeal, pleading that without American support, "[the foreign minister] confesses does not know where it will end." Bowers beseeched Washington to understand that "The issue is clear as crystal – Communism or democracy." This reflected González and Bowers's thinking in Santiago, however, not Truman, Marshall, or Kennan's views in Washington.[50]

Further, although the Truman administration did indeed send coal, the Department of State had to overcome several problems unrelated to Chile before sending it. As Undersecretary of State Robert Lovett explained to Bowers, "possibility obtaining anywhere near 100,000 tons next month extremely remote." The department remained focused on meeting Europeans' coal needs through the winter, and this had led to reductions in all coal allocations elsewhere. The undersecretary never mentioned the PCCh ministers and lower-level officials who had already come and gone in González's government. He did promise to take Santiago's coal problem to "the highest level." Meanwhile, he instructed Bowers to send detailed information on the stoppages, which he claimed to know little about.[51]

Bowers complied and the Truman administration moved quickly after this. The Department of State's Latin American affairs group recommended that the secretary assure González that he would get the coal he needed for November. The department would reassess the situation each month thereafter. Lovett received Ambassador Félix Nieto del Río and told him that he believed that the department could find about 90,000 tons. Assistant Secretary of State for Latin American affairs Norman Armour found that the department could improve this, to approximately 108,000 tons, three days later. González would still have to pay for the coal, but as Armour explained, the department had persuaded the Export-Import Bank to divert up to 4 million dollars from a separate loan to finance construction of a new steel mill to help make ends meet in Chile.[52]

Neither the CIA nor any other department or agency within the intelligence community, moreover, perceived any Soviet threat in Latin America or sounded the alarm in Washington in the late 1940s. According to the Agency's first estimate on the Soviet Union's capabilities and intentions, Moscow remained positioned to use the region's communist parties to complicate and possibly disrupt the flow of strategic materials, such as Chilean copper, during wartime, should another world war occur. Most Latin American governments would not be able to prevent this from happening.

This notwithstanding, the CIA continued, the USSR's influence in the region, as measured by its diminishing diplomatic presence there, was insignificant. The Kremlin was investing far less effort and funds in Latin America than in the past. Local communist parties would back Moscow's overall objectives, especially in propaganda, but would not likely attempt to seize power in the foreseeable future because they lacked the strength to succeed. The Agency cited the González administration's response to the coal strikes when illustrating this point.[53]

The Department of State and the Office of Naval Intelligence found even these assessments "exaggerated." For example, although naval analysts conceded that "Soviet objectives in Latin America are to deny strategic materials to the US in time of war," they found "that the realization of this objective is remote if not impossible," and they faulted the CIA for failing to acknowledge this. Thus, Truman received no alarming reports about Soviet threats or the PCCh, and neither Lovett nor Armour instructed Bowers to press González to turn against Chilean Communists or the labor movement, either.[54]

The Truman administration and the intelligence community were not the only ones within the inter-American and transatlantic communities who disagreed with the González administration, and who found its allegations about foreign intervention in Chile and southern South America far fetched. The British embassy in Santiago and the Foreign Office in London remained skeptical about González's claim to have unmasked Soviet, Yugoslav, and Czech involvement in the stoppages. Ambassador J. H. Leche believed that González and his cabinet were not thinking clearly, that they had succumbed to Cold War paranoia. This was not to suggest that they were acting insincerely. They genuinely thought that they were confronting the Soviet Union and international communism. Holger, for example, was "the straightest man born, and a strong one, but in the tangle of Latin American politics he is an innocent abroad, and all too easily deceived":

> As I have reported before, all "evidence" of Communist activities is seized upon with enthusiasm by the Chilean Government who in their present mood never wait to judge its accuracy . . . Hardly a day passes without fresh proofs of underground activities being discovered . . . with the Government's special powers, it is all too easy for them to dispense with the formalities of providing convincing proofs, and usually little is heard of the ultimate outcome of their investigations beyond the fact that a few more troublemakers have been relegated to the outlying parts of the country.[55]

This coincided with the Foreign Office's impressions. González released documents that Chilean authorities had seized from the Yugoslav diplomats they had expelled, saying that these papers proved that Belgrade was behind the coal strikes. Leche forwarded them to London for translation and comment. They represented correspondence between Yugoslav immigrants and members of the Chilean Communist Party in southern Chile and officials, family, and friends in the Balkans. They spoke of a mix of political and everyday matters. They admired, quite zealously, Marshal Josip Tito (1945–80). One letter from the PCCh's "Marshal Tito section" in Punta Arenas to Belgrade, perhaps the most alarming one to González, promised:

> We shall not give up our fight alongside Comrade Tito while the last traitor remains, and we count it our duty to report every individual and organization, which has relationship with anti-State [that is, anti-Yugoslav] elements, to our state organs, to our people's government, and to our Communist organization with its headquarters in Belgrade.[56]

Another called for "Death to Fascism and Freedom to the Nation!" in its conclusion, which seemed to refer to Tito's anti-Nazi resistance movement in Yugoslavia during the Second World War, not to Chilean politics and the Cold War. Still another insisted that

> We here desire to remain good sons of our old country . . . and loyal citizens of hospitable Chile, our second home, where we . . . have equal rights with the local people, among whom we were born and built our home.[57]

In the Foreign Office's view, these documents, although of interest to the British government, "do not seem to be at all subversive, although it is possible that they have some hidden local significance." London welcomed any additional information Santiago might provide. But it was "rather difficult to see how the Chilean authorities have made a case against these people."[58]

Leche continued to request supplementary evidence from the Chilean government until he finally gave up in January 1948. "We are inclined to think that nothing further will materialise . . . We know there are plenty of Communists here, but we are still vague as to the amount of foreign participation in the present Communist organization." A Foreign Office official, reading this, noted "Rather what we suspected" in the margins.[59]

Notes

1. J. H. Leche to Foreign Office, 26 August 1947, FO 371/61232; Leche to Foreign Office, 4 June 1947, FO 371/61231. British National Archives (BNA); and Claude Bowers to Department of State, 11 June 1947. Department of State, *Foreign Relations of the United States, 1947* VIII: *The American Republics* (Washington, DC: Government Printing Office, 1972), 497.
2. Jody Pavilack, *Mining for the Nation: The Politics of Chile's Coal Communities from the Popular Front to the Cold War* (University Park: Pennsylvania State University Press, 2011), 266–300; Leche to Foreign Office, 30 September 1947, FO 371/61232. BNA; and "Más de 9 mil mineros votaron ya la huelga," *El Siglo*, 24 September 1947. For the PCCh's raising miners' consciousness of their social and economic problems, see "En Lota viven hasta 17 personas en cada casa pero los empresarios se niegan a aumentar salarios," *El Siglo*, 21 September 1947; and "Compañías del carbón tratan a sus obreros como a seres irracionales," *El Siglo*, 14 September 1947.
3. Gabriel González Videla, *Memorias* (Santiago de Chile: Editora Nacional Gabriela Mistral, 1975) I: 707. For the earlier protests, see "El pueblo se unió contra el hambre," *El Siglo*, 22 August 1947; "El P.C. es contrario a todo golpe de estado," *El Siglo*, 20 August 1947; and "El P.C. llama a defender el Régimen Democrático," *El Siglo*, 2 August 1947.
4. "'La gran tarea del momento es hacer la union,' declaró ayer R. Fonseca," *El Siglo*, 29 September 1947; and "A las 10 de la mañana se inician las asembleas del Partido Comunista en todas las comunas de Santiago," *El Siglo*, 28 September 1947.
5. Pavilack, *Mining for the Nation*, 270.
6. Claude Bowers, *Chile through Embassy Windows, 1939–1953* [1958] (Westport: Greenwood Press, 1977), 166–9; Bowers to Department of State, 9 October 1947. Department of State, *FRUS, 1947* VIII: *The American Republics*, 504–5; and "Aumentados en 40 por ciento salarios en la zona del carbón," *La Nación*, 5 October 1947.

7. PCCh, *Ricardo Fonseca, combatiente ejemplar* (Santiago de Chile: Talleres Gráficos Lautaro, 1952), 160.
8. Leonidas Aguirre Silva, ed., *Discursos parlamentarios de Pablo Neruda (1945–1948)* [1996] (Santiago de Chile: Editorial Antártica, 1997), 188–9.
9. Ibid.
10. Pavilack, *Mining for the Nation*, 293–4; González, *Memorias* I: 669–75; and Bowers to Department of State, 21 October 1947. Department of State, *FRUS, 1947* VIII: *The American Republics*, 511–12. For some miners' complaints that the PCCh had threatened to use violence to force noncommunist miners to support the strike, see Pavilack, *Mining for the Nation*, 322, 330.
11. Augusto Pinochet, *Camino recorrido: biografía de un soldado* (Santiago de Chile: Talleres Gráficos del Instituto Geográfico Militar de Chile, 1990) I: 114–23; and Augusto Pinochet, *El día decisivo: 11 de Septiembre de 1973* (Santiago de Chile: Editorial Andrés Bello, 1979), 23–9.
12. Cited in González, *Memorias* I: 667–8.
13. "Acusados de fomenter agitación obrera, son expulsados diplomáticos yugoeslavos," *La Nación*, 9 October 1947; Leche to Foreign Office, 9 October 1947; Leche to Foreign Office, 8 October 1947; Leche to Foreign Office, 7 October 1947, FO 371/61232. BNA; Robert Woodward to Norman Armour, 8 October 1947. Department of State, *FRUS, 1947* VIII: *The American Republics*, 501–3; and González, *Memorias* I: 676–87.
14. CIA, Office of Reports and Estimates, ORE 16/1, "Soviet Objectives in Latin America," 1 November 1947. Papers of Harry Truman, President's Secretary's Files, Research File: Containment in Latin America, Box 1, Folder 1. Harry Truman Library, Independence, Missouri; and Inmanuel Holger, "Exposición del ministro del interior," 28 October 1947. González, *Memorias* II: 1435.
15. "Chile rompió con Rusia y Checoeslovaquia," *La Nación*, 22 October 1947; "Yugoslavia rompió relaciones con Chile," *La Nación*, 12 October 1947; Bowers to Department of State, 24 October 1947; Bowers to Department of State, 21 October 1947; and Bowers to Department of State, 8 October 1947. Department of State, *FRUS, 1947* VIII: *The American Republics*, 513–14, 511–12, 503–4. Also see Director General of *Policía de Investigaciones* (PDI) Luis Brun D'Avoglio to González, 27 October, 20 October, 20 October, and 22 September 1947. González, *Memorias* II: 1407–12.

16. Cavendish Wells Cannon to Department of State, 11 October 1947. Department of State, *FRUS, 1947* VIII: *The American Republics*, 512–13.

17. Germán Vergara Donoso, "Discurso del ministro de relaciones exteriores," 28 October 1947. González, *Memorias* II: 1417–19.

18. Ibid., 1418.

19. Ibid., 1422, 1428.

20. Lawrence Steinhardt to Department of State, 31 October 1947. Department of State, *FRUS, 1947* VIII: *The American Republics*, 514–15. For the Brazilian government's severing relations with the Soviet Union, see ibid., 391–406.

21. Ibid., 514–15

22. González, *Memorias* I: 707. González's emphasis.

23. Pablo Neruda, "Carta íntima para millones de hombres," *El Nacional*, 27 November 1947. Matilde Neruda and Miguel Otero Silva, eds., *Passions and Impressions* [1978], trans. Margaret Sayers Peden (New York: Farrar, Straus and Giroux, 1983), 276, 281.

24. Ibid., 281.

25. Ibid., 269, 274, 277.

26. Pablo Neruda, "I Accuse," 6 January 1948. Neruda and Otero, *Passions and Impressions*, 284–307.

27. Pablo Neruda, *Memoirs* [1974], trans. Hardie St. Martin (New York: Farrar, Straus and Giroux, 1977), 171–220; "La Corte Suprema desaforó a Pablo Neruda," *La Nación*, 4 February 1948; "Por unanimidad fué desaforado Pablo Neruda," *La Nación*, 6 January 1948; "Será procesado el senador Pablo Neruda, por injuriar a S.E. y denigrar a Chile," *La Nación*, 25 December 1947.

28. Pablo Neruda, *Canto general* [1950], trans. Jack Schmitt (Berkeley and Los Angeles: University of California Press, 2011), 7.

29. Pablo Neruda, "González Videla, Chile's Traitor." Neruda, *Canto general*, 200–1. Neruda's emphasis.

30. González, *Memorias* I: 758–65.

31. Harry Truman, "Address before the Rio de Janeiro Inter-American Conference for the Maintenance of Continental Peace and Security," 2 September 1947, at <http://www.trumanlibrary.org>.

32. George Marshall to US ambassadors in Latin America, 9 March 1948. Department of State, *Foreign Relations of the United States, 1948* IX: *The Western Hemisphere* (Washington, DC: Government Printing Office, 1972), 11–16.

33. For private and public investment, see Stephen Rabe, *Eisenhower and Latin America: The Foreign Policy of Anticommunism*

(Chapel Hill: University of North Carolina Press, 1988), 6–25, 64–99.

34. Willard Beaulac to Department of State, 4 April 1948. Department of State, *FRUS, 1948* IX: *The Western Hemisphere*, 31–2. For Chileans' draft proposal, see "Minuta defensa y preservación de la democracia en América," undated. 01 Vol. 27 & Histórico 2772, Fondo organismos internacionales, Archivo Nacional, Archivo del Ministerio de Relaciones Exteriores (AMRREE), Santiago de Chile. For additional background on Chileans' proposal, "Bloque Americano anti-comunista propician Chile y EE.UU.," *La Nación*, 3 April 1948; and "Chile no es indiferente ni neutral: está con los países que defienden la democracia y la libertad," *La Nación*, 1 April 1948. For González's wish to run an off-the-books liaison operation, where invited members of the inter-American community would exchange information pertaining to the location, movements, and activities of communists throughout the region, including within communist-controlled or communist-friendly nations, and Marshall's advising him to remain within legal, diplomatic channels and to respect the OAS charter, see Marshall to US ambassadors in Latin America, 7 December 1948. Department of State, *FRUS, 1948* IX: *The Western Hemisphere*, 204.

35. For reports of this backing, see Juvenal Hernández to Vergara, 2 April 1948; Hernández to Vergara, 30 March 1948 (two cables, same date). 01 Vol. 27 Cables recibidos, parte 1, Fondo organismos internacionales, AMRREE; and Vergara to Hernández, 29 March 1948. 01 Vol. 27 Cables enviados, parte 1, Fondo organismos internacionales, AMRREE. For Marshall and Hernández's meeting, Hernández to Vergara, 4–5 April 1948. 01 Vol. 27 Cables recibidos, parte 1, Fondo organismos internacionales, AMRREE; and "Acerca de la estrategia anticomunista conferenciaron Marshall y Hernández," *La Nación*, 4 April 1948.

36. Marshall to US ambassadors in Latin America, 21 June 1948; Policy Planning Staff, PPS-26, "To Establish U.S. Policy Regarding Anti-Communist Measures Which Could Be Planned and Carried out within the Inter-American System," 22 March 1948. Department of State, *FRUS, 1948* IX: *The Western Hemisphere*, 193–4, 194–201.

37. Hernández to Vergara, 8–9 April 1948; Hernández to Vergara, 8 April 1948. 01 Vol. 27 Cables recibidos, parte 1, Fondo organismos internacionales, AMRREE; Beaulac to Department of State, 4

April 1948; and Marshall to Department of State, 30 March 1948. Department of State, *FRUS, 1948* IX: *The Western Hemisphere*, 23–4.

38. Hernández to Vergara, 16 April 1948. 01 Vol. 27 Cables recibidos, parte 2, Fondo organismos internacionales, AMRREE; and Beaulac to Department of State, 9 April 1948. Ibid., 39. Also see Herbert Braun, *The Assassination of Gaitán: Public Life and Urban Violence in Colombia* (Madison: University of Wisconsin Press, 1985), 132–99; and Vernon Walters, *Silent Missions* (New York: Doubleday, 1978), 150–69.

39. Beaulac to Department of State, 11 April 1948; and Marshall to Department of State, 10 April 1948. Department of State, *FRUS, 1948* IX: *The Western Hemisphere*, 42, 39–40.

40. Marshall to Robert Lovett, 20 April 1948; Lovett to Marshall, 19 April 1948; and Beaulac to Department of State, 12 April 1948. Ibid., 53, 49, 42–3. Also see Walters, *Silent Missions*, 156.

41. González, *Memorias* I: 723–6.

42. Final Act of Bogotá, Resolution XXXII, "The Preservation and Defense of Democracy in America." Marshall to US ambassadors, 21 June 1948; "Texto de la Declaración sobre la Defensa de la Democracia," *La Nación*, 1 May 1948; "Enérgica condena al comunismo en Conferencia de Bogotá," *La Nación*, 23 April 1948; and "Proyecto anticomunista presentó Chile," *La Nación*, 22 April 1948. For González and Vergara's congratulations to Hernández's mission, see Vergara to Hernández, 23 April 1948. 01 Vol. 27 Cables enviados, parte 3, Fondo organismos internacionales, AMRREE; and González to Hernández, 1 April 1948. 01 Vol. 27 Cables enviados, parte 1, Fondo organismos internacionales, AMRREE.

43. "Fué rechazada moción chilena acerca de Checoeslovaquia por doble veto de Rusia," *La Nación*, 25 May 1948; "El Consejo de Seguridad, por 9 votos contra 2, acogió la moción chilena sobre Checoeslovaquia," *La Nación*, 18 March 1948; and "Chile hace suya la denuncia de [Jan] Papanek contra el golpe ruso en Checoeslovaquia," *La Nación*, 13 March 1948.

44. Leche to Foreign Office, 24 May 1948, FO 371/68200. BNA; and "S.E. inauguró período legislativo," *La Nación*, 22 May 1948.

45. "Plan de 8 puntos para mantener la paz mundial propusó S.E.," *La Nación*, 25 April 1950. Also see British Embassy Santiago to Foreign Office, 6 May 1950, FO 371/81315; British Embassy Washington, DC to Foreign Office, 28 April 1950, FO 371/81323.

BNA; "Democracia deben defenderse de la nueva 5.a columna," *La Nación*, 18 April 1950; "Senado Norteamericano, de pie, ovacionó al Presidente," *La Nación*, 14 April 1950; and "'Hablaré con Truman sobre nuestros problemas,' declare S.E.," *La Nación*, 11 April 1950.

46. González, *Memorias* I: 710; and Ministerio del Interior, "Ley de Defensa Permanente de la Democracia," 30 September 1948, at <http://www.memoriachilena.cl>. Also see Pavilack, *Mining for the Nation*, 301–36; Carlos Huneeus, *La guerra fría chilena: Gabriel González Videla y la ley maldita* (Santiago de Chile: Random House Mondadori, 2008), 197–353.

47. PPS, "Policy Regarding Anti-Communist Measures," 195.

48. Huneeus, *Guerra fría chilena*, 15–16, 355–71; Pinochet, *Camino recorrido* I: 114–23; and Pinochet, *Día decisivo*, 23–9.

49. Pavilack, *Mining for the Nation*, 257–8; Huneeus, *Guerra fría chilena*, 117; and Vergara, "Discurso del ministro de relaciones exteriores," 28 October 1947. González *Memorias* II: 1428. For arguments that the United States controlled or pressed González, see Lubna Qureshi, *Nixon, Kissinger, and Allende: U.S. Involvement in the 1973 Coup in Chile* [2009] (Lanham: Lexington, 2010), 22; Margaret Power, *Right-Wing Women in Chile: Feminine Power and the Struggle against Allende, 1964–1973* (University Park: Pennsylvania State University Press, 2002), 39; Brian Loveman, *Chile: The Legacy of Hispanic Capitalism* [1979], 3rd edn (New York: Oxford University Press, 2001), 217–21; Julio Faúndez, *Marxism and Democracy in Chile: From 1932 to the Fall of Allende* (New Haven: Yale University Press, 1988), 71–6; and Carmelo Furci, *The Chilean Communist Party and the Road to Socialism* (London: Zed Books, 1984), 63.

50. Bowers to Department of State, 9 October 1947; and Bowers to Department of State, 13 October 1947. Department of State, *FRUS, 1947* VIII: *The American Republics*, 505–6.

51. Lovett to Bowers, 7 October 1947. Ibid., 501.

52. Woodward to Norman Armour, 8 October 1947; Lovett to Bowers, 14 October 1947. Department of State, *FRUS, 1947* VIII: *The American Republics*, 508–9; and Armour to Marshall, 17 October 1947. Ibid., 509.

53. CIA, "Soviet Objectives in Latin America."

54. "Dissent of the Office of Naval Intelligence, Navy Department." CIA, "Soviet Objectives in Latin America."

55. Leche to Foreign Office, 14 February 1948, FO 371/68199. Also see Leche to Foreign Office, 4 May 1948, FO 371/68200. BNA.

56. British Embassy Santiago to Foreign Office, 28 October 1947, FO 371/67482. BNA.

57. Ibid.

58. Foreign Office to British Embassy Santiago, 27 November 1947, FO 371/67482. BNA.

59. British Embassy Santiago to Foreign Office, 6 January 1948, FO 371/72598. BNA.

5   The Frei Administration

On Saturday, 21 December 1968, the Chilean ambassador to London, Victor Santa Cruz, announced his government's decision to buy a British-made nuclear research reactor. This closely followed the signing of an Anglo-Chilean agreement to share peaceful nuclear science and technology. Santa Cruz explained that these agreements would "allow the country to be fully incorporated into nuclear science and technology, and to be placed among the best equipped countries of this Continent in this matter." Chileans were constructing a national nuclear center that would coordinate research, disseminate information, and train engineers. They hoped to explore nuclear science's potential to develop their country.[1]

Britons, for their part, intended to cultivate a commercial relationship that would lead to lucrative contracts throughout Latin America, as more in the region, they hoped, embraced nuclear technology in the 1970s. They were quite optimistic. As *The Guardian* reported, "Chile thus will found its peaceful nuclear programme on British technology and – though there is no immediate promise of orders – on British hardware." This advanced Prime Minister Harold Wilson's (1964–70) strategy of attempting to slow and possibly counter the United Kingdom's (UK) declining influence as a global power through exports of British technology.[2]

This chapter reconstructs Chile's early nuclear history. It contributes to historians' ongoing endeavors to map the world's nuclear landscape by showing how nuclear science and technology spread from industrial nations in North America and Europe to countries like Chile in the Global South. Chileans encountered the international nuclear-science community, headquartered in the United Nations' (UN) International Atomic Energy Agency (IAEA) in Vienna, in the mid-1950s. This community included 171 members at the time of this writing, the vast majority representing small nations from the developing world. The creation of the IAEA opened new channels for international cooperation in the 1950s and 1960s and influenced the nature and conduct of the Cold War. Chileans remained an integral part of these processes from the beginning.[3]

This advances the book's central arguments in three ways. First, President Eduardo Frei (1964–70) and the Christian Democratic Party (PDC) arose and acted independently of American backing, which was, of course, substantial. Frei and the PDC had committed themselves to a course of development, modernization, and further democratization before the Cuban Revolution and the Alliance for Progress. Their plans also remained more scientifically and technologically ambitious than the Alliance. Second, Frei and the PDC did this as internationalists operating simultaneously within inter-American and transatlantic contexts, primarily the latter – although never in a way that minimized the importance of the United States and Latin America in Chile. As historian Joaquín Fermandois has recognized, Frei's thinking was simply "more oriented to Western Europe" than the US. Third, foreign intervention and intelligence operations, including the CIA's covert support of the PDC, did not play a decisive part in Chile in the 1960s. That is, Chileans would likely have elected Frei even without the Agency's backing. This will become clear, below.[4]

Chile and the International Nuclear-Science Community

The international nuclear-science community emerged within the framework of the Eisenhower administration's (1953–61) Atoms for Peace proposal. Dwight Eisenhower became president of the United States as nuclear weapons were becoming central to the Cold War. Americans had already used them against Japan at the end of the Second World War. They continued researching, improving, and stockpiling them thereafter. Indeed, Eisenhower's massive-retaliation doctrine became an enduring feature of the United States' strategy against the Soviet Union (USSR). The USSR and UK, too, had developed their own nuclear weapons by the early 1950s. France and the People's Republic of China (PRC) would soon produce them as well – as would Israel, India, Pakistan, and the Democratic People's Republic of Korea (North Korea) decades later. This trend seemed dismal, and even apocalyptic, to many.

Eisenhower was among them. The president wanted to get on top of this problem and turn it around while outmaneuvering Soviets on the peace issue at the same time. He addressed the UN in December 1953. He said that he hoped "to shake off the inertia imposed by fear, and . . . make positive progress toward peace." He proposed that the international community restructure the nuclear field to serve humanity's constructive interests rather than warfare. He believed that nuclear science and technology could become "a great boon, for the benefit of all mankind." He recommended that the nuclear powers share this science and technology with others. These powers should also cooperate in arms control, first containing nuclear weapons' proliferation, then reducing, and ultimately eliminating, them.[5]

The UN created the IAEA three years later. The IAEA's mission was "to accelerate and enlarge the contribution of atomic energy to peace, health and prosperity throughout the world." It shared Eisenhower's special interest in the Global South.[6]

Chile's Dr. Eduardo Cruz-Coke, an influential Conservative senator and internationalist who had come within a whisker of winning the presidential election in 1946, suggested that Chileans form a national nuclear energy authority and join the IAEA in 1955. This quickly gained traction. An interdisciplinary group of researchers, who had started working in nuclear science and technology in the University of Chile's Medical School as early as 1941 and subsequently branched out into the Department of Mathematics and Physics, had already built a nuclear physics laboratory, complete with its own linear accelerator, by the early 1950s. They began working with imported radioactive isotopes in the early 1960s. They envisioned many potential applications – for example, in medicine and public health, such as cancer research, diagnosis, and treatment.[7]

The Alessandri (1958–64) administration led Chile into the IAEA in 1960, creating the Chilean Nuclear Energy Commission (CChEN) by decree in 1964. Congress formalized this through legislation that directed the commission "to increase scientific and technical knowledge in the peaceful applications of nuclear energy," especially those advancing the nation's political, social, and economic development. It would liaise with the IAEA and serve as the government's advisory body in nuclear affairs and related technical matters. It would coordinate "all problems related to the production, acquisition, transference, transport, and peaceful uses of nuclear energy and productive, fissionable, and radioactive materials" in Chile.[8]

Frei shared Cruz-Coke's enthusiasm. Frei, while still a senator, understood that, in the industrializing and globalizing world in which Chile found itself,

> everything is subject to change. A century ago, the one who dominated the textile industry controlled industrial power. Twenty years ago, a nation with a heavy steel industry led in economic and political domination. Today power resides in nuclear energy, and in time the possession of a steel industry will be no more important than the production of textile fabrics.[9]

He named Cruz-Coke CChEN's first president in 1964. The commission commenced operations in May 1966. Unfortunately for Cruz-Coke and his successors, Chilean, inter-American, and transatlantic politics had become more complicated, and the commission's future less certain, by then.[10]

The Cuban Revolution

The Caribbean, and through it, by common culture, language, and history, all Latin America, became a contested Cold War zone as early as May 1958. Vice President Richard Nixon spent several days touring South America that month. He encountered unexpected hostility. For example, protestors spat all over him before crowds attacked his car with rocks and pipes in Caracas. Venezuelans had only rid themselves of the dictatorship of Marco Pérez Jiménez (1952–8), with whom Eisenhower had been on friendly terms, that January. Pérez had fled to Miami, which only exacerbated their resentment of the United States.[11]

The Venezuelan government's embarrassed foreign minister, Oscar García Velatini, attempted to explain what had happened while they were still in the car. "The Venezuelan people have been without freedom so long that they tend now to express themselves more vigorously perhaps than they should." Nixon rejected this. "Those mobs were communists led by Communists, and they had no devotion to freedom at all." He reported this to Eisenhower, adding, "Latin Americans much prefer to be friends of the United States rather than Russia and that the great problem was how we could best cultivate this friendship." He suggested that the American government broaden its contacts with everyday people and that "we must be dedicated to raising the standard of living of the masses."[12]

Thus, Eisenhower became more aware of a list of Latin American grievances against the United States that included his administration's history of backing repressive regimes while ignoring the region's pleas for economic assistance. Washington remained committed to *de facto* recognition, which meant that it still considered it proper to deal with dictators like Pérez. But Eisenhower now understood that pinning the Legion of Merit on Pérez's chest and sending Nixon to embrace dictator Rafael Leonidas Trujillo (1930–61) had sent the wrong message, signaling not merely recognition but approval.[13]

Eisenhower introduced some changes to the United States' position toward inter-American development after Nixon's trip. The president did not go as far as Brazilian President Juscelino Kubitschek (1956–61), who was proposing that Americans create "Operation Pan-America," Latin Americans' long-desired Marshall Plan. But he did modify Washington's trade policies, allowing for special commodity agreements with regional exporters. He also created the Inter-American Development Bank (IDB). Undersecretary of State C. Douglas Dillon committed the

United States government to these changes at a regional meeting in Bogotá in September 1960.[14]

Then Fidel Castro seized the initiative, changing Latin America, and indeed the Cold War. He overthrew Fulgencio Batista's (1952–9) dictatorship in Cuba in January 1959. This inaugurated a new era of revolution and reaction, quickening the Cold War from the Caribbean and southern South America to Africa and Asia. Castro channeled the same anti-American energy that Venezuelans had marshaled against Nixon, presenting himself as David against the United States' Goliath. His rhetoric resonated with many in the 1960s and 1970s, as the Cold War evolved to include not only issues pertaining to industrialization and globalization, but also new ones such as decolonization and post-independence governance, dependency and underdevelopment, and the rise of the Global South. This was accompanied by intensive American and Soviet intervention.[15]

Eisenhower attempted to moderate Castro's politics through traditional diplomatic devices, but this soon spiraled out of control. When Castro passed an agrarian reform law that enabled Havana to begin expropriating American-owned property without compensation, Eisenhower suspended an agreement to purchase Cuban sugar. Castro brushed this aside and cultivated a commercial relationship with the Soviet Union. When US-owned oil refineries in Cuba refused to process Soviet-imported oil, Castro nationalized them. He seized all remaining American property in 1960. Eisenhower retaliated with a comprehensive embargo.[16]

Then Eisenhower broke relations with Havana. Castro had accused the United States embassy of being little more than a nest of spies. He demanded that the US reduce its presence to an impossible eleven officials or fewer – adding that if every American foreign service officer and clerk left Cuba, it would be "perfectly all right with us." Eisenhower terminated US–Cuban relations in January 1961.[17]

Neither the Eisenhower nor the Kennedy (1961–3) administration persuaded any Latin American government to follow them over the next two years. This remained so even after the Cuban Missile Crisis in October 1962. However, all but the Mexican government voted to do so in the Organization of American States (OAS) after Castro intervened in Venezuela's elections in 1963.[18]

President John Kennedy intensified the covert operations the CIA was already running against Castro. These operations, failing to foment a Cuban resistance movement, became the Bay of Pigs fiasco in April 1961. They also included multiple efforts to assassinate or at least embarrass Castro. He survived them all.

Castro and his comrade-in-arms, the legendary guerrilla fighter Che Guevara, issued a plain directive to their followers in the 1960s: revolutionaries must make revolution today rather than debate about it endlessly or plan for it tomorrow, as pro-Soviet, orthodox communists seemed to prefer. Castro and Guevara offered a simple method: rural guerrilla warfare. A *foco* – a small band of visionaries – should take to the countryside, win peasants' hearts and minds through daring political and military action against the establishment, and create the subjective conditions people needed to rise up, liberate their countries, and create a more just political and socioeconomic order.[19]

This represented Castro and Guevara's strategy against the United States, "the great enemy of mankind." They hoped to create "two, three or many Vietnams." This would force Americans to disperse their forces to put out endless brushfires throughout the Global South, weakening imperialism and hastening world revolution. Guevara led by example, first in the Congo, then in Bolivia, where he met his death in October 1967.[20]

Guevara's treatise on guerrilla warfare hardly offered anything new in the field of insurgent strategy and tactics. Indeed, parts of it – such as his advice that guerrillas should cover their hammocks with a nylon roof and carry good-quality backpacks that contained a plate, fork, and knife – read like something one might find in the *Boy Scout Handbook*. Mao Zedong, Ho Chi Minh, and Gen. Vo Nguyen Giap, and not Guevara, remain the foremost innovators on guerrilla warfare in the twentieth century. But Castro and Guevara's energy, and more importantly, their image and example, contributed something invaluable to would-be revolutionaries everywhere – the confidence that they could succeed.

Thus, all eyes turned to Latin America in the 1960s. This included Soviet eyes. Moscow, which had pursued peaceful coexistence since the 1950s, had perceived only a single, American-dominated continent in the western hemisphere, which it interpreted as a relative backwater in the decade or so before the Cuban Revolution. As the Committee for State Security's (KGB) Nikolai Leonov explained, Castro and Guevara had achieved power based on their own revolution – that is, without Moscow and the Red Army's support – and consequently changed the Soviet leadership's views on Latin America. Soviet officials now approached the region separately. Both the Ministry of Foreign Relations and the KGB established divisions that specialized in Latin American affairs. This went beyond reorganization within the Soviet bureaucracy. The Soviet Academy of Sciences created the Latin American Institute and founded a journal, *Latin America*. Latin American area studies courses began appearing in Moscow State University as well.[21]

Meanwhile, Guevara and Castro's brother, Raúl, continued to press for closer Soviet–Cuban relations. They wanted to improve trade relations, and they wished to forge a formal politico-military alliance as well. Premier Nikita Khrushchev (1958–64) embraced the opportunity. Khrushchev saw Cuba as a Soviet beachhead in the western hemisphere. The Soviet government had lost its embassies in Santiago de Chile and Rio de Janeiro in 1947, and Bogotá in 1948, among others, while maintaining relations with Mexico City, Montevideo, and Buenos Aires into the 1950s. It was now able to add Soviet naval and air bases in Cuba to this list of relationships and assets.[22]

Soviet leaders were also responding to the Sino-Soviet split. The Soviet Union was finding itself increasingly on the defensive in the Global South as Mao's China began challenging it to lead the international communist movement, particularly the so-called wars of national liberation that were appearing in Southeast Asia and sub-Saharan Africa. Khrushchev was also angry after Soviet forces downed an American reconnaissance aircraft over his country's airspace in May 1960. He had become impatient with the Berlin issue as well.

Thus, Khrushchev wished to alter the balance of power, even if only slightly, via Cuba. Let Washington feel the pressure of nuclear weapons deployed in an enemy position near its border for a change. As historians Aleksandr Fursenko and Timothy Naftali have argued, "Khrushchev sensed the value of making a grand gesture to embrace the Cubans, while at the same time compelling the Americans and Chinese to respect him."[23]

Had all gone as planned, Khrushchev would have deployed forty intermediate-range nuclear missiles and more than 50,000 Soviet soldiers and support personnel to Cuba. He would have based two cruisers, four missile destroyers, twelve Komar-class missile boats, and eleven ballistic-missile submarines there. But things did not go as planned. These movements caught the Agency's attention in October 1962. Kennedy forced Khrushchev to remove the missiles before Soviet technicians had fully assembled them.[24]

Kennedy pledged not to invade Cuba and to withdraw the United States' missiles from Turkey in exchange for this. But these promises did not save Khrushchev from the criticism and loss of prestige that followed. Rising Central Committee member Dmitri Polyansky reproached the secretary general's adventurism and brinkmanship in Cuba. "Ask any one of our marshals or generals, and they will tell you that [Khrushchev's] plans for the military 'penetration' of South America were gibberish, fraught with the enormous danger of war." Thus, this crisis remains among the most important of the several factors that explained the Politburo's decision to depose Khrushchev two years later, in October 1964.[25]

This crisis marked the end of Soviets and Cubans' honeymoon. Castro's suggestion that Moscow should launch a preemptive strategic nuclear strike against the United States at the height of the dispute rattled Khrushchev and others in the Kremlin. Likewise, the Politburo's decision to negotiate a solution with Kennedy without consulting Castro irritated the dictator, who felt that Moscow was sacrificing Cuban security, not to mention dignity, to save its own face.

Meanwhile, the Soviet Union still intended to display Cuba as an example of socialist progress in Latin America, but Moscow soon learned that this would cost it more than it had bargained for. The Kremlin bought Cuban sugar at "3, 4, 5 times as much as the sugar price was on the world market and thus enabled Cubans to import in exchange for one ton of sugar up to 7 or 8 tons of oil," Soviet foreign service officer Yuri Pavlov later recalled. "All the military equipment including uniforms came from the Soviets," who also helped Havana construct Kalashnikov plants to produce its own rifles and ammunition.[26]

Soviet and Cuban differences in foreign policy became more apparent, too. Leonov clarified that "Cuba always maintained an independent policy. Cubans never sought Soviet approval in Latin America. They saw it as their area: the same language, the same religion, the same history, the same worldviews." Guevara in Bolivia, for example, "was the Cubans' thing . . . We did not know anything about it." "The Soviet leadership," he continued, "did not share the famous slogan of creating 100 Vietnams . . . 100 Vietnams would cost too much in human and material resources. Thus Soviet and Cuban policies diverged."[27]

The Soviet Communist Party continued to fund Latin American communist parties, as it had for decades, but Soviets took a long view of this and did not expect these parties to participate in or otherwise support Castro's guerrilla wars. These parties, such as the Chilean Communist Party (PCCh), became relatively kinder and gentler in the 1950s. They appeared as moderate voices when juxtaposed against Castro, Guevara, and their sympathizers in the 1960s and 1970s.[28]

The KGB maintained a low profile in Latin America for the remainder of the Cold War as well, even if it still approached the region as an active hunting ground where it might recruit agents to gather information against the United States and work toward weakening American influence there. This risk-averse strategy defined the Soviet Union's Latin American policy until the USSR collapsed in 1991. Moscow's extensive investment in Cuba, and to a lesser extent, in Gen. Juan Velasco's Peru (1968–75) and Sandinista Nicaragua (1979–90) represented the exceptions that proved this rule.[29]

The Kennedy administration's answer to all of this remained just one part of the United States' evolving response to the Cold War in the Global South. Eisenhower's massive-retaliation doctrine had proved insufficient to counter limited, low-intensity conflicts in Matsu and Quemoy, in the Congo, and in Southeast Asia. As Nixon and others in Washington had noted, Americans were losing the battle for hearts and minds in these regions.

Kennedy's flexible-response doctrine solved these problems. The president emphasized counterinsurgency and special operations in foreign military aid and education. He deployed Green Berets to countries like Vietnam, Laos, and Bolivia, where they instructed local forces in unconventional warfare. The Agency for International Development (AID) oversaw civilian programs, including those that trained local police in investigations, interrogations, and riot-control. The Peace Corps recruited enthusiastic college graduates and placed them to assist local governments in the construction of basic infrastructure, and, most importantly, simply to foster people-to-people relations at the community level.

The Alliance for Progress represented the particular form this response took in Latin America. In it, Kennedy pledged to generate approximately 20 billion dollars in public and private investment over the next decade. To qualify, regional governments had to engage in a kind of economic planning and social reform they had not known before. Kennedy called it "a vast cooperative effort, unparalleled in magnitude and nobility of purpose, to satisfy the basic needs of the American people for homes, work and land, health and schools." The president promised that

> if the countries of Latin America are ready to do their part – and I am sure they are – then I believe the United States, for its part, should help provide resources of a scope and magnitude sufficient to make this bold development plan a success, just as we helped to provide, against nearly equal odds, the resources adequate to help rebuild the economies of Western Europe.[30]

Lyndon Johnson (1963–9) assumed the presidency following Kennedy's assassination in 1963 and then won his own election the following year, in November 1964. Johnson remained even more committed to the Alliance than his predecessor. It was personal to him, stemming from his experience as a middle-school teacher in Cotulla, an impoverished Mexican-American community in southern Texas. As historian Waldo Heinrich observed, Cotulla represented "his gateway to empathy for the poor countries of the world. His Mexican-American experience led to an interest in

Mexico, and that to a special claim on Latin American policy and advocacy of an American mission to the Third World."[31]

Johnson signaled his commitment to the Alliance when he merged the Department of State and AID's Latin American operations and granted sweeping authority to the office of the assistant secretary of state to coordinate and oversee regional policy. These assistant secretaries – Thomas Mann (1963–5), Lincoln Gordon (1965–7), and Covey Oliver (1967–9) – enjoyed unprecedented access to the president, as they expanded the Alliance's objectives. The Alliance remained broadly dedicated to problems such as land reform and public health. It became more specific, over time, in areas like economic integration and educational reform, the latter field leading Johnson, Gordon, and Oliver to realize that they had neglected science and technology, which they only rectified during the administration's final year.[32]

Johnson had been slow to recognize science and technology because the president, like his predecessor, was largely reacting to Castro and his sympathizers' worldviews, politics, and agenda. This had drawn almost everyone's attention to basic development, land reform, and counterinsurgency in the countryside, on the one hand, and public health, public housing, and public safety in the cities, on the other. The administration belatedly shifted its focus to include science and technology partly because Frei had brought it up.

The Revolution in Liberty

Frei and the PDC committed to the Alliance early. Indeed, they had anticipated it by several decades. They had splintered from the Conservative Party and formed the *Falange Nacional* in 1938. They were interested in Catholic-based social action, including land reform and organizing the peasantry. This had alienated many Conservatives. But Frei's *falangistas* eventually attracted likeminded members from the party's older generation, including Cruz-Coke, who joined them in founding the much larger PDC in 1957.[33]

Christian Democratic ideology did not derive from the United States' Cold War politics and modernization theories but rather from the Vatican's criticism of industrial capitalism, which had first appeared in papal encyclicals in the late nineteenth century, and from progressive Catholics in Western Europe, such as philosopher Jacques Maritain, who had continued elaborating and applying this criticism in France, West Germany, and Italy. Frei's *falangistas* applied these ideas in Chile. They gained credibility as sincere reformers after they led a peasant protest in the province of Curicó in October 1953. They continued gaining support and growing as the PDC into the 1960s.[34]

The PDC became an influential party that decade because Chilean conditions favored it. Radicals, Socialists, Christian Democrats, and other parties had collaborated in Congress to expand citizenship and to reform Chile's liberal democracy in the late 1950s. They did this to prevent the conservative Chilean establishment, especially landowners, who had controlled peasant voting since independence, from continuing to have a *de facto* veto over the country's political system. Liberals, for example, had used their congressional position to derail President Gabriel González's (1946–52) promised reforms in the countryside before he was even inaugurated. These parties repealed González's ban against the PCCh, which enabled Communists to return to aboveground politics. They passed legislation permitting peasants to freely organize and vote for the first time as well. The PDC, who had already secured a strong base among progressive-minded Catholics, challenged Communists and Socialists for these votes.[35]

The PDC presented itself as an agent of change, an alternative to the establishment, or, as Frei phrased it, "reactionaries with no conscience," on the one hand, and Communists and Socialists, whom he described as "revolutionaries with no brains," on the other. Frei promised substantial structural reform, including "Chileanizing," rather than nationalizing, the copper industry (which meant that the government would buy majority ownership rather than forcing a Cuban-style seizure of the mines), land redistribution, investment in housing and education, and *"promoción popular,"* the further inclusion and empowerment of marginalized people, from women to shantytown dwellers and the peasantry. He premised this Revolution in Liberty on his sincere belief that his party could preempt the left by winning enough of the electorate's loyalty to guarantee a Christian Democratic presidency and legislature into the future.[36]

Frei's distance from the establishment notwithstanding, he also represented continuity. He was but the latest in a line of Chilean leaders interested in stimulating industrialization and production that had begun in the 1930s. Chileans formed such institutions as the *Corporación de Fomento de la Producción* (CORFO), Chile's national development corporation. Frei's predecessors had sought out new energy sources and technologies, too. CORFO founded the *Empresa Nacional de Electricidad* (ENDESA) to construct the national grid and to start tapping into hydroelectric power in 1943. Chileans discovered oil reserves in Magallanes and began refining petroleum the same decade. These fossil fuels not only satisfied some of the country's energy requirements, but they also enabled Chileans to export petroleum byproducts, such as propane. Frei was determined to expand upon this, partly through nuclear development, which he would approach as president with confidence since he could rely on CORFO, ENDESA, and CChEN as competent, national technical experts with solid transatlantic connections to advise him.[37]

The PDC attracted attention in the United States as early as spring 1962, when Frei and Radomiro Tomic traveled to the US "to attend a forum at [Georgetown] University that would deal with certain basic topics, chiefly, 'Christian Democracy in Chile and Latin America,' and 'What is the opinion of the Christian Democrats on the Alliance for Progress?'" They continued this discussion at Columbia University while giving interviews on television and radio in New York. The Senate Foreign Relations Committee hosted them for lunch as they returned to Washington, DC on their way home, where they also met Kennedy White House aide Ralph Dungan.[38]

From Curicó to London

It remains well known that the Kennedy and Johnson administrations backed Frei's campaign from March to September 1964, and that Frei won the election with 55.6 percent of the vote to Socialist Senator Salvador Allende's 38.6 percent. Dungan coordinated this from an interagency task force at the White House, first under the directorship of Kennedy's Special Group, then under Johnson's 303 Committee. These two subcommittees used the CIA to manage this in Chile. The Agency employed the same methods it had used in Italy decades before. It sent Frei an estimated 2.6 million dollars while amplifying the PDC's efforts across multiple media.[39]

The CIA also spent 3 million dollars against Allende. For example, Castro's sister, Juana, appealed to Chilean women through a series of Agency-sponsored radio broadcasts that detailed the horrors of communism. As historian Margaret Power has shown, this was meant to persuade women as mothers, and it reached many of them across class lines.[40]

The CIA seemed more effective than it really was because it benefited from a special election in the central valley that had frightened the establishment in March 1964. This, more than any other factor, led to Frei's victory. When Curicó's Socialist Deputy Oscar Naranjo Jara died in office on 18 December 1963, conservatives approached the by-election called to replace him as a preview of the upcoming presidential contest, which remained a three-way race until then. The Conservative and Liberal parties had united with Radicals to form a coalition, the Democratic Front, in response to the rising challenges from the PDC and the far left. The Democratic Front's leaders felt assured that they controlled approximately half of the vote (Conservatives and Liberals about 15 percent each, and Radicals nearly 20 percent). They believed that their candidate, Rodolfo Ramírez, would prevail against the far left's nominee, Oscar Naranjo Arias, the deceased deputy's son. But they miscalculated. Naranjo won the election with 39 percent of the vote to the Democratic Front's 33 percent.[41]

Both Conservatives and Liberals panicked and threw their weight behind Frei as the lesser of two evils, while Radicals remained on their own. They attempted to influence his platform as the cost of their support. But he refused to grant them any concession on any issue.

Frei and the PDC's confidence came from many sources, mostly from their feeling that they were on the right side of history and their understanding that Conservatives and Liberals had nowhere else to turn. Frei was also gratefully aware that the United States had decided to support his campaign after Curicó, where, as the

Department of State's Ralph Richardson put it, "our 'decision' to swing behind Frei was made for us." Washington preferred the more US-friendly and predictable Democratic Front, but the PDC, which remained liberal and anticommunist, would suffice.[42]

Frei's campaign lost no time in requesting 1 million dollars from the US embassy. The campaign could have continued on its own budget of approximately 100,000 dollars per month through September without it. But with it, it would be able to spend about 300,000 dollars per month. Dungan's task force sent 750,000 dollars in response.[43]

This money continued to flow for the next six months, during which Frei complained that somewhere in the pipeline, after these funds had left American hands, someone was letting it slip that the United States was backing him. He asked US embassy officials to inform Washington and to see whether they could not ensure that this would not happen again. He clarified that he thought the embassy's "activities had been well handled in this regard and implied that he saw no reason why discreet contacts between Embassy and select PDC leaders should not continue to be maintained." He also asked the embassy for information that he could use against Allende.[44]

Frei was inaugurated in November 1964. He began implementing his agenda immediately. He traveled to Western Europe in July 1965, determined to attract European aid. As Chilean officials told their British counterparts, Frei planned to use this European assistance to diversify foreign financial aid. The president intended to keep his government from becoming dependent on American support or on US-influenced international organizations such as the World Bank and the IDB. The Johnson administration encouraged this. While in London, Frei met officials at the Atomic Energy Authority (AEA), where he sought and received detailed briefings on British nuclear science and technology.[45]

The Foreign Office was following developments in both Peru and Chile by the time Frei arrived in London. Both of these countries were inquiring whether dual-use nuclear technology could help them desalinate seawater in the Atacama, where the arid, southern Peruvian coast and the mineral-rich Chilean north met. And both had sought the IAEA's advice.[46]

Two CChEN engineers, Efraín Friedman, who would serve as the commission's executive director from 1966 to 1970, and Sergio Alvarado, who would briefly succeed him, presented a paper that outlined Chile's problem at a desalinization conference in New York in the mid-1960s. This attracted further British interest. Friedman and Alvarado argued that Chilean water requirements in the north were rapidly outpacing the country's capacity to supply it. It would cost too much to import water, either from the well-watered southern provinces or from across the Andes – and so would solar-powered desalinization techniques. They preferred nuclear desalination because it also offered electricity and could thus kill two birds with one stone.[47]

The IAEA dispatched a mission to Chile in March 1966. Its team suggested that Chileans develop either fossil-fueled or nuclear-powered desalinization plants, that it seek new water sources on or below the surface, and that it expand existing pipelines to the north. It also advised the Chilean government to commission a more thorough study before proceeding. The Frei administration contracted Ewbank and Partners, a London consultancy, to conduct it. The British government paid 80 percent of Ewbank's costs.[48]

The Wilson government subsidized Ewbank because it recognized this as a chance to showcase British nuclear expertise in Chile and southern South America. Santa Cruz was also working with Edmond de Rothschild, a British merchant banker from a family long involved in Anglo-Chilean finance. They worked behind the scenes in London to ensure that Wilson and his cabinet saw this chance. A gradual change from what had been cautious British attitudes toward Latin America between the 1930s and 1960s toward a more imaginative and risk-taking posture worked in Rothschild and Santa Cruz's favor.[49]

Rothschild met several mid-level officials at the Ministry of Overseas Development (ODM) in December 1965, months before the IAEA team arrived in Chile. He advised them that Mexico and Israel would soon test nuclear-powered desalinization plants and that, if these were successful, Chile and Iran, among others, would follow. "If Britain were to stand a reasonable chance of exporting desalinization plant to these last named states in the 1970s, then a start in preparing the ground must be made now."[50]

In Washington, Johnson officials were also asking Britons and West Germans "to pay more attention to Latin America." Although the United States and its Western European allies had clashed in the Caribbean, particularly where Britons, French, Spaniards, and others were trading with Cuba against Johnson's protests, the situation was different in southern South America. US power and influence were not as strong there as they were in the Caribbean. And the security situation there, far from Havana, Ciudad Trujillo, and the Panama Canal, seemed less urgent at the time. Johnson sent Gordon to London and Bonn to urge these governments to get more involved.[51]

Thus, Britons found all the right doors open in Chile. Several companies from many nations had bid on the Ewbank study, but Chileans clearly preferred Britain. They had made special efforts to invite the Britons to submit their offer. This affinity came from more than Santa Cruz and Rothschild's endeavors in London. It derived from nearly 150 years of Anglo-Chilean relations, which had cultivated much more than mere goodwill. Chileans identified with Britain so closely that they called themselves the English of South America, and Britons like Rothschild knew this. But Britons still had to deal with their French competitors.[52]

Enter Charles de Gaulle

In addition to the Wilson government, French President Charles de Gaulle (1958–69) also reached out to Latin America. De Gaulle intended to strengthen France's position in the South Pacific, including Pacific South America from Colombia to Chile, following his decision to test nuclear weapons there. This remained part of his larger efforts to restore French greatness through an independent foreign policy and nuclear deterrent. De Gaulle's initiatives coincided with CChEN's expansion, and he was already exploiting the opening this presented by the time Britons began thinking about moving in.[53]

CChEN was growing rapidly. The Frei administration increased the commission's budget from approximately 80,000 escudos in 1965 to 500,000 escudos and 120,000 dollars in foreign aid, mainly from the IAEA and France, in 1966. This rose to 1.5 million escudos and 40,000 dollars in 1968. Then it soared to 5 million escudos and 200,000 dollars, now primarily from the IAEA and Britain. CChEN controlled assets valued at 7 million escudos by 1969.[54]

CChEN's engineers and scientists had also become more visible in the international community by the mid-1960s. They attended conferences in Buenos Aires, Lima, Mexico City, Washington, DC, and Vienna, and several meetings in Norway, France, Austria, and Czechoslovakia in 1966 alone. The commission negotiated partnerships with its counterparts in Argentina, France, and Israel. CChEN still lacked the physical infrastructure it needed. It required a national center and research reactor, trained engineers to operate it, and highly enriched uranium to fuel it.

De Gaulle offered to meet many of these needs. Chilean officials and scientists at the National Health Service, the University of Chile, and the Federico Santa María Technical University started to operate a network of monitoring stations that spanned the country and reached out into the South Pacific via Easter Island. De Gaulle's representatives assisted them as they evaluated the air, water, and food, especially milk, vegetables, and fish, for gamma radiation that the fallout from France's tests was producing. De Gaulle also trained Chilean engineers in France while sending French and Belgian instructors to Chile. Socia, a French company, offered to provide a research reactor on very favorable terms, through a 3 million-franc grant and a 7 million-franc loan via the French government, or 420,000 pounds by British reckoning at the time, repayable over twenty years at 3 1/2 percent.[55]

Fairey Engineering (FEL), a British firm, was also negotiating with CChEN, but the company lacked the government support Socia counted on and its costs remained more than twice as high. Fairey could sell a reactor to the commission for 800,000 pounds. Fairey offered CChEN a private loan which Chileans could repay over five years at 5 1/2 percent, which was the best it could do. The Board of Trade's Export Credits Guarantee Department (ECGD) had ruled that existing policies did not permit it to subsidize Fairey. So CChEN was inclined to accept the French offer and was poised to formally recommend this to the Frei administration by October

1968. But Frei still preferred Britain. Thus, Santa Cruz asked to see Foreign Secretary Michael Stewart to request ministerial intervention in October 1968.[56]

De Gaulle as Leverage

Santa Cruz reconfirmed that the Frei administration was seeking European help in this endeavor, because "It would not be a good thing, he thought, for Chile to become dependent on the U.S. in this field." Frei wanted British support in particular because Britons had experience installing research reactors abroad. The French did not. Britons were offering more long-term support and spare parts than the French. Perhaps most importantly, Santiago was concerned that accepting the French offer would tie its hands with respect to its objections to France's nuclear testing in the future. Stewart agreed that de Gaulle might have been attempting to win Chilean friends and influence Santiago's policy through generous aid and technical support.[57]

Stewart also agreed that the Wilson government could improve Fairey's offer if the circumstances warranted it. Santa Cruz seized this opening. He tantalized Stewart, comparing the benefits of investing in nuclear science and technology to those that followed railroad construction a century earlier. He proposed that the AEA and CChEN negotiate a treaty to cooperate in these matters. He further suggested that the Frei administration might sign such a document and announce its decision to buy British during Queen Elizabeth II's state visit the following month. Stewart agreed to this, too. He pressed Whitehall to reevaluate the situation.[58]

Elizabeth visited Chile in November 1968. Lord Chalfont (Alun Gwynne Jones), a minister who specialized in defense policy, accompanied her. Britain's interests in Chile and southern South America ranged from cultural and educational exchange to arms sales – Chileans were buying three squadrons of Hunters from the Hawker Siddeley Group at the time. The British government was also backing a 4 million-pound line of credit that Baring Brothers,

Rothschilds, and the Bank of London were offering the Chilean government.[59]

Chalfont's brief included all of this, but he primarily came to Santiago to negotiate the nuclear deal. The Foreign Office had advised him that

> we should do our utmost to obtain this order for the U.K., not only because in itself it represents a sizeable piece of business but also because a nuclear centre in Chile containing a British research reactor and equipment together with the Cooperation that would flow from such an arrangement would give the U.K. an excellent lead when the Chileans decide to build their first nuclear power station.[60]

Chalfont and Ambassador Frederick Cecil Mason met Chilean Foreign Minister Gabriel Valdés, Santa Cruz, and Friedman to discuss this during the queen's visit.

Chalfont eventually discovered that the Frei administration had its own plans and was skillfully implementing them. Frei intended to acquire a British and not a French reactor, but on Chilean and not British terms. He also planned to inaugurate a national center before the presidential elections two years hence. Frei's negotiators skillfully pursued this. As the British embassy gradually understood,

> there has been a lot of political steam put behind this project ... the Christian Democrats are anxious to have something to show for themselves in this field before September [1970], i.e. they would like some part of the project to have reached a stage where there could be some opening ceremony and attendant publicity.[61]

Chalfont argued that the British reactor suited Chilean needs better than the French one. An Anglo-Chilean partnership, moreover, offered long-term technical advantages – such as superior fueling techniques – that outweighed any short-term financial gains Chileans might realize from the French offer. Valdés had explained earlier that the Frei administration would consider Chile's overall trading position with potential sellers when reaching its decision. Chalfont reminded him of "the balance of our bilateral trade, which was in the ratio of 3:1 against us." Mason added "that we had also provided a total of about £60 million in credits over the last couple of years."[62]

Friedman conceded that Britain was ahead in such areas as fueling techniques. This notwithstanding, he had already decided that the French reactor better suited CChEN's needs. Further, the technical differences between Britain and France in such areas as reactor construction and radioisotope production remained negligible. "Señor Friedman," the British embassy reported, "concluded that the Commission's assessment at the moment was that they would recommend to the Chilean government that they should purchase the French reactor." Valdés remained silent as Friedman, who sincerely preferred the French offer, pressed these points to a discouraged British negotiating team.[63]

Chalfont cabled Stewart that the Frei administration would likely announce its decision to buy French within days. He elaborated how French engineers had been advising Chileans for more than a year, and that Socia had consequently gained advantages that Fairey simply could not catch up with. The Foreign Office, to avoid further discomfiture, should not sign the agreement that Stewart had drafted for Santa Cruz until a decent interval had elapsed.[64]

But the situation was not as it seemed. Valdés found Chalfont the next day and suggested they sign the agreement immediately. He assured him that the Frei administration would either buy British or delay buying French until after the New Year, sparing Britons embarrassment. Meanwhile, Fairey should send representatives to Santiago to persuade CChEN, and the Wilson government ought to continue improving the company's offer through government subsidies as well. Chalfont signed the agreement right away, reporting that the administration's position "had changed markedly in our favour."[65]

Valdés confirmed that his government was distancing itself from the French offer two days later. The foreign minister told Mason that he had informed the French ambassador that the British government was making an attractive offer, and his government was considering it. The French ambassador protested, citing existing Franco-Chilean understandings. Valdés retorted that

> the French Government could hardly expect special treatment in view of the embarrassment and difficulties caused to Chile by such French actions as the sale of supersonic aircraft [Mirages] and armaments to Peru and Argentina. This indicated a purely commercial approach to Latin American problems ignoring the interests of Chile.[66]

"There seems no doubt whatsoever," Mason further wrote, "that the Chilean Government are now resolved to buy from us if we can go some way to meet their requirements." Fairey responded swiftly. Its representatives planned to depart for Santiago by the second week of December.[67]

Meanwhile, Stewart's earlier instructions had caused the bureaucratic wheels to turn in Whitehall. The ODM prepared to offer the Chilean government a special loan to purchase the Fairey reactor: up to 100,000 pounds to cover the down payment, repayable over fifteen years with a five-year grace period ending in 1974, at 7 3/4 percent. The ECGD pledged to guarantee Fairey's remaining costs for ten years at 5 1/2 percent.[68]

The Frei administration continued using France to press the Wilson government to go even further. Santa Cruz told Chalfont, who had returned to London, that CChEN was advising the administration to accept the French offer. He predicted that if the administration accepted this, Britain would have no place in Chile's nuclear future. The commission would still welcome Fairey's representatives in Santiago, "but naturally with no commitments." He suggested that the Wilson government might improve the company's chances if it granted Chile 100,000 pounds in equipment in addition to ODM's special loan, and then permitted Chileans to repay that loan over twenty years, and the ECGD's loans over fifteen years, both at 5 1/2 percent. Rothschild called Chalfont to convey these terms later that day.[69]

The Foreign Office deemed the Frei administration's new terms "really somewhat unreasonable" and rejected them. Whitehall finally comprehended that Chileans were using France as leverage to force Britons to improve their offer. As one Foreign Office official recognized, "if we improve our terms, this may provide the Chileans with a lever to extract even better terms from the French Government," and so on. Chalfont concurred. He told Santa Cruz that "the terms which we have already offered are exceptionally favourable and it would be very difficult indeed for us to make any further modifications."[70]

CChEN received Fairey's representatives two days later. These harried representatives further reduced their bid, promising to match any French offer. They also satisfied the commission that Fairey's reactor better suited Chile's technical requirements than Socia's. CChEN now advised the Frei administration to buy British. Santa Cruz, as described above, announced this at the Chilean embassy on 21 December. Thus, Frei seized the initiative while adroitly negotiating the most favorable agreement possible from the precise seller he had wanted to do business with from the start. But this merely represented a small success within what was becoming a larger pattern of failure.

Out of Time: The Election of 1970

Frei had grown disappointed with the Alliance for Progress by the late 1960s. He lamented this in *Foreign Affairs* in April 1967. He complained that its earlier idealism had dissipated, that it had lost its focus, and that it was becoming just another foreign-aid program. He cited conflicting priorities and preferences in different Latin American countries, which, as a group and as individual nations, all lacked "a clear ideological direction and determination." Both the far right and far left not only opposed the Alliance, but they sabotaged it when they could – the right criticizing it as "utopian and unrealistic" and the left dismissing it as "an instrument of imperialism." He was speaking of inter-American affairs generally, but he faced the same problems in Chile.[71]

As the Nixon administration's (1969–74) National Security Council (NSC) noted after Chile's congressional elections in March 1969, Chilean politics were becoming polarized, "with the conservative right and the Marxist left coming out the greatest beneficiaries." Frei and the PDC could regain the initiative, but "they must move rapidly to improve the economy and to plan their strategy for the elections" in 1970. Frei's efforts to secure transatlantic cooperation while realizing his nuclear initiatives were very much a part of his attempts to regain the momentum he had lost in Chilean politics.[72]

The Frei administration signed the British promissory note for the reactor loan in March 1969, and the two governments ratified the agreements they had negotiated that October. New problems followed. Some derived from a French backlash, others from Fairey and CChEN's difficulties, mostly resulting from their hasty negotiations, but also from deeper cultural differences and even personality clashes, and still others from the rising Chilean left, which broadly opposed many of Frei's policies. Although these problems did not prevent the commission's eventually completing its projects, Frei would not see any of its successes before leaving office.

The Wilson government solved the first problem easily enough. An angry French government expelled the Chilean engineers it was training when it learned that the Frei administration had accepted the British offer. The Foreign Office simply moved these engineers to Britain and continued their training there. The AEA helped enroll two Chilean military officers in a two-year civilian program in nuclear engineering at Queen Mary College as well.[73]

Fairey and CChEN's worsening relations presented a more serious problem. Indeed, the British embassy was calling them warlike by December 1970. This originated with their governments' thrusting them into poorly prepared, high-pressure negotiations, and with Chileans' conflating the British government and Fairey. The agreement CChEN and the company had produced lacked the clear meeting of the minds the Franco-Chilean contract would probably have had. Fairey's directors interpreted it very narrowly, exactly as it appeared on paper. But CChEN chose a more expansive interpretation, premised on Fairey's last-minute promises to match the French offer, promises which Chileans continued using to press Britons for yet more advantages.[74]

This first appeared when Valdés traveled to London to exchange ratification instruments in October 1969. He also planned to sign what he believed were minor, ancillary agreements in a press conference at the Chilean embassy. But these were not, in fact, minor or ancillary matters. CChEN had modified the reactor's design specifications several times, and the project's costs had increased by 110,000 pounds. Fairey had provisionally accepted these changes, understanding that the commission would pay the new costs directly or that the Wilson government would offer Chileans supplementary, low-interest loans to do so. When Fairey's representatives approached Valdés at the signing ceremony, laying the amended agreement before him, explaining that expected additional modifications were going to incur even more costs as construction continued, "Chileans exploded at this and the signature ceremony was cancelled."[75]

Valdés threatened to nullify all of the agreements unless the Wilson government resolved these differences in CChEN's favor. He would go to Chalfont, Stewart, and even the queen, if necessary. The Foreign Office avoided direct involvement, proposing Fairey and Valdés sign the original contract and set the company's amended agreement aside. If new costs had arisen, Fairey and CChEN should discuss them later. This assuaged tempers that day, but Fairey and CChEN's relations only worsened afterward.

Friedman presented the commission's complaints to the British embassy several months later. CChEN expected the ODM to send more equipment to Chile than it was sending, the commission requested that AEA waive approximately 20,000 pounds in inspection costs it deemed unreasonable, it asked the Foreign Office to extend its engineers' training programs, which would end in May, to September, and it accused Fairey of delaying the project's completion.[76]

Although most at the British embassy and many at the Foreign Office sympathized with Friedman, others in Whitehall, particularly at the AEA, had grown wary of CChEN, and they objected to Friedman's complaints. Dr. Fritz Hinzner, CChEN's senior engineer, had come earlier to London to negotiate the inspection costs. AEA officials found him abrasive, and they compared his continually citing the French offer to get a better deal to blackmail. "When Dr. Hinzner was in this country," one protested, "he tried consistently to force us into additional offers of help by quoting what the French had promised." With respect to the inspection costs, they were not seeking profit or charging Chileans unnecessarily.

Rather, their charges derived from the inspection's actual costs. With respect to Friedman's allegation that Fairey was delaying the project, "This of course is a matter for Faireys themselves."[77]

Fairey's board members were in no mood for this. They personalized it as a dispute with Hinzner, a dispute that became so bitter that the Foreign Office had to intercede. Each side was openly accusing the other of breaching the contract by November 1970, and the company was threatening to walk away. Further complicating this, and perhaps driving Hinzner's desperation, Allende had won the presidential election that year. He was inaugurated the same month the Foreign Office attempted to mediate this problem.

The Allende campaign had made it clear that it regarded some imported technology, particularly from the United States and Western Europe, with suspicion. As Allende explained in more detail when addressing the UN's Conference on Trade and Development in April 1972, imperialism had long exploited and impoverished the Global South through its self-serving use of technology. This had robbed the developing world of its trained professionals, its culture, and its creativity while underdeveloping it. "These conditions must be abolished," he insisted. "We must be able to select technology in relation to our own needs and our own development plans."[78]

Both Frei and CChEN had seen Allende's challenge coming. Indeed, it remained an old argument to them. Many on the Chilean left not only opposed Frei's approach to development, as the president acknowledged in his *Foreign Affairs* piece, but they rejected the commission, its external relations, and its ongoing construction projects, too. Chileans, these critics argued, must devote their limited resources to more pressing problems. They wanted to realign Chilean foreign relations toward the Soviet Union and Cuba while liberating and nationalizing their mineral wealth and financial system from the US and other Western interests. They wanted to see an aggressive land reform program. And they wished to combat poverty in public housing, public health, and the education system as well.

Dr. Benjamín Viel, CChEN's president from 1966 to 1968, had responded to some of this criticism. According to Viel, scientific and technological innovation did not derive from economic growth or social progress. Rather, it drove them. When Europeans had first embraced industrialization, they were less developed than Chile presently was. They had not modernized by investing their resources in literacy campaigns. Rather, they progressed because they boldly invested in the most advanced science and technology of the time, from textile mills to railroads. Socioeconomic improvements, which enabled them to prevent large numbers of needless deaths, solve multiple food-production problems, and improve education, followed and did not precede this. "Transcending underdevelopment and incorporating Chile into the community of nations that offers its citizens a just life requires stimulating scientific innovation," Viel concluded. Chileans should think imaginatively and act ambitiously. Now was not the time to think small.[79]

Viel lost this argument when Allende entered *la Moneda*, the presidential palace. The Allende administration promptly suspended the commission's projects, subject to further review. CChEN's board had resigned during the transition, as was customary in Chilean politics, but the incoming government did not reappoint it, as was also customary. Friedman left his position as executive director, and, like Viel and more than 2,500 other managers and skilled technicians, left the country. Hinzner began acting as director on his own initiative. All of this threw CChEN into disarray, which compounded its problems with Fairey. This landed on the Foreign Office's desks with an unwelcome thud that November.[80]

According to Fairey's board, CChEN was failing to understand the relationship between its modifications, the company's price increases, and the project's delays. The commission was refusing to pay its bills as well. Hinzner, Fairey continued, was not positioned to place legal orders. But he was placing orders anyway, insisting that Fairey accept his "letters of intent." The company's board members feared that if they honored these letters, they would never receive payment. "FEL are being forced to the conclusion that the Comision [*sic*] has no intention of honoring the contract . . . FEL's best course will shortly be to recognize this and end the contract." Fairey asked the Foreign Office to find out what had happened to Friedman, clarify Hinzner's status, and sound out the Allende administration.[81]

According to Hinzner, Fairey was arbitrarily and unfairly increasing costs on items already quoted, it was declining to accept his orders, and it was demanding payments but refusing to submit proper invoices. For example, he and Fairey had previously agreed to install an upgraded water make-up plant in the reactor. But the company, citing a revised estimate, had raised the price more than 40 percent since then. This and other unexplained and unjustified increases concerned him, and he asked the Foreign Office to audit Fairey's pricing.[82]

Hinzner also wrote to Fairey's board directly. He discussed the water make-up plant and several other items. He alleged that the company was acting in bad faith. Unless it justified its prices to his satisfaction, he would bypass it and deal with its subcontractors and even the subcontractors' suppliers instead.[83]

Fairey's board responded in an unmistakably condescending tone. The board told Hinzner that the company was working diligently to control costs. But each modification created new expenses, as reflected in the subcontractors' revised estimates that he already had before him. However this may have been, Fairey did not have to justify its prices or otherwise defend its integrity to Hinzner. The board dismissed most of his complaints as false, and rejected others as irrelevant. It announced that it was withdrawing all outstanding offers and quotations forthwith. Both parties would have to renegotiate everything before proceeding, if they remained interested in proceeding at all. CChEN had a week to respond. If it failed to do so, Fairey would terminate its relationship with the commission.[84]

By this time, the Foreign Office merely wished to salvage what it could. It, too, was serving a new government. Prime Minister Edward Heath (1970–4) had replaced Wilson in June 1970. The Foreign Office no longer regarded Chile's nuclear project as optimistically as it had. The dual-use project in Antofagasta that had been expected to lead to substantial orders in the 1970s was becoming increasingly improbable. ENDESA now proposed to address the northern water problem with larger reservoirs and through recycling. It would purchase and operate conventional electrical power stations there unless nuclear technology proved cheaper, which seemed unlikely. Several European firms, including British ones, were expressing their interest in supplying these needs. But as the British embassy recognized, "we shall not be helped by the fact that Fairey Engineering and the Comisión Nacional de Energia Nuclear have still not entirely resolved their differences."[85]

The Foreign Office had calmly accepted Allende's victory, choosing a position one official characterized as "wait and see." "Certainly we thought it far too early, and particularly where commercial business with the public sector was concerned, to prophesy doom." Still, the Fairey–CChEN conflict worried the embassy:

> Clearly several people here have been very put out by FEL's language. This is a difficult moment with the UP [Allende's coalition] stirring up feelings about economic dependence, and arrogance and exploitation from developed countries. So far the UK has had a good reputation but FEL's telex was in the worst US league.[86]

The Foreign Office believed that it could deescalate the situation if both the company and the commission replaced their negotiators. It asked Fairey's board to revise its response to Hinzner. But it was too late. Fairy clarified that its response had said exactly what it intended to say. It would not change one word. It had already sent all that CChEN had paid for. It was voiding the contract and would supply nothing further.

CChEN languished under the Allende administration, although the government eventually appointed Alvarado executive director, a position he left less than a year later. Three presidents and two more executive directors came and went between early 1971 and late 1973, when the Chilean armed forces overthrew Allende. The three-to-six-month delay Fairey and Hinzner had been haggling over in 1970 became a three-to-six-year delay. CChEN stopped producing annual reports in 1970, and it did not produce them again until 1976. When it reemerged as a functioning agency of the Chilean government, it did so under military direction.

The Significance of Chile's Early Nuclear History

Frei's commitment to CChEN remained but one part of his larger plans to develop, modernize, and further democratize Chile in the 1960s. As this chapter has argued, Frei and the PDC arose as expressions of Chilean politics before the Cuban Revolution, before the Kennedy and Johnson administrations began promoting the Alliance for Progress, and independently of the CIA's substantial intervention in the county's elections. Their thinking and actions were more ambitious and more oriented toward Western Europe than the Alliance, which remained relatively low-technology and narrowly inter-American in scope.

The chapter reconstructed Chile's early nuclear history while illustrating these points. Chileans such as Cruz-Coke and Viel, like their counterparts from the many developing nations that make up the IAEA's membership today, joined the international nuclear-science community as transatlantic internationalists who understood that it represented a world-historical trend that served their interests. This was not a straightforward process in Chile, or elsewhere in the Global South, for that matter, where many, including Chileans, seemed to take one step forward but two steps back throughout the turbulent 1960s and 1970s.

Chileans still shy away from large-scale nuclear power in the twenty-first century, even though it could help them deal with their growing energy issues. They have not yet solved the safety and security problems that earthquakes pose, which the Fukushima incident in Japan highlighted once again in March 2011. This notwithstanding, Chileans have remained involved with the IAEA, which has made several advances in the developing world since it first appeared in the late 1950s. This remains so because Cruz-Coke, Viel, and those who followed them persevered, and their vision eventually prevailed – to the benefit of the larger international community.

The IAEA's research and applications have become, as Deputy Director General David Waller has explained, "a constant factor in daily life" in the Global South. "The Agency's focus . . . has increasingly been the use of nuclear and isotopic techniques to address the daunting challenges in the developing world – disease, poverty, hunger, and a shortage of drinking water." Its projects include expanding radiotherapy to treat cancer, cultivating radiation-induced mutations to improve rice production, and employing discrete irradiation techniques to sterilize insect populations where conventional pesticides have failed. This has resulted in the tsetse fly's eradication in Zanzibar, among other successes. Chileans, whose transatlantic history led them into these endeavors, have long contributed to such projects.[87]

This chapter also argued that foreign intervention and intelligence operations, particularly but not exclusively the CIA's involvement in Chilean politics, did not play a decisive role in Chile in the 1960s. The Agency certainly helped Frei press his advantage after Curicó, and it did so on a massive, multimillion-dollar scale. Frei knew that the CIA was supporting him, and he welcomed it. Indeed, he had explicitly requested it, then thanked the American embassy for "its discretion and cooperation" after the election. But none of this created, controlled, or even influenced very much the ground conditions and trends that elected and sustained him.[88]

Johnson administration and Agency officials failed to understand this. They were exuberant and hubristic in the aftermath of Frei's victory, and they tended to exaggerate the part of the CIA. For example, Director of Central Intelligence (DCI) John McCone, caught up in this mood, remarked that his analysts remained certain that "without the large-scale covert support provided for the campaign, Frei would have gained, at most, a bare plurality." Then he added, apparently as an afterthought, that "the voters, themselves, in Chile deserved some commendation," too.[89]

A more circumspect Tomic headed a delegation to Washington the month after the election, in October 1964. As he explained to Mann and his colleagues at the Department of State, Curicó's elimination of the Chilean establishment's candidate had forced conservatives to support Frei in what became "a choice between Frei's democratic reform program and the Marxist alternative offered by Allende." This turn of events was clearly much more valuable to Christian Democrats than any Agency covert operation, no matter how well planned, lavishly funded, or meticulously implemented. Thus, the CIA's backing merely enabled Frei to press his advantage because it was aligned with favorable ground conditions and trends. Not even 1 billion dollars in Alliance funds and the Agency's continuing support could keep Christian Democrats in *la Moneda*, after Conservatives and Liberals abandoned Frei and the PDC's left wing splintered from the party to join Allende's coalition in the late 1960s.[90]

Notes

1. Chilean embassy press release, attached to Santa Cruz to Foreign Office, 20 December 1968, FCO 55/311; Foreign and Commonwealth Office Chile No. 53, "Exchange of Notes concerning a Development Loan towards the cost of a Nuclear Research Reactor (United Kingdom/Chile Loan 1969)," Santiago, 3 and 11 March 1969, FO 93; and Foreign Office Ratification No. 2523, "Ratification by Chile of the Agreement on Co-Operation in Peaceful Uses of Atomic Energy of 18 November 1968," London, 22 October 1969, FO 94. British National Archives (BNA).

2. Ian Breach, "British reactor bought by Chile," *The Guardian*, 23 December 1968.

3. International Atomic Energy Agency (IAEA), "List of Member States of IAEA," 5 February 2019, at <http://www.iaea.org>. For international cooperation, see Elisabeth Roehrlich, "The Cold War, the Developing World, and the Creation of the International Atomic Energy Agency (IAEA)," *Cold War History* 16 (2016): 195–212. For an early expression of Chilean interest in nuclear science and technology, see "Chile la cabeza de investigación atómica en Sudamérica," *La Nación*, 31 August 1948.

4. Joaquín Fermandois, "The Hero on the Latin American Scene." Christian Nuenlist, Anna Locher, and Garret Martin, eds., *Globalizing de Gaulle: International Perspectives on French Foreign Policies, 1958–1969* [2010] (Lanham: Rowman & Littlefield, 2011), 278.

5. Dwight Eisenhower to United Nations General Assembly, "Atomic Power for Peace," 8 December 1953. Joseph Pilat, ed., *Atoms for Peace: A Future after Fifty Years?* (Washington, DC: Woodrow Wilson Center Press, 2007), 239–46.

6. IAEA, "Statute of the International Atomic Energy Agency," 23 October 1956. Ibid., 247–67.

7. CChEN, "Comisión Chilena de Energía Nuclear, 1964–1989" (Santiago de Chile: CChEN, 1989), 5, 8–10. Centro Nacional de Estudios Nucleares, La Reina (CNEN); Marta Cruz-Coke Madrid, *Eduardo Cruz-Coke: testimonios* (Santiago de Chile: Fundación Procultura, 2015), 376–82; and "Chile la cabeza de investigación atómica en Sudamérica."

8. CChEN, "Comisión Chilena de Energía Nuclear, 1964–1989," 8.

9. Eduardo Frei Montalva, *Pensamiento y acción* (Santiago de Chile: Editorial del Pacífico, 1958). Paul Sigmund, *The Ideologies of the Developing Nations* [1963], 2nd edn (New York: Praeger, 1972), 456.

10. CChEN, *Memoria anual 1966: la energía nuclear en Chile* (Santiago de Chile: CChEN, 1967), 7. CNEN.

11. Eisenhower to Nixon, 9 May 1958. Department of State, *Foreign Relations of the United States, 1958–1960* V: *American Republics* (Washington, DC: Government Printing Office, 1991), document 45; and Roy Rubottom, Memorandum of telephone conversation, 13 May 1958. Ibid., document 46.

12. Richard Nixon, *RN: The Memoirs of Richard Nixon* (New York: Grosset & Dunlap, 1978), 190, 192; Vernon Walters, *Silent Missions* (New York: Doubleday, 1978), 313–37; and Cabinet meeting minutes, White House, 16 May 1958. Department of State, *FRUS, 1958–1960* V: *American Republics*, document 55.

13. Stephen Rabe, *Eisenhower and Latin America: The Foreign Policy of Anticommunism* (Chapel Hill: University of North Carolina Press, 1988), 102.

14. Rabe, *Eisenhower and Latin America*, 134–52; Department of State, "Promoting Economic and Social Advancement in the Americas," *Department of State Bulletin* 43 (3 October 1960): 533–41; and Department of State, "President Pledges U.S. Cooperation to Promote Social Progress and Economic Growth in the Americas," *Department of State Bulletin* 43 (1 August 1960): 166–70.

15. For these changes in Latin America and the Global South, see Thomas Wright, *Latin America in the Era of the Cuban Revolution and Beyond* [1991], 3rd edn (Santa Barbara: ABC-CLIO/Praeger, 2018); Jonathan Brown, *Cuba's Revolutionary World* (Cambridge, MA: Harvard University Press, 2017); Piero Gleijeses, *Visions of Freedom: Havana, Washington, Pretoria, and the Struggle for Southern Africa, 1976–1991* (Chapel Hill: University of North Carolina Press, 2013); Hal Brands, *Latin America's Cold War* (Cambridge, MA: Harvard University Press, 2010); Odd Arne Westad, *The Global Cold War: Third World Interventions and the Making of Our Times* [2005] (Cambridge: Cambridge University Press, 2007); Piero Gleijeses, *Conflicting Missions: Havana, Washington, and Africa, 1959–1976* (Chapel Hill: University of North Carolina Press, 2002); and Brian Loveman and Thomas Davies, eds., *Guerrilla Warfare* [1985], 3rd edn (Wilmington: Scholarly Resources, 1997).

16. For this escalation, see Wright, *Latin America in the Era of the Cuban Revolution*, 61–65.

17. For Eisenhower's breaking relations with Cuba, see Livingston Merchant, Memorandum of conversation, 29 December 1960. Department of State, *Foreign Relations of the United States, 1958–1960* VI: *Cuba* (Washington, DC: Government Printing Office, 1991),

document 627; Carlos Olivares to Daniel Braddock, 3 January 1961, enclosed in Braddock to Department of State, 3 January 1961. Department of State, *Foreign Relations of the United States, 1961–1963* X: *Cuba, January 1961–September 1962* (Washington, DC: Government Printing Office, 1997), document 1; and Christopher Herter to Cuban *Chargé d'affaires* in Washington, 3 January 1961, enclosed in Department of State to Braddock, 3 January 1961. Ibid., document 7. Also see Wayne Smith, *The Closest of Enemies: A Personal and Diplomatic History of the Castro Years* (New York: W.W. Norton, 1987), 42–67.

18. For Cuban intervention in Venezuela, see Brown, *Cuba's Revolutionary World*, 250–79; Loveman and Davies, *Guerrilla Warfare*, 209–31; and Harold Eugene Davis, John Finan, and F. Taylor Peck, *Latin American Diplomatic History* (Baton Rouge: Louisiana State University Press, 1977), 248–50.

19. For Guevara's strategy and tactics, see Che Guevara, *Guerrilla Warfare* [1960]; and Che Guevara, "Guerrilla Warfare: A Method" [1963]. Loveman and Davies, *Guerrilla Warfare*, 41–162.

20. Che Guevara, "Message to the Tricontinental," 16 April 1967. Loveman and Davies, *Guerrilla Warfare*, 164–76. For Guevara in Bolivia, see Brown, *Cuba's Revolutionary World*, 413–50; and Loveman and Davies, *Guerrilla Warfare*, 311–34.

21. Nikolai Leonov, "La inteligencia soviética en América Latina durante la guerra fría," *Estudios Públicos* 73 (1999), 50.

22. See Aleksandr Fursenko and Timothy Naftali, *"One Hell of a Gamble": The Secret History of the Cuban Missile Crisis* [1997] (New York: W.W. Norton, 1998).

23. Ibid., 52. The Chinese presence in Latin America was minimal in the 1960s, and this remained so for the duration of the Cold War. Most Latin American communist parties remained closely tied to the Soviet Union, as they had been since the 1920s. None but a few individuals broke with Moscow and sided with Beijing in the Sino-Soviet split. See Directorate of Intelligence, Memorandum No. 1110/65, "Chinese Communist Activities in Latin America," 30 April 1965. Papers of Lyndon Johnson, National Security Files, Country Files: Latin America, Box 2a, "Latin America Volume 3: 1/65–6/65." Lyndon Johnson Library, Austin, Texas (LBJ).

24. Fursenko and Naftali, *"One Hell of a Gamble"*, 188–9.

25. Ibid., 353.

26. Interview with Yuri Pavlov, Roll 10842. CNN, Cold War (1998). Transcript courtesy of the National Security Archive, at <http://www.nsarchive.gwu.edu>.

27. Leonov, "La inteligencia soviética en América Latina," 35, 51.
28. For example, see Olga Ulianova and Eugenia Fediakova, "Algunos aspectos de la ayuda financiera del Partido Comunista de la URSS al comunismo chileno durante la guerra fría," *Estudios Públicos* 72 (1998): 113–48.
29. For example, see Kristian Gustafson and Christopher Andrew, "The Other Hidden Hand: Soviet and Cuban Intelligence in Allende's Chile," *Intelligence and National Security* 33 (2017), published online on 1 December 2017, at <http://www.tandfonline.com>; Christopher Andrew and Vasili Mitrohkin, *The World Was Going Our Way: The KGB and the Battle for the Third World* (New York: Basic Books, 2005); Leonov, "La inteligencia soviética en América Latina"; Nikolai Leonov, Eugenia Fediakova, Joaquín Fermandois, et al., "El General Nikolai Leonov en el CEP," *Estudios Públicos* 73 (1999): 65–102; and Nicola Miller, *Soviet Relations with Latin America, 1959–1987* (Cambridge: Cambridge University Press, 1989).
30. John Kennedy, Address to the Latin American diplomatic corps at the White House, 13 March 1961. Department of State, *Department of State Bulletin* 44 (3 April 1961), 472.
31. Walter Heinrichs, "Lyndon B. Johnson: Change and Continuity." Warren Cohen and Nancy Tucker, eds., *Lyndon Johnson Confronts the World: American Foreign Policy, 1963–1968* (Cambridge: Cambridge University Press, 1994), 27. Also see Thomas Mann oral history, 4 November 1968, 4–5. LBJ.
32. Department of State, "The Department of State during the Administration of President Lyndon B. Johnson, November 1963–January 1969" I: Administrative History, Chapter 6, Inter-American Relations, Section B: The Alliance for Progress. LBJ.
33. Simon Collier and William Sater, *A History of Chile, 1808–2002* [1996], 2nd edn (Cambridge: Cambridge University Press, 2004), 305–8; Brian Loveman, *Chile: The Legacy of Hispanic Capitalism* [1979], 3rd edn (New York: Oxford University Press, 2001), 230–7; and Biblioteca Nacional de Chile, "La Falange Nacional (1891–1957)," at <http://www.memoriachilena.cl>.
34. David Mutchler, *The Church as a Political Factor in Latin America: With Particular Reference to Colombia and Chile* (New York: Praeger, 1971); Frei, *Pensamiento y acción*; and Pius XI, "Quadragesimo Anno," 15 May 1931; and Leo XIII, "Rerum Novarum," 15 May 1891, at <http://w2.vatican.va>.
35. Julio Faúndez, *Marxism and Democracy in Chile: From 1932 to the Fall of Allende* (New Haven: Yale University Press, 1988), 116–32.

36. Collier and Sater, *History of Chile*, 308. Also see Jadwiga Pieper Mooney, *The Politics of Motherhood: Maternity and Women's Rights in Twentieth-Century Chile* (Pittsburgh: University of Pittsburgh Press, 2009), 71–101; Wright, *Latin America in the Era of the Cuban Revolution*, 144–7; and Faúndez, *Marxism and Democracy*, 133–58.

37. For Chilean development, see Collier and Sater, *History of Chile*, 226–302; Loveman, *Chile*, 196–229; and Faúndez, *Marxism and Democracy*, 42–50.

38. Eduardo Frei to Ralph Dungan, 17 April 1962, with press clippings attached. Papers of President Kennedy, National Security Files, Countries, Box 20A, "Chile: General: 1/62–6/62." John Kennedy Library, Boston, Massachusetts (JFK).

39. For the election's results, see Ricardo Cruz-Coke, *Historia electoral de Chile, 1925–1973* (Santiago de Chile: Editorial Jurídica de Chile, 1984), 107–10. For US intervention, see United States Senate, *Covert Action in Chile, 1963–1973* (Washington, DC: Government Printing Office, 1975).

40. Margaret Power, *Right-Wing Women in Chile: Feminine Power and the Struggle against Allende, 1964–1973* (University Park: Pennsylvania State University Press, 2002), 71–98.

41. Biblioteca del Congreso Nacional de Chile, Reseña Biográfica Parlamentaria, "Oscar Alfredo Naranjo Jara," at <http://historiapolitica. bcn.cl>; and Biblioteca del Congreso Nacional de Chile, Reseña Biográfica Parlamentaria, "Oscar Gastón Naranjo Arias," at <http:// historiapolitica.bcn.cl>. Also see Collier and Sater, *History of Chile*, 261–3; Power, *Right-Wing Women in Chile*, 73–4; Cruz-Coke, *Historia electoral*, 109; Paul Sigmund, *The Overthrow of Allende and the Politics of Chile, 1964–1976* (Pittsburgh: University of Pittsburgh Press, 1977), 29–30; and Directorate of Intelligence's Latin American division to Sherman Kent, "An Old Fear Revived," 17 March 1964. CIA Records Search Tool (CREST), National Archives, College Park, MD (NA).

42. Editorial note. Department of State, *Foreign Relations of the United States, 1964–1968* XXXI: *South and Central America; Mexico* (Washington, DC: Government Printing Office, 2004), document 248. For the Johnson administration's preference for the Democratic Front, see J. C. King to John McCone, "Political Action Program in Chile," 3 January 1964. Ibid., document 245.

43. "Support for the Chilean Presidential Elections of 4 September 1964," 1 April 1964. Ibid., document 250.

44. Charles Cole to Department of State, 29 July 1964; and Joseph Jova to Mann, 5 May 1964. Ibid., documents 263 and 254, respectively.

45. D. E. N. Peirson, AEA, to J. McAdam Clark, Foreign Office, 11 August 1965, FO 371/183314. BNA; and William Dentzer, "The Secretary's Second Meeting with the Mission of President-Elect Frei of Chile," 17 October. Department of State, *FRUS, 1964–1968* XXXI: *South and Central America; Mexico*, document 275.

46. Enrique Monge Gordillo, Junta de Control de Energía Atómica del Perú to A. H. Spire, British embassy Lima, 26 May 1965, FO 371/183322; and British embassy Santiago, "Nuclear Power in Northern Chile," 31 August 1965, FO 371/183314. BNA.

47. British embassy Santiago summarized this paper in British embassy Santiago to Foreign Office, 7 April 1966, FO 371/189469. BNA.

48. "Resumé of Statement of Sr. Ole Pedersen, Head of the scientific mission that visited the North," 25 March 1966, attached to ibid.; and ODM to Ewbank and Partners, Ltd., 19 November 1966, FO 371/189469. BNA.

49. For this gradual change in British attitudes, see Bevan Sewell, "'We Need Not Be Ashamed of Our Own Economic Profit Motive': Britain, Latin America, and the Alliance for Progress, 1959–63," *International History Review* 37 (2015): 607–30.

50. "Record of a conversation between the Parliamentary Secretary and Mr. Edmond de Rothschild," 1 December 1965, FO 371/183314. BNA.

51. Lincoln Gordon oral history, 10 July 1969, 69; Department of State, Administrative History of the Johnson Administration, Chapter 6 (Inter-American Relations): Section B: The Alliance for Progress; and ibid., Section C: Western Hemisphere Security. LBJ. For the Anglo-American clash in Cuba, see Christopher Hull, "'Going to War in Buses': The Anglo-American Clash over Leyland Sales to Cuba, 1963–1964," *Diplomatic History* 34 (2010): 793–822.

52. British embassy Santiago to Foreign Office, 6 June 1966, FO 371/189469. BNA.

53. France lost its testing ground in the Sahara when it withdrew from Algeria. Paris moved into the South Pacific from there, where it tested nuclear weapons from 1966 to 1996. See Jean-Marc Regnault, "France's Search for Nuclear Test Sites, 1957–1963," *Journal of Military History* 67 (2003): 1223–48; and "France Ending Nuclear Tests That Caused Broad Protests," *New York Times*, 30 January 1996, at <http://www.nytimes.com>.

54. CChEN, *Memoria anual 1966*; CChEN, *Memoria anual 1967: Centro Nacional de Estudios Nucleares* (Santiago: CChEN, 1968); CChEN, *Memoria anual 1968* (Santiago de Chile: CChEN, 1969); and CChEN, *Memoria anual 1969* (Santiago de Chile: CChEN, 1970). CNEN.

55. Jeffery Ling, "Visit of the Chilean Ambassador on 23 October," 22 October 1968, FCO 55/310; Graham, Foreign Office, to Hawkins, Treasury, 28 October 1968, FCO 55/310; and Drucker, Foreign Office, to Hawkins, Treasury, 31 October 1968, FCO 55/310. BNA.

56. Santa Cruz to Stewart, 11 October 1968, FCO 55/310; and Dennis Allen, "Atomic Reactor for Chile," 19 November 1968, FCO 55/310. BNA.

57. "Record of a Conversation between the Foreign Secretary and the Chilean Ambassador Held at the Foreign and Commonwealth Office on Thursday, 24 October, 1968, at 4.30 p.m.," attached to Ling to Diggines, 24 October 1968, FCO 55/310. BNA.

58. Ibid.

59. "State Visit to Chile: November 1968: Supplementary Brief for Lord Chalfont," undated, FO 73/71. BNA; and Alun Chalfont, *The Shadow of My Hand: A Memoir* (London: Weidenfeld & Nicolson, 2000), 141–6.

60. Jeffry Ling, "Background Brief for Lord Chalfont's Visit Accompanying the Queen to South America: Sale of Nuclear Reactor to Chile," undated, FCO 55/310. BNA.

61. British embassy Santiago to Foreign Office, 9 January 1970, FCO 55/556. BNA.

62. Mason to Foreign Office, Telegram 395, 17 November 1968, FCO 55/310; and British embassy Santiago, "Record of a Meeting at the Chilean Ministry of Foreign Affairs between Señor Valdés, Minister of Foreign Affairs, and Lord Chalfont," 18 November 1968, FCO 55/311. BNA.

63. British embassy Santiago, "Record of a Meeting at the Chilean Ministry of Foreign Affairs."

64. Chalfont to Foreign Office, Telegram 399, 18 November 1968, FCO 55/310. BNA.

65. Mason to Foreign Office, Telegram 395, 17 November 1968; and Chalfont to Stewart, Telegram 401, 19 November 1968, FCO 55/310. BNA.

66. Mason to Foreign Office, Telegram 403, 21 November 1968, FCO 55/310.

67. Ibid.; and Jeffery Ling, "Sale of a Nuclear Reactor to Chile," 29 November 1968, FCO 55/311. BNA.

68. Rednall, ODM, to Blagden, Foreign Office, 5 December 1968, FCO 55/311; and "Dictated over the telephone by Mr. Edmond de Rothschild on Thursday, 5 December 1968, at 2.30 p.m. at the termination of a meeting between the Chilean Ambassador, Mr. Bray of Faireys and Sir Charles Cunningham, UKAEA," undated, FCO 55/311. BNA.

69. Santa Cruz to Chalfont, 5 December 1968, FCO 55/311; and "Dictated over the telephone by Mr. Edmond de Rothschild on Thursday, 5 December 1968." BNA.

70. C. D. Wallace, "Atomic Reactor for Chile," 6 December 1968, FCO 55/311; and Chalfont to Santa Cruz, 6 December 1968, FCO 55/311. BNA.

71. Eduardo Frei Montalva, "The Alliance That Lost Its Way," *Foreign Affairs* 45 (1967), 441, 443.

72. NSC, "Final Report: March 1969 Chilean Congressional Election," 14 March 1969. Department of State, *Foreign Relations of the United States, 1969–1976* XXI: *Chile, 1969–1973* (Washington, DC: Government Printing Office, 2014), document 3.

73. British embassy Santiago to Foreign Office, 21 January 1969, FCO 55/311; British embassy Santiago to Foreign Office, 7 February 1969, FCO 55/311; AEA to Foreign Office, 13 February 1969, FCO 55/311; ODM to Foreign Office, 24 February 1969, FCO 55/311; Ministry of Defense to Foreign Office, 31 March 1969, FCO 55/311; and British embassy Santiago to Foreign Office, 2 July 1969, FCO 55/312. BNA.

74. British embassy Santiago to Foreign Office, 22 December 1970, FCO 55/556. BNA.

75. Wiggin to Graham, "Chilean Foreign Minister's Visit – Nuclear Training Reactor," 21 October 1969, FCO 55/312; and C. C. Vinson, Chairman, Fairey, to Chilean embassy London, 20 October 1969, FCO 55/312. BNA.

76. Efraín Friedman, "Aid Memoire of Discussions Held the 6th of January 1970 between Mr. McQuade (British Embassy), Mr. Lavercombe (British Embassy), Mr. Friedman (CCEN), Mr. Alvarado (CCEN), Dr. Hinzner (CCEN)," attached to British embassy Santiago to Foreign Office, 9 January 1970. BNA.

77. B. D. MacLean, AEA, to P. J. Kelly, Ministry of Technology, 6 February 1970, FCO 55/556. BNA.

78. Salvador Allende, "Address to the Third United Nations Conference on Trade and Development (UNCTAD)," April 1972. James Cockcroft, ed., *Salvador Allende Reader: Chile's Voice of Democracy* (Melbourne and New York: Ocean Press, 2000), 172.

79. Benjamín Viel, "Introducción," CChEN, *Memoria anual 1966*, 5–6.

80. Lewis Diuguid, "Allende Reassures Fearful Chileans," *Washington Post*, 23 October 1970.

81. Fairey Engineering, "Contract with the Government of Chile," undated summary, stamped 25 November 1970, FCO 55/556, enclosure 1. BNA.

82. Hinzner to British embassy Santiago 5 November 1970, attached to British embassy Santiago to Foreign Office, 9 November 1970, FCO 55/556. BNA.

83. Hinzner to Whittaker, Fairey, 5 November 1970, FCO 55/556, enclosure 2. BNA.

84. Fairey to Hinzner, 13 November 1970, FCO 55/556, enclosure 3. BNA.

85. British embassy Santiago to Foreign Office, 15 June 1970, FCO 55/556. Also see British embassy Santiago to Foreign Office, 9 March 1970, FCO 55/556; and "Antofagasta Nuclear Project," undated memorandum attached to British embassy Santiago to Foreign Office, 18 June 1970, FCO 55/556. BNA.

86. C. D. Wiggin, FO, to British embassy Santiago, 6 December 1970, FCO 55/556; and British embassy Santiago to Foreign Office, 18 December 1970, FCO 55/556. BNA.

87. David Waller, "Atoms for Peace and the International Atomic Energy Agency." Pilat, *Atoms for Peace*, 23.

88. Editorial note. Department of State, *FRUS, 1964–1968* XXXI: *South and Central America; Mexico*, document 270.

89. Editorial note. Ibid., document 270.

90. Harry Lunn, "Meeting of Mr. Mann with the Mission of President-Elect Frei of Chile," 12 October 1964. Ibid., document 274.

6   The Viaux Movement

This chapter reconstructs the rise of Brig. Gen. Roberto Viaux, whose activism helped to create the grassroots military movement that destabilized civilian-dominated civil–military relations in Chile in the late 1960s. The Viaux movement, which began forming within the Chilean army around issues relating to defense policy, military spending, and pay and benefits, evolved to focus on communism while explicitly calling for the overthrow of civilian government in the early 1970s. Along the way, it attracted Chilean politicians, Viaux's attorney Pablo Rodríguez, and large numbers of conservative women and youths. Indeed, Rodríguez's *Frente Nacionalista Patria y Libertad* was actively involved in the coup that occurred in September 1973.

President Eduardo Frei (1964–70) lost the initiative to govern effectively after Viaux's *acuartelamiento*, or his political mobilization, of the Tacna Artillery Regiment fizzled out in October 1969. Neither Frei nor his successor, President Salvador Allende (1970–3), were able to restore discipline within the ranks after this incident, which Chileans called the *Tacnazo*. This was so even though three successive chiefs of staff – Gen. Sergio Castillo, Gen. René Schneider, and Gen. Carlos Prats – diligently, even desperately, tried to restore it.

Viaux's movement represented a continuing expression of Chilean anticommunism, which dated back to the Ibáñez dictatorship (1927–31) and flared up again during the González administration (1946–52). Viaux, Rodríguez, and those who joined them were part of Chilean politics and traditions. They operated on their own initiative and on their own terms. They did this for their own purposes and on their own schedule. And they made their own history as internationalists.

Viaux's Early Career

Viaux earned his commission as a twenty-year-old lieutenant in 1937. He followed a career path in conventional ground warfare that led to high command. He completed specialized training in artillery and then served as an instructor in the *Escuela Militar* in the 1940s. He was promoted to captain in 1947.[1]

Capt. Viaux reported to Lota as part of the González administration's response to the coal strikes in October 1947. He was granted complete authority to pacify the area. As he saw it, he occupied a neutral position between the mining company and its workers. He supervised new union elections, from which he excluded Communists, and he negotiated improvements in pay and benefits for the miners there.

Viaux learned two lessons from this experience. First, it reconfirmed his understanding that the army's most important missions remained defending national sovereignty, independence, and honor, on the one hand, and guaranteeing internal order during moments of national crisis, on the other. Second, he became an anticommunist. He, like his colleague Capt. Augusto Pinochet, saw the Chilean Communist Party (PCCh) as "under the control of a foreign power – Soviet power" from then forward. His thinking and vocabulary on these issues thus represented a continuation of President Gabriel González's anticommunism.[2]

Viaux and Pinochet were not the only ones to learn these lessons. Many within the army did. As political scientist Carlos Huneeus has found, most of those officers ranked colonel and above who served the Pinochet dictatorship (1973–90) in its early years had participated in the repression in Lota and Coronel, or they had, like Pinochet, guarded internment camps such as Pisagua.[3]

Viaux attended the Chilean army's War College, the *Academia de Guerra*, from 1951 to 1953. He was promoted to major when he graduated. He came back as an instructor in 1957, teaching courses in combined operations in support of ground warfare. Viaux served the army's senior staff as a lieutenant colonel, and then at the Ministry of Defense's National Defense Council – analogous to the US Joint Chiefs of Staff – in 1960 and 1963, respectively. The army promoted him to full colonel and sent him to Bogotá as military attaché in 1966. When he returned in February 1969, he was promoted to brigadier general and placed in command of the First Division in Antofagasta. This gave him jurisdiction over the Atacama. He was fifty-two years old, and he had grown deeply dissatisfied with the course his country had taken.

Latin American Military Affairs and the Chilean Army in the Late 1960s

Viaux began complaining of the army's deteriorating conditions when he assumed command of the First Division. Civilian governments had been reducing the service to a poor state of readiness since 1958. The general feared that this undermined the army's capability to perform its missions, and that this was weakening Chilean security.[4]

This partly derived from the United States' changing strategic posture in Latin America. Washington had been leading a conventional, inter-American defense since the Second World War. This prepared the region's armed forces to protect the hemisphere against a Soviet attack should a third world war occur. This would secure its sea lines of communication and its strategic raw materials while freeing American warships and support services for deployment elsewhere. The US government passed the Mutual Security Act in 1951, following the Truman administration's (1945–53) enacting NSC 68 the year before. It granted Latin American governments more than 38 million dollars the first year, adding nearly 52 million dollars in 1952.[5]

United States military strategy and aid remained conventional through the 1950s. The Department of Defense's military and naval missions coordinated interoperability all over Latin America. The

Pentagon also granted equipment while selling surplus warships and other systems. For example, Brazil, Argentina, and Chile bought two light cruisers each, and Peru and Uruguay several destroyers, in 1951. The Cuban Revolution changed this in 1959.[6]

The Castro regime (1959–present) exported revolution into the Global South, where multiple guerrilla movements tried to follow its example in the 1960s. The Kennedy (1961–3) and Johnson administrations (1963–9) refocused United States military assistance on counterinsurgency in response to this. US officials and congressional budget committees appreciated that several of Latin America's border disputes, many of them dating back to the nineteenth century, remained unresolved, and that this contributed to its armed services' concerns. But they wished to avoid provoking a costly arms race that would divert investment from the Alliance for Progress's social and economic initiatives to support the acquisition of more warships, tanks, and guns. Although Chileans received approximately 1 billion dollars in Alliance aid, they got only about 93 million dollars for military spending, or approximately 9 percent of the total.[7]

Thus, American advisory groups gave increased attention to special forces and tactical police units, such as the *Carabineros' Grupo Móvil* in Chile, thereafter. They assigned the region's conventional armies civic-action missions, hoping to transform them into something akin to the US Army's Corps of Engineers. This meant much less attention to heavy infantry, artillery, and armor. Viaux spoke of the tasks that Chilean soldiers now had to perform in dismissive language such as "taking out civilians' trash, caring for hospitals, preparing meals for the sick and then cleaning their chamber pots, burying the dead in cemeteries, etc., etc."[8]

The Frei administration's military spending consumed no more than approximately 10 percent of the national budget (2–2.5 percent of Gross National Product [GNP]) through 1966. Peruvians and Argentines, however, were spending more – averaging about 15–20 percent of the national budget (and 2–4 percent of GNP). These disparities worsened after the French government, seeking to expand its influence in the South Pacific and southern South

America, began selling Mirage aircraft to Peru and Argentina. This marked the first appearance of supersonic fighters in Latin America, and the mere suggestion of these fighters heightened pre-existing tensions, which complicated Frei's efforts to keep military spending down.[9]

Chilean buyers turned to Britain when responding to this. British defense contractors such as the Hawker Siddeley Group remained trusted arms dealers in southern South America. Brazilians, Argentines, and Chileans purchased British-made aircraft carriers, destroyers, frigates, minesweepers, oilers and salvage ships, bombers and fighters, helicopters, missiles, and spare parts well into the 1980s.[10]

The offices of Queen Elizabeth II were involved in some of these problems. The queen herself traveled to Brazil and Chile on a state visit in November 1968. Lord Chalfont (Alun Gwynne Jones), a minister who specialized in defense policy, accompanied her. Chalfont discussed Hawker Hunters with his Chilean counterparts. They had purchased twenty-one of them in 1966. They pressed him to convince Hawker Siddeley to sell them at least nine additional aircraft, to form three full squadrons as soon as possible. Chalfont explained that many clients were awaiting Hunters, and they were on backorder. Chileans would either have to wait until September 1973 to receive the whole complement they required or accept substitutions.[11]

Frei, however, remained committed to reducing the military budget, particularly the army's spending. He took exception to "the assertion that to stop subversion we must purchase fifty-ton tanks, supersonic aircraft and battleships." He called on the inter-American community "to establish a quantitative limitation on arms purchases." Defense spending, at its current level, was encouraging nationalism and sowing the seeds of mistrust. This undermined the Alliance's plans for Latin American integration. It also diverted "important resources which should be utilized to satisfy the urgent need for economic and social development." But, as he soon learned, he would have to take into account the interests of the Chilean armed forces whether he wanted to or not.[12]

The Politicization of the Professional Officer Corps

Frei lost the initiative to govern as Chileans divided, his opposition broadened, and the professional officer corps was politicized in the late 1960s – something civilian politicians and army commanders had kept at bay since the early 1930s. Officers at the highest levels had become concerned that a Marxist-Leninist government might come to power, and they started to discuss what, if anything, they should do about it. These fears combined with the army's deteriorating ability to do its job, as they saw it. This created a powder keg that Viaux would set off in October 1969.

Meanwhile, the far left remained loosely together in the *Frente de Acción Popular* (FRAP) coalition and the *Central Única de Trabajadores* (CUT) labor confederation, but differences remained. Although the PCCh still followed the peaceful road it had embarked upon as it returned to legal politics in the late 1950s, rising leaders within the Socialist Party (PS), such as Senator Carlos Altamirano, believed that they would eventually have to resort to armed revolution, which they proclaimed inevitable in November 1967. A group of Cuban-inspired university students, following Miguel Enríquez at the *Universidad de Concepción*, had already broken with the PS leadership. They created the Movement of the Revolutionary Left (MIR), an urban guerrilla movement that declared itself Chile's true vanguard in August 1965.[13]

Further complicating matters, Frei's Christian Democratic Party (PDC) splintered into left, right, and center factions (*rebeldes*, *oficialistas*, and *terceristas*, respectively). The *rebeldes* eventually formed the *Movimiento de Acción Popular Unitario* (MAPU) and joined FRAP's successor, the *Unidad Popular* (UP) coalition. Further, Frei's policies and style of governing alienated Conservatives and Liberals. They united and reinvented themselves as the National Party (PN) in 1966. They ran their own candidates in congressional elections in 1969, where they earned 20 percent of the vote (thirty-three deputies). Based on this outcome, they believed that they could regain a significant voice in Congress and possibly retake the presidency in 1970.[14]

Chile and other nations in the Global South were experiencing the same dissidence that was shaking the status quo all over the northern hemisphere in the late 1960s. Chile's politics and society – which had seen the conservative establishment, particularly landowners, gradually lose its privileged access to power and influence while women and millions from the urban poor and peasantry gained the vote from the late 1940s into the 1960s – became unstable. Chile's college-educated middle class also grew during these decades. This had created an entirely different country by the late 1960s. As political scientist Brian Loveman has phrased it, by the time Allende won the presidency, he had "inherited the political mythology and constitutional legitimacy of a system no longer viable without substantial modifications."[15]

The streets and countryside became rowdy. Students seized the *Universidad Católica*, peasants rose against landowners, and the MIR unleashed a campaign of assaults, bank robberies, and airline hijackings. A fifteen- and eighteen-year-old pair of *miristas* perpetrated one of these hijackings. They seized a LAN Chile domestic flight from Santiago to Punta Arenas and attempted to reroute it to Havana. The flight crew apprehended the two boys in midair and then returned to the capital, where authorities arrested them. Another attempt resulted in a firefight at the airport that left one dead and several wounded. These were but a few examples of the activism and violence that engulfed Chile in the late 1960s.[16]

These mounting problems affected the army. In May 1968, the instructors and students of the War College and noncommissioned officer school resigned in protest at the army's low pay, its lack of adequate housing, its poor medical services, and what Prats later characterized as "the decay of an institution that offered them no professional future." Officers from units deployed throughout the country joined them. They timed this to coincide with the visit to Chile by the chief of staff of the army of the Federal Republic of Germany to maximize its impact.[17]

The Frei administration relieved the minister of defense and chief of staff of the army, replacing them with retired Gen. Tulio Marambio and Castillo. The latter persuaded the agitated officers to withdraw their resignations and return to their posts, promising to redress the army's problems within six to nine months. They agreed. Then a year passed, and nothing happened.[18]

In March 1969, Frei told Ambassador Edward Korry that the armed forces' senior commanders had approached him through intermediaries on at least three separate occasions to sound him out about a coup. They were concerned about leftist Gen. Juan Velasco's (1968–75) military government in Peru, and they worried about Argentine arms purchases, but they were mostly upset about the increasingly likely prospect that the far left would come to power in Chile. They floated a hypothetical suggestion – "more an attitude than a plan" – that they could seize power, send Frei to Europe for a time, then invite him back to resume his presidency, which would somehow extend beyond the expiration of his six-year term. Korry reported that Frei discouraged this, but he found it significant that the president never explicitly rejected it.[19]

Thus, Frei knew that "the three commanding officers of the three services had discussed this contingency among themselves," and that they were continuing to do so. Adm. Fernando Porta, chief of naval operations, had privately let the ambassador know that "under no rpt no conditions would the Navy permit a Marxist government." Korry claimed that he did not "make any comment of any kind," while listening to Frei and the admiral. He was merely forwarding the former's warning to Washington that "there was a facile tendency to consider the Chilean military as frozen in its apolitical posture . . . [and that] he was no longer so persuaded."[20]

The army's apolitical posture was indeed thawing and in transition. Officers and senior noncoms began forming a movement around Viaux. As it took shape, the general made it clear that he sided with the nation, the service, and its soldiers against the government and the high command. He took on the air of Julius Caesar marching on Rome.

The Department of State took note. The Bureau of Intelligence and Research (INR) predicted that Viaux would attempt a coup that October. INR cited CIA reports that Marambio was planning to relieve Viaux from his command while elaborating that this would likely precipitate it. The bureau understood that Viaux intended to either depose the president or force him to fire the minister of defense and then name himself as his replacement.[21]

Viaux attempted to convey his concerns to Castillo several times. Castillo promised to address these concerns, then ignored them. When Viaux proposed that the army should construct a military hospital in the north, Castillo shot the proposal down. Consequently, Viaux explained, he, the professional officer corps, and the soldiers they commanded lost their respect for the high command – "which they accuse of having become an inept bureaucracy."[22]

Maj. Arturo Marshall, who led a battalion in the Yungay Regiment – one of the Chilean army's elite units, consisting of infantry, airborne, and special forces – showed that this loss of respect extended to Frei in September 1969. Marshall kept the president waiting at an independence-day celebration, where he was to review the troops. The major later told journalists "that it was not his fault, that it just had not been his day." But all understood that he had meant to express contempt. Frei, Marambio, and Castillo interpreted it as such, and they retired him immediately. Many in the Chilean press raised their eyebrows, wondering whether this had not represented a failed coup.[23]

Castillo dealt with Viaux two weeks later. The army's senior officers gathered to conduct the service's *Junta Calificadora*, or annual promotion board, in Santiago that October. It was routine that Viaux should return to the capital. The general, however, felt that something was amiss. The government placed him under close surveillance, but Castillo denied knowing anything about it when he asked him to explain it.[24]

Viaux's efforts over the following two to three weeks in Santiago represented his final attempt to resolve his grievances through normal channels. The Chilean army allowed any officer to bring an issue up the chain of command all the way to the minister of defense and even the president through what Chileans called *el conducto regular*, although it rarely went that far. The general tried to take it that far. Castillo told him that the high command was studying the problem. Marambio heard him out and promised to respond at some unspecified time in the future. Frei refused to see him. Nothing resulted from any of this.

Viaux persisted. He asked several senators to bring him to Frei. The president remained unavailable. Viaux sent him a letter, complaining that the Chilean government's military assistance agreements with the United States and the administration's defense budget were creating "a criminal crisis of war material" in the army. The service's Table of Organization and Equipment, and more importantly, its personnel, had dramatically shrunk since 1961. This was overloading the remaining officers and noncoms with work just to keep the army minimally functional.[25]

These officers and noncoms, Viaux continued, earned the lowest salaries in government service. The Chilean economy continued to suffer from chronic inflation, and these men's salaries had steadily lost purchasing power, which had reduced them and their families to poverty. Many were working second jobs simply to make ends meet. Conscripts required family support just to eat regularly. Some contracted debts that followed them after their service. This caught up with many of them when they retired and had to spend their old age living in *callampas*, or shantytowns. The army's morale and the service itself seemed to be collapsing.

Viaux insisted that he was not merely speaking for himself or even the First Division "but for the vast majority of soldiers in the army." Frei must redress these problems. The president should change his administration's defense policies and increase servicemen's pay and benefits. The general also demanded that he replace Marambio and Castillo. Frei continued to ignore him.[26]

Then, suddenly, on 16 October, Castillo summoned Viaux to a private meeting, where he announced Viaux's immediate retirement. The chief of staff allowed him one day to return to Antofagasta, relinquish command of his division, and then come back to Santiago to muster out of the service. According to Prats, a pale Viaux walked back into the conference room, collected his papers, and left without a word. Castillo later told Prats and the others there that Viaux had engaged in political deliberations and lost the government and the high command's confidence.[27]

The *Tacnazo*

Viaux explained what had happened during a hasty farewell to the First Division over the weekend of 18 and 19 October. Then he departed for Santiago, where he arrived, as journalist Eugenio Lira phrased it, "in the style of a field marshal" on Monday afternoon. The press, aware that something was up, met him at the airport. He told them that he did not recognize the high command's authority to retire him. He did not recognize his relief in Antofagasta, either. He handed out an open letter that the officers of his former command had signed, urging Frei to reinstate him. The administration promptly used Chile's internal security laws to move against *La Segunda*, the newspaper that had published the letter.[28]

Viaux took command of the Tacna Artillery Regiment, located on the northern rim of *Parque Cousiño* – now *Parque O'Higgins* – late that night. He secured his position there before the sun rose on Tuesday, 21 October. All three classes from the War College, instructors and men from the noncommissioned officer school, the school of infantry, the special forces school, tanks from the Second Armored Regiment, and the guard unit at the Ministry of Defense suited up and joined him between 6:00 and 8:00 a.m. The general claimed that the First Division had also communicated its support, and that some air force and *Carabineros* officers were with him as well.[29]

Marshall attempted to mobilize the Yungay Regiment, too. But Frei, having quickly declared a state of emergency, arrested the retired major before he could get to his former unit that morning. Marshall, undeterred, warned the police officers assigned to him that they were failing to understand the situation. "You are following orders from the minister of interior, right? Who says that, come tomorrow, Gen. Viaux will not find himself installed in *la Moneda* [the presidential palace] with me as his minister of interior? What would you say then?"[30]

Meanwhile, Castillo ordered Brig. Gen. Alfredo Mahn, who commanded the Santiago garrison, to deploy forces to *Parque Cousiño* and put down Viaux's movement. But many of the officers and men under his authority refused to follow his orders. When those troops who did respond positioned themselves in front of the Tacna Regiment's headquarters building, they stopped there and it seemed unclear whether they had chosen neutrality or had actually sided with Viaux. As the American embassy's Deputy Chief of Mission Harry Shlaudeman reported, "considerable fraternization between the two sides" ensued, and no action followed.[31]

Frei began to fear that Viaux, who claimed that "85 percent of the army is with us," was not exaggerating. The administration cut the electricity, water, and telephone lines at the Tacna building. But the general and his men possessed sufficient provisions to last at least several days, and they had their own communications equipment as well. Frei's spirits rose when the cabinet received a report that six trucks filled with soldiers from another province were arriving in Santiago. Then Marambio asked, "*¿Vienen a favor o en contra?*" – Whose side are they on? No one knew.[32]

Frei learned that the divisions outside of Santiago – for example, Prats's Third Division south of the capital and Schneider's Fifth Division in Punta Arenas – remained loyal. But they were far away and he felt vulnerable in *la Moneda*. He turned to popular support to stop Viaux. PDC Senator Benjamín Prado appeared in the *Plaza de la Constitución*, in front of the presidential palace, where crowds and journalists were gathering. The senator urged Chileans to come out into the streets. "Chileans! Paralyze the country! Paralyze industry and its factories! Paralyze transportation! Paralyze the mines! Come out to protest, to defend freedom! . . . We must save the country."[33]

The *Unidad Popular* coalition and the CUT's leaders promised to mobilize a general strike in response. But the *Tacnazo* ended before they could set this in motion and test its effectiveness. Meanwhile, Frei received several municipal garbage trucks, which the president and his supporters christened "people's tanks." A crowd of student protesters came, too, for what it was worth.[34]

Frei sent Mahn to warn Viaux that he would arm the population to defend the government if he did not capitulate. This puzzled him. He pointed out that he had already secured the armory. Further, "I knew that he was counting on the garbage trucks," he asked, rhetorically, later, "but do you really believe that this would have stopped the army?"[35]

These people's tanks and student protesters, and the Tacna Regiment's response to them, provided the day's comic relief before leading to serious injuries. A column of garbage trucks appeared at *Parque Cousiño* in the afternoon, its drivers chanting, "*¡Frei sí, gorilas no!*" The officer in charge invited the lead garbage man to come into headquarters to meet Viaux, as the general remained eager to demonstrate the apolitical nature of his movement. The garbage man declined, explaining that he did not talk to *gorilas*. So, the officer instructed him to turn his trucks around and leave. He refused. Then the officer ordered the tanks to reposition themselves to attack the garbage trucks, prompting the trucks to return to *la Moneda*.

Students arrived next, blocking the Tacna building so that no one could enter or leave it. The officer in charge ordered the tanks, which were old, from the Second World War, to intimidate the students. The first tank lurched forward, but the second one sputtered and caught fire, its excited crew running out of it, shouting that its ammunition was going to cook off. Senior officers on the scene calmly observed that this validated Viaux's complaints that the army was in poor condition. But others there, including Lira, just laughed at the soldiers while they scrambled to put the fire out. This broke the tension, and everyone backed down for the moment.[36]

Both Frei and Viaux held several press conferences as the day wore on. The defiant president affirmed that he had already been working on the army's pay issues and would continue to do so. The general and his movement had nothing to do with it. He also insisted that he had always honored the service as one of the nation's pillars. He referred to the army's democratic traditions several times throughout the day, too. But this only created the impression, as Shlaudeman remarked, "that president not entirely sure of his ground." And the fact that garbage trucks and students were the only ones who came to defend *la Moneda* had sharpened the embassy's perception that Viaux indeed had many from the service with him.[37]

Frei agreed to Viaux's demands late that evening, after a firefight of sorts had erupted in *Parque Cousiño*. Students had remained near the soldiers in the park, taunting them as night fell. They started throwing rocks. Apparently, an angry soldier fired on them in reprisal. Others, perhaps fearing they were being fired upon, joined him. Confusion followed. Mahn and Viaux issued cease-fire orders, immediately regaining control. But the incident left fourteen civilians wounded.[38]

Mahn helped Frei and Viaux broker their agreement later that night, before taking the general into custody around 3:30 a.m. on

Wednesday, 22 October. Frei, who had already retired Marambio, promised to replace the high command and introduce special legislation to pass a pay raise for all servicemen right away. Viaux would submit to military justice. Mahn, whom Viaux expected to become the next chief of staff, would ensure that no one would retaliate against anyone who had participated in the *Tacnazo*. Then Mahn checked Viaux into the military hospital, where the administration kept him under house arrest.[39]

Aftermath

Sweeping changes ensued. As Lira wrote, "There is a saying that goes 'After the battle, everyone is a general.' But in the *Tacnazo*'s case, we should say 'a retired general.'" Frei retired Castillo, the entire high command, and even the army attaché in Washington. Unexpectedly, he also retired Mahn. He promoted Schneider to full general and named him the new chief of staff. In this reshuffle, Prats, now a major general, suddenly became the second highest-ranking officer in the army, and he, too, moved up into the high command. Brig. Gen. Camilo Valenzuela took charge of the garrison in Santiago.[40]

Schneider spent the next year trying to restore discipline while overseeing pay raises and efforts to reequip the army. The Frei administration put down another uprising in March 1970, the so-called Easter *Putsch*. Just after this, Schneider felt it necessary to explicitly instruct the professional officer corps to ensure a clean presidential election the following September. In what became known as the Schneider doctrine, he ordered his subordinates to guarantee that the candidate who won that election, regardless of party affiliation, assumed office.[41]

Schneider also declared that while he sympathized with Viaux's complaints, he disagreed with the way he and his followers had expressed them. He disavowed whatever agreement Mahn and Viaux may have negotiated, explaining that he had not been a party to it. He subjected some of those who had joined the uprising to military justice. As INR's Ray Cline recognized, the Frei administration and the high command's response never really resolved the issues that separated the government and high command, on the one hand, and Viaux's movement, on the other.[42]

Viaux's movement represented the most salient manifestation of the break in civilian-dominated civil–military relations that occurred in an increasingly polarized Chile in the late 1960s. As Frei understood, the senior leadership of all three branches of the armed forces, concerned about a possible Marxist-Leninist ascent in Chile, had already returned to political deliberations by the time Viaux carried out the *Tacnazo*. This would continue to destabilize Chilean politics into the early 1970s.

The CIA and other foreign intelligence services remained passive observers and peripheral to these particular events. But this did not stop rumors, centered on what Korry called "that old familiar scapegoat," from circulating to the contrary. Talk began in the *Washington Post*, which ran a story the day the *Tacnazo* ended that cited an unattributed source at the Agency who had bragged that "the CIA was aware of the situation for six weeks." This brought immediate protests and demands for clarification from the Frei administration, the Chilean foreign ministry, and the Chilean embassy in Washington. Frei and other Christian Democrats, particularly Foreign Minister Gabriel Valdés and the Foreign Ministry's Patricio Silva and Eduardo Palma, in addition to Chile's leftist parties and press, started suggesting that the US government was agitating for a coup and was even somehow responsible for the *Tacnazo*.[43]

These concerns were reasonable, given Frei's intimate knowledge of the Agency's involvement in Chilean politics. But they nevertheless remained untrue. The Nixon administration (1969–74), Korry, and Shlaudeman vigorously denied them. These officials reminded Frei that "US friendship and support for Frei administration and Chilean democracy too clearly established over long years to allow responsible govt. officials entertain such notions." Privately, Shlaudeman advised Washington that this reflected the administration's increasing "nervousness and intemperance" with respect to the problems that seemed to be overwhelming it. He also spoke for many in government when he expressed his frustration with whoever it was who had leaked such a statement to the press, acknowledging that "we made this particular trouble for ourselves." All of this grew dramatically worse over the following year.[44]

Notes

1. Viaux's service record summarized in Florencia Varas, *Conversaciones con Viaux* (Santiago de Chile: Impresiones EIRE, 1972), 11–13.
2. Ibid., 48.
3. Carlos Huneeus, *La guerra fría chilena: Gabriel González Videla y la ley maldita* (Santiago de Chile: Random House Mondadori, 2008), 15–16, 355–71.
4. Varas, *Conversaciones con Viaux*, 53–109.
5. Department of State, "Military Assistance to Latin America," *Department of State Bulletin* 28 (30 March 1953): 463–7.
6. Ibid.
7. For examples of the Kennedy and Johnson administrations' awareness of this, see Directorate of Intelligence, Weekly Summary Special Report No. 0320/66A, "Assessment of Latin American Military and Arms Needs," 23 December 1966; Directorate of Intelligence, Office of Current Intelligence No. 0285/63D, "The Bolivian–Chilean Dispute," 21 June 1963. CIA Records Search Tool (CREST), National Archives, College Park, MD (NA); and White House memorandum of conversation between John Kennedy and Jorge Alessandri, "US Military Assistance Programs, and Chilean Relations with Bolivia," 11 December 1962. Papers of President Kennedy, National Security Files, Countries, Box 20A, "Chile: General: 1/63–6/63." John Kennedy Library, Boston, Massachusetts (JFK). For Alliance funds and military aid to Chile, see United States Senate, *Covert Action in Chile, 1963–1973* (Washington, DC: Government Printing Office, 1975); and Department of State, "The Department of State during the Administration of President Lyndon B. Johnson, November 1963–January 1969" I: Administrative History, Chapter 6, Inter-American Relations, Section B: The Alliance for Progress, and Section C: Hemispheric Security. Lyndon Johnson Library, Austin, Texas (LBJ).
8. Varas, *Conversaciones con Viaux*, 77.
9. Directorate of Intelligence, "Assessment of Latin American Military and Arms Needs."
10. Directorate of Intelligence, "The Chilean Military Establishment," 15 August 1969. Department of State, *Foreign Relations of the United States, 1969–1976* E-16: *Documents on Chile, 1969–1973* (Washington, DC: Government Printing Office, 2015), document 8. Also see Mark Phythian, *The Politics of British Arms Sales since 1964* (Manchester: Manchester University Press, 2000), 105–45.

11. "State Visit to Chile: November 1968: Supplementary Brief for Lord Chalfont," undated, FO 73/71. Also see "State Visit to Brazil: November, 1968: Supplementary Brief for Lord Chalfont," undated, FO 73/71. BNA; and Alun Chalfont, *The Shadow of My Hand: A Memoir* (London: Weidenfeld & Nicolson, 2000), 141–6. The last Hunters arrived in Chile just days after the coup in September 1973, creating controversy in Britain.

12. Eduardo Frei Montalva, "The Alliance That Lost Its Way," *Foreign Affairs* 45 (1967), 446.

13. Biblioteca Nacional de Chile, "El Movimiento de Izquierda Revolucionaria (MIR, 1965–1990)," at <http://www.memoriachilena. cl>; José Díaz Nieva, *Patria y Libertad: el nacionalismo frente a la Unidad Popular* (Santiago de Chile: Ediciones Centro de Estudios Bicentenario, 2015), 22; Julio Faúndez, *Marxism and Democracy in Chile: From 1932 to the Fall of Allende* (New Haven: Yale University Press, 1988), 159–76; and Carmelo Furci, *The Chilean Communist Party and the Road to Socialism* (London: Zed Books, 1984), 82–104.

14. Ricardo Cruz-Coke, *Historia electoral de Chile, 1925–1973* (Santiago de Chile: Editorial Jurídica de Chile, 1984), 85–7. For American reporting on these developments, see National Intelligence Estimate 94–69, "Chile," 28 January 1969. Department of State, *FRUS, 1969–1976* E-16, document 1; William Bowdler to Walt Rostow, "Chile: Frei Suffers another Setback," 18 December 1967. Department of State, *Foreign Relations of the United States, 1964–1968* XXXI: *South and Central America; Mexico* (Washington, DC: Government Printing Office, 2004), document 297; Walt Rostow to Lyndon Johnson, 20 July 1967. Ibid., document 296; Ralph Dungan to Lincoln Gordon, 19 April 1967. Ibid., document 293; and Bureau of Intelligence and Research (INR) to Dean Rusk, "Frei Moves to Break Political Impasse in Chile," 25 January 1967. Ibid., document 290.

15. Brian Loveman, *Chile: The Legacy of Hispanic Capitalism* [1979], 3rd edn (New York: Oxford University Press, 2001), 248. For grassroots dissidence in the northern hemisphere in the late 1960s, see Jeremi Suri, *Power and Protest: Global Revolution and the Rise of Détente* [2003] (Cambridge, MA: Harvard University Press, 2005).

16. Alejandro San Francisco, ed., *La toma de la Universidad Católica de Chile (Agosto de 1967)* (Santiago de Chile: Globo Editores, 2007); Cristián Pérez, "Guerrilla rural en Chile: la batalla del Fundo San Miguel (1968)," *Estudios Públicos* 78 (2000): 181–208; "56 minutos permanenció en Pudahuel avión argentino desviado a

Cuba," *La Nación*, 9 October 1969; "Otro avión desviado a Cuba estuvo 2 horas en Pudahuel," *La Nación*, 5 November 1969; and "La tripulación del avión LAN Chile, desviado a Cuba, apreso a los asaltantes en pleno vuelo," *La Nación*, 13 November 1969. Also see "Boeing 'LAN' secuestrado en vuelo y conducido a la Havana," *La Nación*, 20 December 1969; and "Fracasó secuestro de avión LAN," *La Nación*, 7 February 1970.

17. Carlos Prats, *Memorias: testimonio de un soldado* (Santiago de Chile: Pehuén Editores, 1985), 110.

18. Ibid., 109–11; Varas, *Conversaciones con Viaux*, 86; and Eugenio Lira Massi, *¡Ahora le toca al golpe!* (Santiago de Chile: Abumohor Impresores, 1969), 10–11.

19. Edward Korry to Department of State, 25 March 1969. Department of State, *Foreign Relations of the United States, 1969–1976* XXI: *Chile, 1969–1973* (Washington, DC: Government Printing Office, 2014), document 6. For Gen. Juan Velasco's government, see Thomas Wright, *Latin America in the Era of the Cuban Revolution and Beyond* [1991], 3rd edn (Santa Barbara: ABC-CLIO/ Praeger, 2018), 121–39; and Stephen Gorman, "Antipolitics in Peru." Brian Loveman and Thomas Davies, eds., *The Politics of Antipolitics: The Military in Latin America* [1978], 3rd edn (Wilmington: Scholarly Resources, 1997), 300–26.

20. Korry to Department of State, 25 March 1969.

21. George Denney, "Chile: Military Unrest Serious, But Frei Administration Should Survive," 3 October 1969. Department of State, *FRUS, 1969–1976* XXI: *Chile, 1969–1973*, document 19.

22. Viaux to Frei, 2 October 1969. Varas, *Conversaciones con Viaux*, 64.

23. Paul Sigmund, *The Overthrow of Allende and the Politics of Chile, 1964–1976* (Pittsburgh: University of Pittsburgh Press, 1977), 85; and Lira, *Ahora le toca*, 10–11.

24. Varas, *Conversaciones con Viaux*, 88–94.

25. Viaux to Frei, 2 October 1969, 57.

26. Ibid., 65.

27. Mario Valdés Urrutia and Danny Monsálvez Araneda, "Recogiendo los pasos: los movimientos deliberativos al interior de las filas del Ejército (1969–1973)," *Notas Históricas y Geográficas* 13–14 (2002–3), 192–4; Prats, *Memorias*, 121–2; Sigmund, *Overthrow of Allende*, 86; and Varas, *Conversaciones con Viaux*, 94–8.

28. Valdés and Monsálvez, "Recogiendo los pasos," 193; Sigmund, *Overthrow of Allende*, 86; and Lira, *Ahora le toca*, 20.

29. Valdés and Monsálvez, "Recogiendo los pasos," 194; and Varas, *Conversaciones con Viaux*, 98–101.

30. Lira, *Ahora le toca*, 114; and Henry Kissinger to Richard Nixon, "Reported Military Revolt in Chile," 21 October 1969. Department of State, *FRUS, 1969–1976* XXI: *Chile, 1969–1973*, document 20. Viaux's insistence that his movement was apolitical and that he never wished to seize *la Moneda* notwithstanding, he acknowledged being urged by his followers do so before, during, and after the *Tacnazo*, which the Frei administration and many in the press interpreted as an attempted coup.

31. Harry Shlaudeman to Department of State, 21 October 1969. RG 84, Foreign Service Posts of the Department of State: Chile/U.S. Embassy Santiago, Box 30, "POL 23–9 Rebellion Coups 1969." NA.

32. Lira, *Ahora le toca*, 66, 77.

33. Ibid., 29.

34. Ibid., 33–42.

35. Varas, *Conversaciones con Viaux*, 104–5.

36. Lira, *Ahora le toca*, 104–7.

37. Shlaudeman to Department of State, 21 October 1969; and Shlaudeman to Department of State, 25 October 1969. RG 84, Foreign Service Posts of the Department of State: Chile/U.S. Embassy Santiago, Box 30, "POL 23–9 Rebellion Coups 1969." NA. For one of Viaux's press releases, see Lira, *Ahora le toca*, 47.

38. Lira, *Ahora le toca*, 119–23; and Shlaudeman to Department of State, 22 October 1969. RG 84, Foreign Service Posts of the Department of State: Chile/U.S. Embassy Santiago, Box 30, "POL 23–9 Rebellion Coups 1969." NA.

39. Roberto Viaux and Sub-Secretary of Health Patricio Silva, "Acta," 21 October 1969. Varas, *Conversaciones con Viaux*, 107–8. Also see Valdés and Monsálvez, "Recogiendo los pasos," 194–5; Lira, *Ahora le toca*, 123; and Shlaudeman to Department of State, 22 October 1969.

40. Sigmund, *Overthrow of Allende*, 87; Prats, *Memorias*, 126–9; Lira, *Ahora le toca*, 127–30; and Shlaudeman to Department of State, 25 October 1969.

41. Valdés and Monsálvez, "Recogiendo los pasos," 199–203; and Prats, *Memorias*, 130–61, 169.

42. Ray Cline to William Rogers, "Chile: Causes of Army Discontent Seem Likely to Persist," 4 November 1969. Chile Declassification Project (CDP), at <http://www.state.gov>. Also see Varas, *Conversaciones con Viaux*, 110–15.

43. Shlaudeman to Department of State, "CIA and the Golpe," 20 November 1969; Shlaudeman to Department of State, "Statement of CIA Spokesman," 23 October 1960; and Viron Vaky to Henry Kissinger, "CIA Press Comments on Chilean Situation," 22 October 1969. Department of State, *FRUS, 1969–1976* XXI: *Chile, 1969–1973*, documents 21, 22, and 23. Josh Goshko, "2 Units Revolt in Chile: Frei Claims Army Support against Rebels," *Washington Post*, 22 October 1969.

44. Shlaudeman to Department of State, "Statement of CIA Spokesman."

7   Plan Alfa

Salvador Allende (1970–3), leading the Marxist-Leninist *Unidad Popular* (UP) coalition, won a plurality of 36.6 percent in Chile's presidential election on 4 September 1970. Independent, conservative-leaning Jorge Alessandri (1958–64), the former president who had come out of retirement to represent the National Party (PN), closely followed him with 34.9 percent. The Christian Democratic Party's (PDC) Radomiro Tomic, running to the left of the Frei administration, came in a distant third with 27.8 percent. Per constitutional procedure, and since Alessandri declined to concede, Congress would decide between the top two candidates – who remained separated by about 40,000 votes – on 24 October.[1]

Congress had faced similar scenarios three times since 1945 – during the elections of Gabriel González in 1946, Gen. Carlos Ibáñez in 1952, and Alessandri in 1958. President Eduardo Frei's (1964–70) victory in 1964 represented a rare, decisive vote – achieved because Conservatives and Liberals had dropped out of the race and backed the PDC. In each of the above elections, after the most influential parties compromised and negotiated agreements among themselves, Congress selected the candidate who garnered the most votes. For example, Liberal congressmen supported González in 1946 on condition that he admit their party into the cabinet, where they pressed him to disregard his campaign promises on land reform and rural labor.

But this election was different. Allende presented the specter of a Marxist administration that would invite Chilean Communists, who had long cultivated Soviet ties, into the government – an outcome that the pro-Western, conservative Chilean establishment, the professional officer corps, and other anticommunists had dreaded since the 1920s. This triggered six weeks of fear, intrigue, and violence. Most eyes turned toward Frei and the PDC, the Chilean armed forces, and retired Brig. Gen. Roberto Viaux, whose activism only increased after the *Tacnazo*.

This chapter approaches these six weeks through Chilean, inter-American, and transatlantic perspectives that balance and integrate the Chilean high command, the Nixon administration (1969–74), and Viaux into a comprehensive narrative that unfolded during a particularly tense time in the Cold War. It highlights President Richard Nixon's churlish refusal to accept Allende's victory and Frei's subtle attempts to manipulate the high command while reconstructing Viaux's *Plan Alfa* from the ground up. This broad and multifaceted conspiracy remains more commonly known by its White House name, Track II, or its Agency codename, Project FUBELT, but it was nevertheless Chilean in conception, planning, and execution.[2]

These six weeks remain somewhat clouded, even when work-ing with the massive trove of declassified documents available today. Frei and those in his cabinet who participated in the conspiracy carefully and deliberately remained off the record. Thus, the record remains incomplete, not to mention heavily redacted. Although this chapter clears up much about *Plan Alfa*, its findings remain provisional. This notwithstanding, it remains clear that Chileans made this history, and that they did so as internationalists. Foreign intervention and intelligence operations – particularly the CIA's – remained limited to support and encouragement, which was often frantic in this period, but still not decisive. Further, as will become clear by the end of this chapter, the Agency, duly carrying out Nixon's ill-conceived and emotional commands, attempted to swim against the current in Chile and were entirely ineffective.

The Frei Administration and the Election

A flurry of activity occurred around and within the highest ranks of the armed services – particularly in the office of the army's chief of staff, the National Defense Council, and *Primera Zona Naval*

(PRIZONA), the Chilean navy's fleet headquarters at Valparaíso – after 4 September. All understood that these officers could have supported the election's results, influenced them in Alessandri's favor, or entered the cabinet, seized power, and then called for another round of voting, depending on the decisions they took in the coming weeks. This activity left Schneider dead and Adm. Fernando Porta, the chief of naval operations, forced into retirement. It also resulted in the exiling of Adm. Hugo Tirado, who succeeded Porta, and Brig. Gen. Camilo Valenzuela, who commanded the army's garrison in Santiago.

Gen. René Schneider, the army's chief of staff, met with Maj. Gen. Carlos Prats, his deputy and the chair of the National Defense Council, on 5 September. He identified the four most likely ways that this would end. First, the PDC could vote for Alessandri. Alessandri had declined to concede, but he had also made it clear, because he had not won a clear majority, that he would not accept the presidency if Congress elected him. Rather, he would resign to allow for new elections. He would do this to deny victory to Allende. Schneider believed that Allende's agitated supporters would reject this and that civil war would ensue. Second, the PDC might vote for Allende in exchange for the latter's promise to respect the constitutional order. Schneider predicted that a protracted conflict between the executive branch, under Allende's control, and the legislative and judicial branches, largely in conservative and Christian Democratic hands, would follow. Third, Allende could refuse to compromise with the PDC or any other party and force his way into power on the strength of his plurality. Schneider thought that this would produce a proletarian dictatorship or anticommunist reaction, probably spearheaded by military intervention. Finally, Viaux might seize power before Congress voted. Schneider feared that this, too, would drag the country into civil war.[3]

Schneider and Prats agreed that the army should stay out of this mess, which civilian politicians had created, and leave it to them to clean it up. The two generals had worked hard, although not as successfully as they would have liked, to restore professionalism and respect for the chain of command within the ranks since Viaux's *Tacnazo* had destabilized civilian-dominated civil–military relations and their institution itself in October 1969. They believed that their best course of action was to maintain discipline and remain strictly constitutionalist. This was both what the army needed and what Chile required as well. They explained this to their subordinates, including Valenzuela, hoping to inoculate them against Viaux, who they believed, rightly, it turned out, was already making overtures to key officers.[4]

On the same day, Schneider and Prats joined a larger group, including Porta, Gen. Carlos Guerraty, who commanded the air force, Gen. Vicente Huerta, director general of *Carabineros*, and Valenzuela, at Guerraty's residence. According to Guerraty, who described this meeting to a CIA informant after it broke up, these officers had sounded each other out on the possibility of organizing a coup. They talked about forming a military cabinet, removing Frei to a third country, and holding new elections. Schneider opposed this, Prats remained silent, and the gathering ended inconclusively.[5]

Valenzuela, who seems to have played the leading part in this meeting, saw Viaux the following day, on 6 September. Just afterward, he asked the US military attaché to solicit Ambassador Edward Korry's position on the discussion at Guerraty's residence and to see whether the ambassador might be willing to use his influence with Frei to persuade him to back or at least passively acquiesce to this still nascent plan. Korry sent word to Valenzuela that he was "very satisfied" to learn that these officers had reached the same conclusions he had with respect to what an Allende administration would entail. Korry insisted that these were his personal views, and not Washington's, when he advised the Department of State that the situation was more or less stalemated, with a despondent Frei apparently looking for the generals to move on their own while the wary generals waited for Korry to persuade Frei to take responsibility and issue orders to them.[6]

Frei, Minister of Defense Sergio Ossa, and other PDC cabinet members and party leaders sent confusing and contradictory signals to Schneider and Prats in the days that followed. It appears that Frei, his closest advisors, and the intermediaries they used feared to cross their Rubicon and sat on its banks in indecision. This notwithstanding, they hoped that the two generals would somehow get the message and then act on their own. They painted dark portraits of a Marxist-Leninist future, particularly with respect to Chile's economy, while hinting that US military assistance could end, which would complicate the armed forces' pending acquisitions. They seemed to want them to take responsibility for "saving the country," as they phrased it, and they became increasingly desperate as the days passed. But Schneider and Prats wanted nothing to do with it. This remained a civilian, not a military, problem, and they would do nothing that would endanger the standing of the army, whose professional detachment from politics they deemed their institution's, and indeed Chile's, last line of defense.

For example, a retired officer approached Prats, complaining that Schneider was preventing the other service commanders, who could not succeed without the army, from taking action. He wondered whether Prats might not retire Schneider, then seize power and save the day. A well-known but anonymous Christian Democrat sought Prats out more than a week later. Frei worried that Schneider had failed to understand what he must do. The army should take *la Moneda*, the presidential palace, by night, send the president abroad, stabilize the situation through emergency powers, close Congress, suspend political parties for a time, put trustworthy people in strategic positions, and then supervise new elections. Prats reported these and other conversations to Schneider. Schneider in turn brought this up, first with Ossa and then with Frei. Both of them, when confronted, denied knowing anything about it.[7]

Meanwhile, in the first week of October, Allende, who was negotiating an agreement to guarantee the constitutional order in exchange for the PDC's support, as Schneider's second scenario anticipated, reached out to the high command. The Frei administration had granted the service commanders leave to brief Alessandri and Allende's campaigns on military and naval affairs during the weeks before the congressional runoff. Schneider, Prats, and the others believed that this remained standard procedure and uncontroversial. Most of these conversations related to pressing practical matters, such as continuing budgetary support for the navy's fuel requirements with respect to the fleet's ongoing maneuvers and training exercises.

Alessandri's people, who already had experience in government, did not take advantage of these meetings, but Allende's staff did.

Allende reserved the right to appoint ministers of defense and their deputies, and to name service commanders as well. But he would not politicize the professional officer corps, bypass the chain of command, or interfere with promotions or other internal matters. He would respect existing laws and contracts, including military assistance agreements. Schneider and Prats, both anticipating that they would be among those soon retired, accepted Allende's assurances while encouraging their subordinates to do so as well.[8]

Allende also reached out to Porta, Vice Adm. Raúl Montero, Rear Adm. José Toribio Merino, and others in the navy. His campaign had perhaps distressed these officers more than the others. Indeed, Merino's first instinct had been to resign his commission. Allende had promised to withdraw from the Organization of American States (OAS) and the Inter-American Defense Board, and to break all defense relations with the United States, from the Rio Pact to the UNITAS antisubmarine warfare exercises the Chilean navy participated in every year. Porta and his colleagues were concerned that Allende would reorient Chilean foreign policy in a pro-Soviet and anti-US direction and that this would weaken Chilean security. They, like many others within the armed forces, worried that Allende might create people's militias – he was already using a private, Cuban-trained protection detail rather than Chilean police – and use them to subject the navy to party discipline.[9]

Allende reassured these admirals that his administration would respect the navy's wishes. Chile would remain within the Western community of nations and the OAS while maintaining existing military relationships with the United States, from whom the navy was currently purchasing seven warships. This satisfied Porta, Merino, and the others, and they came to share Schneider's position that the armed services should remained focused on national security, internal order, and institutional integrity while leaving politics to politicians, although they remained concerned that Allende and others on the left would eventually politicize the navy.

Porta's relationship with Frei and Ossa collapsed after these meetings. Rumors appeared in the press that Allende had compromised Porta and the navy's integrity with promises of a new aircraft carrier, among other material rewards. Ossa confronted Porta, characterizing his behavior as offensive to the administration. He suggested he take time off, leaving Tirado, who commanded PRIZONA, as acting chief of naval operations. No sooner had he done this than the navy sent "five men armed with submachine guns, under orders not to leave me alone, not even in the bathroom," while his *Carabinero* escort of one suddenly became five. Porta interpreted this as a form of house arrest, and he complained to Frei about it. Frei formally retired him and officially named Tirado his successor, effective 15 October.[10]

Schneider and Prats had warned Porta that he should be careful, as they suspected that something was going on, that some in the administration seemed to be trying to manipulate the armed forces. Porta agreed, characterizing his falling out with Frei and Ossa as "a maneuver to get me to retire and replace me with Tirado, who, together with Viaux and Valenzuela . . . and others were working with certain politicians to produce an *autogolpe*," a coup from within. As will become clear, below, Viaux, Tirado, and Valenzuela shared the admiral's interpretation, but responded much more favorably to it.[11]

"Higher authority had no intention of conceding": Nixon and the Election

In Washington, the Nixon administration's National Security Council (NSC) staff was surprised, since the latest polls had indicated an Alessandri victory, but still unperturbed when the election results came in. Viron Vaky, the NSC's Latin American specialist, summarized the intelligence community's views at the time. The United States had "no vital interests within Chile . . . The world military balance of power would not be significantly altered." Allende's election "would represent a definite psychological set-back to the U.S. and a definite psychological advance for the Marxist idea . . . There would be tangible economic losses." But Allende did not presently threaten United States security.[12]

The NSC had been considering such questions since late July 1970, when Nixon first took an interest in the election. He asked

National Security Advisor Henry Kissinger to look into the possibility of an Allende presidency in order to offer alternatives should he win. On 18 August, the interdepartmental committee that responded to this proposed four options. The administration could seek a *modus vivendi* with Allende; it might adopt a cool, correct, and restrained posture toward him; it could try to isolate him, diplomatically and economically; or, if Allende were deemed a threat, it might attempt to overthrow him. The committee preferred the second option for its flexibility while warning that the fourth entailed high risks. Kissinger deferred further discussion on these recommendations the day he received them. Korry's back-channel reporting, which contained a stream of unverified but dramatic impressions, rumors, and speculation from Santiago, had distracted him.[13]

Although Korry saw "very little possibility of a duly-elected and inaugurated Allende being overthrown," he believed it possible to influence Chilean affairs before the inauguration. He explained that the president of the senate, Christian Democrat Tomás Pablo, had come to his residence on Sunday, 9 August. The senator told the ambassador that Congress could elect Alessandri, Alessandri could refuse to accept the presidency, and then Congress would have to call new elections, which Frei would likely win. "In other words," Korry reported, "there would be a deal between [the PN] and PDC to block Allende and to reelect Frei."[14]

Korry did not know exactly what Frei's intentions were, and he was not familiar with Frei's relationship with Schneider, either. He understood that the president wished to keep Allende out of power, but he could only guess at what precisely he was prepared to do. Pablo appeared to be seeking American intervention to support the deal to reelect Frei – possibly but not necessarily at Frei's urging. He emphasized that "the critical time frame will be the first fortnight after the elections when the bidding for congressional votes begins." Korry agreed, suggesting to Washington that "If we are to influence that bidding we shall have to be prepared to act promptly on Sept 5 and to take our decision now." This persuaded Kissinger, who set the NSC's calm policy deliberations and the intelligence community's reasoned views aside while following Korry down the rabbit hole.[15]

Korry had been asking the Nixon administration to increase its investment in the anticommunist propaganda operations the CIA was running against the UP since March 1970. He had also been urging the administration to back Alessandri and/or Tomic, and to start planning to buy congressional votes in the event of a runoff, since June. The 40 Committee – Nixon's sub-cabinet, interagency authority to oversee covert operations – had denied Korry and the Agency permission even to explore this with their Chilean contacts for fear of exposure. Kissinger disagreed. The CIA could at least plan such operations. He overruled Vaky and the Department of State, instructing Director of Central Intelligence (DCI) Richard Helms to begin planning for this on 19 August.[16]

The Agency cited "ample precedent for the purchase of congressional favors" when advising that, if Alessandri came in first and Allende a close second, it could probably bribe enough Chilean legislators to tip the balance in Alessandri's favor. But it could only buttress "courses of action upon which Chileans themselves have already decided to embark," and would play no more than an ancillary role. This might cost approximately 500,000 dollars. The CIA judged that, were Allende to come in first, even by a slight margin, "popular forces rallying to his support may soon prove to be overpowering." The election rendered this discussion moot before the committee could discuss it.[17]

The 40 Committee met again on 8 September. Kissinger asked Korry and Chief of Station Henry Hecksher to assess the likelihood that American backing for a military coup before 24 October would succeed. They replied that such action remained "impossible" and "nonexistent." Korry was still exchanging views with Ossa, Pablo, and Raúl Sáez, a former minister of finance, on the maneuver that could lead to Frei's reelection. The Agency described this maneuver as promising – but it remained "a very long shot."[18]

The 40 Committee talked about this once again on 14 September, deciding to concentrate its efforts on backing what it was now calling "the Frei reelection gambit" or "the Rube Goldberg scheme." Korry and Hecksher were to make contact with Christian Democrats and the Chilean military in order to confirm that they understood that, if they went through with this, the United States would support them.

As Under Secretary of State for Political Affairs U. Alexis Johnson, the Department of State's representative on the committee, put it to Korry, Washington was instructing him to stay on the safe side of a fine line while backing the right people. "We do not want you to get out in front and we do not want you to 'take over.' Yet we do not want their will to flag for lack of support."[19]

Johnson had carefully chosen his words, particularly those that ordered Korry not to take over. Secretary of State William Rogers and Vaky, among others who were reading Korry's cables, worried about his reliability, even his emotional stability. Rogers told Kissinger that Korry's messages seemed "frenetic and somewhat irrational." Vaky found them overwrought, "as if he is under too much stress, almost hysterical." He speculated that Korry might have been anticipating McCarthyistic-like accusations for losing Chile at some point in his future, and he wondered whether he was trying to position himself to parry this. He feared that he was exceeding his instructions, that he had already committed the Nixon administration to courses of action it had not yet authorized, and he wanted to rein him in.[20]

Vaky fought a rearguard action over the next several weeks to refocus Kissinger's attention on proper policy deliberations. He wanted "to stop mucking around." "We stand vulnerable," he warned, "to the charge that we did not reach policy decisions through the reasoned NSC system of examination of the situation and alternatives on which we have prided ourselves." He implored Kissinger to reach "*a policy decision . . . and a controlled implementation of that decision.*"[21]

Assistant Secretary of State for Inter-American Affairs Charles Meyer raised the issue again, before the 40 Committee. Kissinger shot it down, explaining that

> this presumed total acceptance of a fait accompli and higher authority [that is, Nixon] had no intention of conceding before the 24th; on the contrary, he wanted no stone left unturned . . . He went on to note the inevitable contrast of higher authority advising heads of state in Europe of the absolute undesirability of an Allende regime in Chile while back home the bureaucracy performed a slow gavotte over what our posture should be.[22]

Nixon was closely reading Korry's cables, too. He underlined several sentences in Korry's first post-election report – "We have been living with a corpse in our midst for some time and its name is Chile"; "Chileans like to die peacefully with their mouths open"; and "The political right depend upon the economic right" – before pronouncing it "An excellent perceptive job of analysis." By the following week, Nixon was following Korry in comparing Chile to Czechoslovakia and Cuba. The president seemed to be getting just as worked up as the ambassador.[23]

Other information and opinions came to Nixon's increasingly agitated White House. Donald Kendall, a campaign contributor who occasionally offered unsolicited foreign policy advice, brought Chilean publisher Agustín Edwards to Washington on 14 September. Kendall, Edwards, and an unlisted, apparently Chilean, associate breakfasted with Kissinger and Attorney General John Mitchell before being debriefed by Helms later in the day. Both Kissinger and Helms later cited Edwards, who had come to warn Nixon about the consequences of an Allende government, when explaining the outburst that followed.[24]

The declassified record only contains part of what Edwards and his associate said. They described the political dispositions of the commanders of the Chilean armed forces while outlining each of the services' state of readiness. Schneider and Porta would not act against the constitutional order, but all of the other commanders wanted to block Allende's inauguration. Valenzuela was prepared to back Prats as Schneider's successor, provided the latter was given an honorable exit. He was even ready to move alone, if necessary. Edwards and his associate clearly wanted Nixon's support for a coup, and they preferred "a serious effort" rather than one led by Viaux "or some other nut." Edwards thought there was just too much to lose to remain cautiously uninvolved or to rely on the Frei reelection gambit. This seems to have triggered Nixon's wrath.[25]

Nixon summoned Kissinger, Mitchell, and Helms to his office the next day. He directed Helms to do everything possible to instigate a military coup in Chile regardless of the costs and risks involved. He told him to do this outside of the 40 Committee and without the knowledge of the Department of State, Korry, and the embassy. Kissinger later characterized this as "a passionate desire, unfocused and born of frustration, to do 'something.'" He also testified that no one who knew the president would have paid attention to this rant, particularly his pledge of 10 million dollars. Chief of Staff H. R. Haldeman wrote much the same thing in his diaries. However this may have been, Kissinger failed to speak up at the time. Indeed, he acted as Nixon's enforcer on the NSC, in the 40 Committee, and at the Agency.[26]

Helms objected to Kissinger's remarks in his memoirs. "I do not consider myself to have been an unwary or even casual recipient of instructions by the President from behind his desk in the Oval Office," he wrote. "President Nixon had ordered me to instigate a military coup in Chile ... By what superior judgment was I to leave the White House and then decide that the President did not mean what he had just said?" He returned to Langley and formed a task force to carry out Nixon's directive the following day.[27]

The CIA codenamed the operation Project FUBELT. It was a task force of one. Its chief, David Atlee Phillips, worked and slept in Deputy Director for Plans Thomas Karamessines's offices. Karamessines and Phillips reported to Kissinger from 16 September to 3 November 1970, when they shut the task force down. Meanwhile, Kissinger and his assistant, Brig. Gen. Alexander Haig, subjected Karamessines, William Broe, the Agency's director of Latin American operations, and Phillips to "just constant, constant ... Just continual pressure." The CIA's Santiago Station, whose case officers had found their mission an impossible one from the beginning, duly combed the professional officer corps to find anyone willing to overthrow the government. Using Edwards's intelligence and the military attaché's contacts with the Chilean military, these officers soon found their only viable option: the Valenzuela, Tirado, and Viaux group and the so-called Viaux Solution.[28]

The Viaux Solution

Viaux had remained in the political arena since the *Tacnazo*. A Viaux-for-president campaign, consisting of active and retired officers, noncoms, and conservative civilians, coalesced around him in late 1969. As the Department of State's Director of Intelligence and Research (INR) Ray Cline reported, "an aura of achievement" surrounded the general, and he and his supporters had grown conscious of it. He canvassed the country from the Atacama to Chiloé, hearing what people had to say and making his own views clear in the months that followed.[29]

When Viaux spoke at a dinner in his honor in February 1970, he reminded his audience of the misgovernment and chaos that had preceded Gen. Carlos Ibáñez's anticommunist dictatorship (1927–31). He called for the reestablishment of a strong government that would promulgate a new constitution. More than 500 active and retired officers and their wives attended this event. Still more sent cables and letters to express their support. Viaux disliked all three of the candidates who were running for president. But he found an Allende presidency particularly intolerable.[30]

Valenzuela and Viaux sought each other out on 6 or 7 September. They agreed that they could not permit "the enthronement of communism in Chile." They found Tirado, Gen. Joaquín García, the second ranking officer in the air force, Capt. Raúl Lopez, another naval officer, and the *Carabineros'* Huerta after Valenzuela had met with Schneider, Prats, Porta, and Huerta at Guerraty's house. These officers feared that Frei was playing the role Alexander Kerensky had in the Bolshevik Revolution. But they also understood that several members of the administration, including the minister of interior, to whom Huerta reported, Ossa in defense, and the minister of economy were passively encouraging them to act. Thus, Viaux and his colleagues believed that they were conceiving a *coup d'état* not only with implied consent, but with vague and unspoken prodding from senior cabinet members.[31]

Two scenarios – consistent with what Schneider, Prats, and Porta, on the one hand, and Korry, on the other, understood – emerged in Valenzuela and Viaux's discussions by the third week of September. In the first one, several of Frei's cabinet members would resign, provoking a crisis. The president would appoint the commanders of the armed forces to replace them. This would allow him to keep his hands clean while enabling army, navy, and air force commanders to seek emergency powers. In the second one, the armed services would seize power, with unspoken permission. Then Frei would leave the country. After a reasonable time, he could return and run in new elections, as President Arturo Alessandri (1920–4, 1925, and 1932–8), albeit under different circumstances, had done in the 1920s and again in the 1930s.[32]

As Viaux acknowledged, however, "the problem of the army's chief of staff remained." Schneider would not support any of the above scenarios and he ordered his subordinates to stay out of the election. Valenzuela and Viaux's friends tried to change his mind to no avail. Schneider refused even to listen to them, prompting one frustrated conspirator to remark to a CIA informant that plotters did not need US support or money; they needed "a general with balls."[33]

Viaux reached out to Prats via an intermediary, asking for a private meeting. Prats turned him down, telling him,

> Nothing personal, but I have never shared his attitudes, which I consider offensive to the army. If he wants to discuss some plot to change the election's results, I will be obligated to report it immediately. If he wants to talk about some other, non-political business, he can come to my office.[34]

Viaux sent word back that there must have been a misunderstanding. He had thought that Prats was asking to meet with him.[35]

It became clear that Schneider was not going to move under any circumstances by mid-October. This weakened Valenzuela, who "preferred to act only under the orders of a superior officer," and it left Viaux a retired general who remained willing to act unilaterally, but who had no actual forces to command. The navy, air force, and *Carabineros*, moving individually or jointly, could not accomplish much without the army. These problems notwithstanding, these officers continued to meet and discuss the situation into October.[36]

Valenzuela and Viaux remained the ones driving most of this. They had developed relationships with Army Attaché Col. Paul Wimert and Santiago Station's cutouts. Viaux was requesting covert arms drops and money to back what was shaping up as his own desperate act against Schneider. Santiago Station reported these developments through 10 October, when a frustrated Hecksher settled on the Viaux Solution as the only remaining way to produce Nixon's coup:

> *Alto Mando* [Schneider] Solution cannot be achieved . . .
> Frei plus *Alto Mando* Solution. See subpara A . . .
> Regimental Commander Solution . . . lack requisite leverage . . .
> Navy or Air Force Solution. Neither jointly nor singly, neither by persuasion nor by coercion, will they be able to sway *Alto Mando* . . .
>
> . . . You have asked us to provoke chaos in Chile. Thru Viaux Solution we provide you with formula for chaos which unlikely to be bloodless. To dissimulate U.S. involvement will clearly be impossible. Station [redacted] team, as you know, has given most serious consideration to all plans suggested by hqs counterparts. We conclude that none of them stand even remote chance of achieving [redacted] objective. Hence, Viaux gamble, despite high risk factors, may commend itself to you.[37]

The Agency understood that Valenzuela's will was slackening and that Viaux was planning to abduct Schneider on his own. The general proposed to blame militants in the Socialist Party (PS) and the Movement of the Revolutionary Left (MIR) for it. Then he would exploit this "leftist coup attempt" to rally the professional officer corps around him as he declared a state of emergency and formed a new government. He believed that this would start a chain reaction and that Valenzuela and the others, possibly even Prats, would quickly join him. Hecksher and his colleagues in Santiago found the general's assumptions untested and his scheme farfetched, reckless, and likely not only to fail, but to worsen the overall situation. As the chief of station sarcastically wrote Langley, "We somehow feel that this whole operation so unprofessional and insecure that, in Chilean setting, it could stand fair chance of succeeding."[38]

Karamessines met Kissinger and Haig at the White House to discuss this on 15 October. They agreed that Viaux's plan would not only fail, but that it would compromise Valenzuela and the others. As Kissinger told Nixon that evening at 6:00 p.m., "I saw Karamessines today. That looks hopeless. I turned it off. Nothing would be worse than an abortive coup." He still wanted to keep Viaux in reserve, however, and so he instructed the CIA to tell him to preserve his assets and await a more favorable time, for what it was worth.[39]

It was not worth much. Viaux ignored Kissinger's message. Tirado's promotion carried more weight with him, Valenzuela, and the others. As the Defense Intelligence Agency (DIA) recognized, this "may have made the navy more likely to participate in a coup." Valenzuela, now optimistic, approached Hecksher's cutouts and asked for a handful of untraceable submachine guns, ammunition, and teargas canisters the next evening, 17 October. This puzzled Karamessines, Broe, and Phillips, who still seemed to think that Viaux and Valenzuela were leading two separate groups of plotters. They urgently queried Hecksher "What happened between morning 17 October and evening 17 October to change [redacted] from despondency to measured optimism? Who exactly is involved in coup attempt? Who are leaders and which units will support them?"[40]

The answer that neither Langley nor Santiago Station understood at the time, was that Viaux, Valenzuela, Tirado, García, and Huerta had hastily gathered after learning of the admiral's promotion. They unanimously voted to execute Viaux's plan on Saturday evening, 17 October. They would kidnap Schneider. Then Huerta's *Carabineros* would reveal several of the MIR's arms caches around Santiago while Viaux alerted Chileans to the communist danger that was upon them. They understood that Frei would declare a state of emergency while mobilizing forces in Santiago, which would place them directly under Valenzuela's command. Once this happened, Tirado would form a military government and name Viaux the minister of defense. The president would leave the country. Valenzuela would present Schneider with a *fait accompli* and then release him.[41]

There remained only one complication. Valenzuela insisted, as a matter of honor, that someone other than Chilean soldiers grab Schneider. It was too much for him to consent to a military operation directed against a sitting chief of staff. Viaux was ready for this. He had maintained close relations with the PN, which had led him and attorney Pablo Rodríguez into each other's arms just days after the election.

Rodríguez and approximately 200 conservative professionals had formed the *Movimiento Cívico Patria y Libertad* immediately after Allende's victory for the express purpose of pressing Congress to either vote for Alessandri or call for a new election. PL's first activities were in support of a group of anticommunist women who held nighttime vigils in front of *la Moneda*, mourning the coming death of Chilean democracy. Rodríguez apparently participated in *Plan Alfa* as well.[42]

Viaux recruited Juan Diego Dávila and Luis Gallardo from the PN, and "several others, the majority of whom I did not know," sometime around 11 September. Dávila, Gallardo, and some of these others, including Jaime Melgoza, had come from the Alessandri campaign. Melgoza, a self-professed martial arts expert, had driven a bus and sold cars before joining the conspiracy. The others were probably associated with Rodríguez and PL.[43]

Gallardo rented a downtown apartment from a friend. He and his group called it "*la pecera*" – the fish tank – and made it their safehouse. From there, they followed Schneider to learn his routine and whatever security arrangements he may have had in place. They practiced target shooting at a site just outside Santiago and they guarded Viaux's residence by night.[44]

Viaux saw Gallardo and the others late on 17 October. He instructed them to execute *Plan Alfa*. They would abduct Schneider and take him to "a place only Dávila and I knew about." Then "a message would be sent to Frei, in the name of an imaginary organization, demanding that he designate a military cabinet as a condition of the general's release." Gallardo understood that unnamed Christian Democratic leaders had given Viaux assurances that the president was aware of the operation and that he was waiting for the note. They had several handguns, chloroform, and pepper. They expected everything to be over within a smooth 48 hours.[45]

Viaux told Gallardo's group that Valenzuela had arranged a dinner on the pretext of celebrating Schneider's one-year anniversary as chief of staff. This would lure the general to his official residence in Las Condes on Monday evening, 19 October. Valenzuela would ensure that the festivities ended around 1:00 a.m. and that the other officers lingered for about twenty minutes while Schneider left alone. Huerta would clear the patrol cars away from the neighborhood, leaving him in the open and unprotected.[46]

Gallardo and his accomplices waited outside the residence at the correct time, but Schneider thwarted them, unknowingly. Gallardo's surveillance team had correctly reported that Schneider arrived in his official Mercedes. Both Schneider and Prats, however, opted to drive themselves home in their private cars. They lived nearby and did not wish to trouble their drivers. So, Gallardo's snatch-and-grab team, which was watching Schneider's official vehicle, never saw him leave that night. Gallardo tried improvising the following day, on 20 October. He planned to stop Schneider on the street, but no one in his group had a car that could keep up with the general.[47]

Viaux met Gallardo's group again, passing teargas canisters and possibly submachine guns to them, which they had probably acquired from the CIA via Wimert, and Valenzuela on Wednesday evening, 21 October. They assembled a larger group, consisting of approximately twenty cars, including a Jeep. The other vehicles would create the appearance of a traffic jam the following morning, forcing Schneider's car onto a side street near Américo Vespucio and Martín de Zamora. The Jeep would crash into the rear of the Mercedes, and then three or four other vehicles would surround it. Melgoza would disable Schneider's driver "with a karate chop" while the kidnapping unfolded. Others would use sledgehammers to intimidate the general while moving him to the secure location.[48]

Plan Alfa proved a catastrophic failure in the execution on Thursday morning, 22 October. Schneider resisted and someone from within Gallardo's group shot him before the others panicked and scattered. Gallardo blamed Melgoza, alleging that he was working for the MIR and had somehow sabotaged the operation. But Gallardo's group more likely failed because they were amateurs who had no idea what they were doing.[49]

Frei declared a state of emergency while Ossa, Prats, and the other service commanders denounced the attack, promising swift justice. Prats placed army units on standby throughout the nation, and Valenzuela became *jefe de la plaza*, assuming command of all forces in and around the capital. Prats described "a general feeling of indignation" among the army's senior commanders in Santiago, "not only for the seriousness such an attack against our respected superior and colleague represented, but because it was also an attack against the army itself." When he contacted Valenzuela, he found him demoralized and depressed.[50]

Viaux believed that his moment had finally arrived, however, and Nixon, Kissinger, and everyone following these events at the CIA sat up and leaned forward to see what would happen next. They were all disappointed. Hecksher flatly turned down Viaux's request to tell Frei that this had been a communist move, and Valenzuela would not even take his calls. The Agency and the *Washington Post*'s correspondent in Santiago reported that one of the assailants was in hiding and offering to name everyone involved in the botched kidnapping. These names included high-ranking government and military officials who had allegedly promised "that if Schneider was kidnapped there would be a coup," but who had failed to follow through and were "desperately trying to find a way to prevent public revelation of their involvement." Schneider died three days later, on 25 October. The CIA found "no indications that Valenzuela's or Viaux's group are planning a coup" after this. It was over, at least for the moment.[51]

Chilean authorities arrested Viaux, who surrendered, Rodríguez, who was taken into custody while boarding a flight from Santiago to La Serena, and approximately 150 others, including those from Gallardo's group who had not gone into hiding or left the country, within several days. Gallardo and his associates had used their own names, driven their own cars, and knew all of the others, whom they seem to have quickly identified under interrogation. Valenzuela, still *jefe de la plaza*, issued a gag order to all of those detained and silenced all media. Retired Gen. Emilio Cheyre, who led the investigation, eventually charged Tirado and Valenzuela in addition to Viaux while keeping Frei and the cabinet out of it. The information that would detail and explain this remains incomplete, heavily redacted, and inconclusive in the declassified record today, although Karamessines, Broe, and Phillips commented that "Frei was aware of the main elements of [Valenzuela and Viaux's] plan as were a few cabinet members" in their after-action report.[52]

To this day, *Plan Alfa* remains known by its White House name, Track II, or its CIA codename, Project FUBELT. Yet it was Chilean in conception, planning, and execution. Valenzuela, Viaux, and their coconspirators clarified this when they showed Hecksher's cutouts the door during one of their strategy sessions, explaining that "this [was a] Chilean matter." As Hecksher dryly reported, neither he nor his people "share[d] in planning of professionally executed military coup." Santiago Station was not even able to persuade Viaux to await a more propitious moment after 15 October. Thus, the Agency remained about as influential as those who cheer from the sidelines and in the stands at football games – and they were poorly directed cheerleaders and fans at that.[53]

Nixon, Kissinger, and Korry's confused leadership undermined whatever influence the CIA may have been able to exercise had it been properly supported. As Vaky repeatedly warned Kissinger, the Nixon administration was neither carefully determining its policy nor clearly communicating it to the government's departments and agencies. Further, Korry was behaving erratically, as an unguided missile, proposing a bold course of action one day, and then criticizing it or even taking an entirely different course the next. This confusion in Washington and within the walls of the embassy led to crossed wires on several occasions.[54]

For example, Korry unknowingly discouraged Frei and Ossa from supporting *Plan Alfa* at the precise moment that Nixon, Kissinger, and the Agency wanted to encourage and reassure them that Washington did indeed back it. On the evening of 6 October, Ossa asked Korry whether the US government supported the plotting that was occurring within the army and around Viaux. Korry explicitly told them that he remained responsible for all American policies and actions in Chile, and that he opposed it. He advised Kissinger and Johnson that the 40 Committee should "end all indirect contacts . . . with Viaux, [Maj. Arturo] Marshall, [Ricardo] Claro, et al., even if it signifies an informational sacrifice." He so instructed Hecksher and Wimert, reasoning that it would look better if Washington were "totally surprised by whatever might develop." Kissinger quickly rescinded this instruction, but he could not retract the words Korry had spoken to Ossa, words that Frei almost certainly heard, too.[55]

The Nixon administration's confused leadership and the Agency's ineffectiveness notwithstanding, there was little Broe, Phillips, and Hecksher could have done to prevent Allende's election, as they advised their superiors from the beginning, in any case. Had Chilean conservatives, moderates, center-leftists, and independents rallied together around either Alessandri or Tomic against Allende as they had rallied around Frei six years earlier, the CIA might have been able to support them. If Frei had decisively and openly backed Valenzuela and Viaux's group, or had Schneider or Prats acquiesced to or joined it, the Agency may have been positioned to support them. But none of these conditions existed, and no covert operation, no matter how angry or determined Nixon was, and no matter how well funded, could have got around these obstacles. As Vaky phrased it when describing Korry's frantic moves and urging Kissinger to return to proper policy deliberations, "The fact of the matter is that Frei refuses to move or lead any action. Korry is grabbing at straws, but each one breaks when he grabs it . . . we are kidding ourselves to believe that there are any more gambits that can work."[56]

Thus, Allende assumed the presidency on 5 November 1970. The CIA's inability to stop this did not mean that Allende was in a strong position in Chile. The Soviet delegation to the inauguration surveyed the situation after the dust had settled from *Plan Alfa*. They saw a minority presidency based on a less-than-united coalition, with some in the new administration committed to the peaceful road while others preferred, and were already perpetrating, revolutionary violence. They saw an entrenched, if currently divided, anticommunist opposition in Congress and the courts, the armed forces, and the press. "This is not going to end well," one of them remarked.[57]

Notes

1. Ricardo Cruz-Coke, *Historia electoral de Chile, 1925–1973* (Santiago de Chile: Editorial Jurídica de Chile, 1984), 109–13.
2. With respect to this period's terminology, the NSC and Ambassador Edward Korry spoke of Phase I when referring to the CIA's anticommunist propaganda operations directed against Salvador Allende's campaign during the normal election period, from March through

September 1970. Korry introduced Phase II, a proposal to influence Eduardo Frei's thinking and congressional voting during the runoff stage, in September and October. President Richard Nixon, Attorney General John Mitchell, and National Security Advisor Henry Kissinger split Phase II into Tracks I and II after 15 September. Korry's Phase II continued as Track I. The 40 Committee, Korry, and the Agency collaborated on it. However, only Nixon, Mitchell, Kissinger, and the CIA knew of Track II, which the Agency codenamed Project FUBELT. It represented the president's secret order that the CIA instigate a military coup on its own, regardless of its cost. Brig. Gen. Roberto Viaux was already working within a larger Chilean conspiracy, which included leading Christian Democrats and many within the Chilean high command, to accomplish this objective before the Agency's task force found him. Viaux's inner circle referred to this plot as *Plan Alfa*.

3. Carlos Prats, *Memorias: testimonio de un soldado* (Santiago de Chile: Pehuén Editores, 1985), 165–6.
4. Mario Valdés Urrutia and Danny Monsálvez Araneda, "Recogiendo los pasos: los movimientos deliberativos al interior de las filas del Ejército (1969–1973)," *Notas Históricas y Geográficas* 13–14 (2002–3), 198–208; and Prats, *Memorias*, 165–89.
5. Santiago Station to CIA, 8 September 1970. Department of State, *Foreign Relations of the United States, 1969–1976* XXI: *Chile, 1969–1973* (Washington, DC: Government Printing Office, 2014), document 67.
6. Edward Korry to NSC, 7 September 1970. Ibid., document 65.
7. Prats, *Memorias*, 169–74.
8. Ibid., 178–80.
9. José Toribio Merino, *Bitácora de un almirante: memorias* (Santiago de Chile: Editorial Andrés Bello, 1998), 72–9. Adm. Fernando Porta's account of his retirement, dated June 1973, in ibid., 104–20. For Salvador Allende's Cuban-trained security detail, which he downplayed as his "group of personal friends," see Cristián Pérez, "Salvador Allende, Apuntes sobre su dispositivo de seguridad: el grupo de amigos personales (GAP)," *Estudios Públicos* 79 (2000): 31–81. The US Navy had organized annual hemispheric antisubmarine warfare exercises as part of the American-led conventional defense in the 1950s.
10. Merino, *Bitácora de un almirante*, 116; and Prats, *Memorias*, 180–2. Also see DIA, Intelligence Summary, Chile, 16 October 1970. Chile Declassification Project (CDP), at <http://www.state.gov>.
11. Merino, *Bitácora de un almirante*, 113; and Prats, *Memorias*, 172.

12. Viron Vaky, "Chile – 40 Committee Meeting, Monday – September 14," 14 September 1970; and CIA, "Situation Following the Chilean Presidential Election," 7 September 1970, attached to Vaky, "40 Committee Meeting, September 8 – Chile," 7 September 1970. CDP. Chief of Naval Operations Adm. Elmo Zumwalt dissented, suggesting that a Soviet presence in Chile could threaten the US. See Zumwalt to Thomas Moorer, "Chile (U)," 15 September 1970. Department of State, *FRUS, 1969–1976* XXI: *Chile, 1969–1973*, document 91.

13. Special Review Group, "Chile (NSSM 97)," 19 August 1970; Charles Meyer to U. Alexis Johnson, "NSSM 97 – Chile: Recommendation of Option," 18 August 1970; and Henry Kissinger to William Rogers, Melvin Laird, Richard Helms, and Moorer, "Chile," 24 July 1970. Department of State, *FRUS, 1969–1976* XXI: *Chile, 1969–1973*, documents 53, 52, and 46. For the committee's arguments, see Meyer to Kissinger, "Chile – Response to NSSM 97," 18 August 1970; and "Annex NSSM-97," 18 August 1970. Department of State, *Foreign Relations of the United States, 1969–1976* E-16: *Documents on Chile, 1969–1973* (Washington, DC: Government Printing Office, 2015), documents 13 and 14.

14. Korry to John Crimmins, 11 August 1970. Department of State, *FRUS, 1969–1976* XXI: *Chile, 1969–1973*, document 50.

15. Ibid.

16. Special Review Group, "Chile (NSSM 97)," 19 August 1970. For the CIA's anticommunist propaganda operations against the UP, see Margaret Power, *Right-Wing Women in Chile: Feminine Power and the Struggle against Allende, 1964–1973* (University Park: Pennsylvania State University Press, 2002), 126–37; United States Senate, *Covert Action in Chile, 1963–1973* (Washington, DC: Government Printing Office, 1975); and "Options in Chilean Presidential Election during the Congressional Run-Off Phase (5 September–24 October 1970)," 31 August 1970. Department of State, *FRUS, 1969–1976* E-16: *Documents on Chile, 1969–1973*, document 16.

17. Acting director of Latin American operations, CIA, "Phase II Planning," 23 August 1970. Department of State, *FRUS, 1969–1976* XXI: *Chile, 1969–1973*, document 55.

18. Vaky to Kissinger, "Chile – 40 Committee Meeting, Monday – September 14"; Korry to 40 Committee, "Ambassador's Response to Request for Analysis of Military Option in Present Chilean Situation," 11 September 1970; Korry to 40 Committee, 12 September 1970; and Frank Chapin, "Minutes of the Meeting of the 40

Committee, 8 September 1970," 8 September 1970. Department of State, *FRUS, 1969–1976* XXI: *Chile, 1969–1973*, documents 79, 78, and 70.

19. Johnson to Korry, 15 September 1970. Department of State, *FRUS, 1969–1976* XXI: *Chile, 1969–1973*, document 92. The NSC's executive secretary was absent and none of those in attendance took notes at this meeting.

20. William Rogers and Kissinger telephone transcript, 14 September 1970; and Vaky to Kissinger, "Chile," 10 September 1970. Ibid., documents 88 and 76.

21. Vaky to Kissinger, "40 Committee Meeting – Chile – October 6, 1970," 5 October 1970; Vaky to Kissinger, "Chile," 1 October 1970; and Vaky to Kissinger, "Chile – Our Modus Operandi," 16 September 1970. Ibid., documents 134, 130, and 95. Vaky's emphasis.

22. Peter Jessup, "Minutes of the Meeting of the 40 Committee, 6 October 1970," 6 October 1970. Ibid., document 138.

23. Richard Nixon and Kissinger telephone transcript, 12 September 1970; and Korry to Department of State, 5 September 1970. Ibid., documents 82 and 62.

24. Kenneth Millian, "Discussion of Chilean Political Situation," 14 September 1970. Ibid., document 89. Also see Peter Kornbluh, "Agustín Edwards: A Declassified Obituary," 25 April 2017, at <http://www.nsarchive2.gwu.edu>; Henry Kissinger, *White House Years* (Boston: Little, Brown, 1979), 673–4; and United States Senate, *Alleged Assassination Plots Involving Foreign Leaders* (Washington, DC: Government Printing Office, 1975), 228, n. 1.

25. Millian, "Discussion of Chilean Political Situation."

26. Kissinger, *White House Years*, 673; and Editorial note. Department of State, *FRUS, 1969–1976* XXI: *Chile, 1969–1973*, document 93. H. R. Haldeman wrote of "a challenge I faced frequently . . . whether or not to follow a specific Presidential order. I sometimes decided not to, on the basis that it was not an order that was really intended to be carried out, but rather a letting off of steam, or that it was clearly not in the P's interest that it be carried out." Haldeman also related how Nixon had learned to bypass him and go directly to officials like Helms, who lacked the rank to delay or disregard such orders. H. R. Haldeman, *The Haldeman Diaries: Inside the Nixon White House* [1994] (New York: Berkley Books, 1995), 77–8.

27. Richard Helms, *A Look Over My Shoulder: A Life in the Central Intelligence Agency* (New York: Random House, 2003), 405.

28. United States Senate, *Alleged Assassination Plots Involving Foreign Leaders*, 235; and William Broe, "Genesis of Project FUBELT," 16 September 1970. Department of State, *FRUS, 1969–1976* XXI: *Chile, 1969–1973*, document 94. Also see David Atlee Phillips, *The Night Watch: 25 Years of Peculiar Service* (New York: Atheneum, 1977), 219–23.

29. Ray Cline to William Rogers, "Chile: Causes of Army Discontent Seem Likely to Persist," 4 November 1969. CDP.

30. Florencia Varas, *Conversaciones con Viaux* (Santiago de Chile: Impresiones EIRE, 1972), 119; and Arturo Olivarría Bravo, *Chile bajo la Democracia Cristiana: sexto y último año (3 de noviembre de 1969–3 de noviembre de 1970)* (Santiago de Chile: Editorial Salesiana, 1971), 49–73.

31. Varas, *Conversaciones con Viaux*, 127–8.

32. Ibid., 132–3.

33. Ibid., 133; Santiago Station to CIA, 16 October 1970; and Santiago Station to CIA, 22 September 1970. CDP.

34. Prats, *Memorias*, 182.

35. Ibid.

36. Varas, *Conversaciones con Viaux*, 133.

37. Santiago Station to CIA, 10 October 1970. CDP.

38. Santiago Station to CIA, 19 October 1970. CDP.

39. Kissinger and Nixon, Telcon, 15 October 1970, 6:00 p.m. Henry Kissinger telephone conversation transcripts (TELCONS), Box 7, "12–16 October 1970." Richard Nixon Library, Yorba Linda, California (RN). "The Coup That Failed: The Effects on Allende and His Political Posture, with Special Emphasis on His Stance before U.S. Positions, Moderate or Tough," 15 October 1970; and "Dr. Kissinger, Mr. Karamessines, Gen. Haig at the White House – 15 October 1970," 15 October 1970. CDP.

40. Varas, *Conversaciones con Viaux*, 134; CIA to Santiago Station, 19 October 1970; and DIA, Intelligence Summary, Chile, 16 October 1970. CDP.

41. Varas, *Conversaciones con Viaux*, 134–40.

42. Nathaniel Davis to Department of State, "Patria y Libertad," 23 December 1971. CDP. For *Patria y Libertad*'s creation and politics, see José Díaz Nieva, *Patria y Libertad: el nacionalismo frente a la Unidad Popular* (Santiago de Chile: Ediciones Centro de Estudios Bicentenario, 2015), 19–70. Korry complained to Washington that he was "appalled to discover that there is liaison for terrorist and coup plotting among Pablo Rodríguez, leader of the post-electoral

Patria y Libertad organization, Viaux, Major [Arturo] Marshall and several well-known discredited rightists." Korry to Kissinger and U. Alexis Johnson, 9 October 1970. Department of State, *FRUS, 1969–1976* XXI: *Chile, 1969–1973*, document 144. But as Davis acknowledged, the exact nature of their relationship remained "fuzzy." Chilean authorities arrested Rodríguez, who was trying to board a flight from Santiago to La Serena two days after the assault against Gen. René Schneider. They found a handgun on him. But he was not among those imprisoned for the attack. See "Track II," 26 October 1970. CDP.

43. Varas, *Conversaciones con Viaux*, 137.
44. Gallardo's testimony, in ibid., 148–70
45. Ibid., 159, 162, 165.
46. Gallardo's testimony; Prats, *Memorias*, 183–4; Santiago Station to CIA, 20 October 1970; and the station's second cable the same day. CDP.
47. Gallardo's testimony; Prats, *Memorias*, 183–4; Santiago Station to CIA, 20 October 1970; and the station's second cable the same day. CDP.
48. Varas, *Conversaciones con Viaux*, 167. Santiago Station used US Army Attaché Col. Paul Wimert to pass three untraceable, .45 caliber sub-machine guns, ammunition, six teargas canisters, and 50,000 dollars to Valenzuela around this time. The CIA had sent the weapons from Washington to Santiago via diplomatic pouch. Wimert recovered these weapons, reportedly unused, and threw them into the Pacific Ocean after Gallardo's group shot Viaux. United States Senate, *Alleged Assassination Plots Involving Foreign Leaders*, 243–5. For reports that the submachine guns, ammunition, and cash never left Valenzuela's residence, see Peter Kornbluh, *The Pinochet File: A Declassified Dossier on Atrocity and Accountability* [2003], 2nd edn (New York: The New Press, 2013), 30. All agree that those who murdered Schneider used weapons other than these submachine guns.
49. Juan Enrique Prieto, Jaime Melgoza's lawyer, denied these allegations. See his interview in Varas, *Conversaciones con Viaux*, 172–201.
50. Prats, *Memorias*, 184–6.
51. "Special Report," 26 October 1970; "Track II"; Lewis Diuguid, "Chilean Army Chief Dies; Right-Wing Plot Described," *Washington Post*, 26 October 1970; and Santiago Station to CIA, 24 October 1970. CDP.
52. CIA, "Report on CIA Chilean Task Force Activities, 15 September to 3 November 1970," 18 November 1970; Korry to Department of

State, "Viaux Gives Up: Beginning of Another Chapter?" 29 October 1970; "Track II." For text of Viaux's declaration when he surrendered, see Santiago Station to CIA, 27 October 1970. CDP.

53. Santiago Station to CIA, 19 October 1970.

54. Vaky to Kissinger, "Chile – Our Modus Operandi."

55. Jessup, "Minutes of the Meeting of the 40 Committee, 6 October 1970"; and Korry to Johnson, 6 October 1970. Department of State, *FRUS, 1969–1976* XXI: *Chile, 1969–1973*, document 136.

56. Vaky to Kissinger, "40 Committee Meeting – Chile – October 6, 1970," 5 October 1970.

57. Olga Ulianova, "La Unidad Popular y el golpe militar en Chile: percepciones y análisis soviéticos," *Estudios Públicos* 79 (2000), 90.

8   Cool and Correct

This chapter highlights President Salvador Allende's (1970–3) inter-nationalism, including his relationship with the United States and the Soviet Union, and his objectives in Chile, Latin America, and the Global South. It clarifies President Richard Nixon's (1969–74) intentions with respect to Allende, paying particular attention to any influence the American business community may have had in the Nixon White House and National Security Council (NSC). It finds that Nixon intended to disrupt and weaken Allende's govern-ment and to support Allende's opposition, but he did not seek to overthrow Allende after his inauguration.

Nixon did not do this because he was driven by "a ruthlessly imperial disdain for Latin America" or because he was feeling "the pressure of U.S. business interests," which many have suggested. Neither Nixon and National Security Advisor Henry Kissinger nor the CIA intended to destabilize Chilean democracy or the Chilean economy. Nixon and Kissinger grudgingly acknowledged that they lacked the influence they required to overthrow Allende. They hoped that the Chilean armed forces would eventually do so, and this indeed occurred, as the following two chapters show.[1]

Salvador Allende and the World

As historian Tanya Harmer has found, Allende had "clear, long-standing ideas about what was wrong with the world and what position he wanted Chile to assume within it." He had been attracted to communism and radicalized while studying medicine at the University of Chile in the late 1920s and early 1930s, where he avidly read Karl Marx, Frederick Engels, and Vladimir Lenin, among others. He thus entered politics as an idealist who helped to create the Socialist Party (PS) in the aftermath of Col. Marmaduke Grove's short-lived socialist republic in 1932, which he regarded as the beginning of the Chilean revolution.[2]

Allende believed that such a revolution was necessary because industrialization and globalization had ensured that Chile and many countries like it in Latin America had merely gone from colonial to neocolonial status, while others throughout Africa and Asia had experienced annexation or colonization from the late nineteenth century onward. The bourgeoisie, an international class of investors, bankers, and financiers, had arisen, cast aside their previous roles as merchant intermediaries, and were now dominating the modern political economy. They had underdeveloped entire continents, unjustly depriving many nations of their sovereignty and natural resources while enslaving the majority of those who lived and worked there.

This, of course, derived from Allende's reading of Lenin, which he affirmed in conversations with journalist Régis Debray, and which remains worth repeating here:

> I think that when one has read Lenin, particularly Imperialism, the Highest Stage of Capitalism, one has a grasp of the theory. The issue of imperialism has a great deal of meaning in under-developed countries, particularly in Latin America. We Socialists have proclaimed that imperialism is our number one enemy, and we therefore gave and still give first priority to national liberation.[3]

With respect to aspiration and ideological orientation, Allende's Chile would join Cuba's struggle for national liberation and revolution against imperialism. Together, Santiago and Havana would "constitute the vanguard of a process that all Latin American countries will reach. And I would say more: the rest of the exploited peoples of the world . . . this is why the confrontation goes beyond our own frontiers and acquires a universal meaning."[4]

Allende's campaign denounced US-led Pan-Americanism and targeted the Organization of American States (OAS) "as an agent and tool of American imperialism." It rejected Chile's commitment to hemispheric defense and bilateral military-assistance agreements that had taken form in the 1940s and 1950s. These agreements penetrated and manipulated the armed forces and "limited our sovereignty." As president, Allende would work "to create an organization which is really representative of Latin American countries" while breaking free from these institutions and agreements.[5]

Still, Allende did not wish to provoke a confrontation with the United States. He thought that the Cold War was winding down, that the Soviet Union's strategy of peaceful coexistence was prevailing, and that the American government was coming out on the losing side, as had been inevitable from the beginning. Washington was experiencing "deep-seated internal problems" relating to its conduct in Vietnam, and this had complicated its ability to operate in Latin America. Further, Allende's democratic victory had tied Americans' hands. As Debray crowed, "bourgeois legality has been turned against the bourgeois themselves." Thus, a direct confrontation would not only be counterproductive, but unnecessary.[6]

Allende promised sweeping constitutional and domestic reform within Chile. He would promulgate a new political order where a people's government and unicameral People's Assembly would represent the true people of Chile, subordinate bourgeois judicial power to the popular will, bypass private landowners to deal directly with peasants, and place education in its service through the *Escuela Nacional Unificada* (ENU) plan, announced in 1973. This would reify "a new culture and a new type of man" in Chile.[7]

Allende's coalition, which included Communists, Socialists, Radicals, and splinter factions from the Christian Democratic Party (PDC), among others, was quite enthusiastic as Allende entered office. The Chilean left had come a long way since the labor movement and PCCh had emerged. Communists had started as combative militants, fiercely loyal to the Soviet Union and the Comintern, committed to assaulting the bourgeoisie in the 1920s. Anticommunists had persecuted them and driven them underground in the late 1920s and again in the 1940s. Socialists, who initially distrusted and feared the PCCh because of its subordination to Moscow, and whom Communists, in turn, denounced as

Trotskyists or worse, accounted for some of this opposition into the 1950s.

Much of this changed in the mid-1950s, particularly after Joseph Stalin (mid-1920s–1953) died, and Nikita Khrushchev, who eventually succeeded him, announced that peaceful roads to socialism were permissible – indeed, they were preferable in the nuclear age. According to Khrushchev,

> the forms of social revolution vary. And it is not true that we regard violence and civil war as the only way to remake society . . . the working class . . . has an opportunity . . . to win a firm majority in parliament and to turn the parliament from an agency of bourgeois democracy to an instrument of genuinely popular will.[8]

These changes eased tensions, particularly within Chile. Christian Democrats, Socialists, and others took note when Secretary General Oyarzun Galo González (1948–58) informed his comrades that revolution

> is not necessarily always followed in every circumstance by political action involving civil war, armed insurrection and violent and extreme change. In our country there are examples that encourage us to think of the possibility of transforming the actual regime by peaceful means, i.e. by parliamentary action.[9]

Galo's successor, Secretary General Luis Corvalán (1958–90), also known as "Shorty" (*patas cortas*), recalled that the party conformed to this new strategy "without problems." This remained Chilean Communists' thinking when Allende assumed office in 1970.[10]

Communists and Socialists became more willing to cooperate with each other in the 1950s and 1960s, when they combined their efforts to capture the presidency through the *Frente de Acción Popular* (FRAP) and UP coalitions. The Soviets' Committee for State Security (KGB) even recruited Allende as a paid, confidential informant – which would have been quite problematic for a Socialist leader only a decade or two earlier. KGB case officer Svyatoslav Kuznetsov met him in 1953, after which he passed information on

Chilean politics to Moscow in a mutually beneficial relationship that continued through his presidency.[11]

According to the KGB's Nikolai Leonov, the Soviet Union did not regard any Latin American nation as a threat or an enemy. So, finding informants like Allende, meeting American informants in cities like Acapulco, Rio de Janeiro, and Santiago, and recruiting other sources who had access to American science and technology that Soviets could not acquire in the USSR or Eastern Europe, accounted for the majority of the KGB's activities in the region. But Soviet intelligence officers did not target Latin American governments *per se*.[12]

Neither the KGB nor its risk-averse superiors in the Kremlin believed that Latin America fell within the Soviet Union's sphere of influence, either. They feared that if they ran covert or paramilitary operations in the region, they would fail and possibly provoke dangerous American responses similar to those that followed the Cuban Missile Crisis of October 1962. Leonov encountered this hesitancy when he proposed a daring seaborne raid using cargo ships, assault helicopters, special-operations forces, and a submarine to rescue Corvalán from Dawson Island, where the Pinochet dictatorship (1973–90) held him after the coup. The Politburo "looked at us as if we were half-crazy, and all our efforts to persuade them to at least study the plan proved fruitless."[13]

The Soviet Communist Party (CPSU), however, was another matter. It contributed more than 3 million dollars to the PCCh between 1955 and 1973, including a 100,000 dollar contribution to the UP's campaign in 1970. Allende asked Moscow for this contribution himself. But, as Olga Ulianova and Eugenia Fediakova explained, the CPSU declined to support political campaigns, and it did not pass such funds to noncommunists, friendly or otherwise, either. The party still sent the PCCh 100,000 dollars more that year than it had previously. Chilean Communists gave that amount to Allende's campaign on behalf of the USSR.[14]

The Politburo and KGB continued to cultivate Allende's friendship into the 1970s. They paid him another 50,000 dollars during the election year. They also indirectly supported his coalition by passing 18,000 dollars to an unlisted leftist senator to persuade him not to run against him. It remains impossible to assess the effectiveness of this 18,000 dollars, but it may have kept the difference of the 40,000 votes or so that separated Alessandri and Allende from growing smaller by however many this leftist senator might have taken with him.[15]

Meanwhile, Chilean Communists and Socialists' new cooperativeness notwithstanding, differences remained. Mostly, they disagreed on strategy and tactics. While the PCCh remained firmly behind Soviet foreign policy and was committed to the peaceful road, PS leaders were less certain. Indeed, Socialists had declared political violence "inevitable and legitimate" at their party congress in 1967. The PS's Cuban-style, urban guerrilla offshoot, the Movement of the Revolutionary Left (MIR), whose leadership included Allende's nephew, was already waging a campaign of expropriation against banks and other bourgeois interests in Santiago – which most others just saw as robbing financial institutions and kidnapping lucrative targets for ransom.[16]

Allende tried to find and hold a common, moderate ground within this fractious and restless coalition, but he never acted decisively, never used the power of the presidency to resolve these differences. Further, he himself raised eyebrows from time to time – such as when he praised the People's Republic of China's Chairman Mao Zedong and the Cultural Revolution in interviews with Debray. Allende and his coalition partners nevertheless believed that their moment had finally arrived. Although their victory at the polls surprised them and the Soviet government, they entered office as idealistic and as confident of the future as ever.[17]

The Nixon Administration's Response

The NSC had begun identifying policy options toward a possible Allende administration in July 1970, when Nixon asked Kissinger to look into it. An interdepartmental committee drafted National Security Study Memorandum 97 (NSSM 97) in response. As mentioned in the previous chapter, the committee offered three overt options with a covert annex the following month. Nixon could seek a *modus vivendi* with Allende; he might adopt a cool, correct, and restrained posture toward him; he could try to isolate him, diplomatically and economically; or, if Allende threatened the United States, he might try to overthrow him. The committee preferred the second option for its flexibility while cautioning that the fourth entailed the highest risks.[18]

Kissinger had set these deliberations aside to support Nixon's flailing efforts to prevent Allende's victory in September and October. Nixon instructed the CIA to instigate a coup in Chile, but this proved impractical, and it failed. Kissinger acknowledged that there "appeared to be little the U.S. can do to influence the Chilean situation one way or another," and he refocused the NSC's attention on NSSM 97 in mid-October.[19]

Both Nixon and Kissinger sought advice and received suggestions from inside and outside government that September and October. For example, campaign contributor Donald Kendall, Chilean publisher Agustín Edwards, and another, unlisted Chilean seem to have triggered Nixon's response in mid-September. Director of Central Intelligence (DCI) John McCone, now a board member at International Telephone and Telegraph (ITT), whose investments in Chile totaled approximately 150 million dollars, sent Kissinger a letter pledging "a minimum of $1,000,000" to help prevent Allende's taking office while urging Nixon to intervene.[20]

No one seems to have influenced Nixon's thinking on Chile more than Maj. Gen. Vernon Walters (USA), however. The president's friendship with the general went back to his trip to Latin America in 1958. Walters had been with Nixon in his car in Caracas, when Venezuelans attacked him. The general was gifted in languages, had cultivated close relations with his counterparts in Brazil and several other nations in the region, and the president valued his views.

Walters reminded Nixon that the United States remained involved in "a mortal struggle to determine the shape of the future of the world," and that Latin America was "a key area" that the president could not afford to neglect. Allende's Chile threatened to undermine the region's security. Walters recommended that the administration give leading southern South American nations such as Brazil and Argentina "a sense of participation in the defense of freedom" while emphasizing the inter-American community's common destiny and encouraging them to cooperate with each other in this larger endeavor. He regarded American military sales to these countries as vital. Nixon returned a heavily underlined copy of Walters's letter to Kissinger, instructing him to "see that it is implemented in *every* respect."[21]

Kissinger took all of this into account while summarizing the NSC working committees' discussions on NSSM 97. He recommended that the administration "oppose Allende as strongly as we can and do all we can to keep him from consolidating power, taking care to package those efforts in a style that gives us the appearance of reacting to his moves." He implored the president to "make it crystal clear where you stand on this issue."[22]

Nixon accepted these recommendations at the NSC's formal meeting. When he clarified where he stood, he may as well have been reading from Walters's message, to which he added a list of typical Nixonian grievances:

> I will never agree with the policy of downgrading the military in Latin America. They are power centers subject to our influence . . . We want to give them some help. Brazil and Argentina particularly. Build them up with consultation. I want Defense to move on this. We'll go for more in the budget if necessary.
>
> We'll be very cool and very correct, but doing those things which will be a real message to Allende and others . . . No impression should be permitted in Latin America that they can get away with this, that it's safe to go this way. All over the world it's too much the fashion to kick us around . . . There must be times when we should and must react, not because we want to hurt them but to show we can't be kicked around . . . We must be proper on the surface with Allende, but otherwise we will be tough.[23]

Kissinger sent out National Security Decision Memorandum 93 (NSDM 93), the Nixon administration's policy toward the Allende government, on 9 November. The government would remain cool and correct while seeking to maximize pressure against Allende. This pressure was meant to assure anticommunists throughout Europe and Latin America, including within Chile, that the United States opposed the consolidation of any Marxist-Leninist government in the region, and that it welcomed others' opposition. The administration would consult with Brazilian and Argentine political and military leaders. And it would work with international financial institutions such as the World Bank, the International Monetary Fund, and the Inter-American Development Bank. As Nixon explained it, "If Allende can make it with Russian and Chinese help, so be it – but we do not want it to be with our help."[24]

Such financial concerns were never far from the thoughts of American policymakers before, during, and after the Cold War. They nevertheless remained less central than the United States' credibility as an anticommunist leader in global affairs, particularly within the transatlantic and inter-American communities. Nixon and Kissinger both confirmed this while formulating NSDM 93.

Kissinger dealt with this issue explicitly. He knew that private American investments in Chile amounted to about 1 billion dollars, and that public and private loans totaled another 1.5 billion dollars, of which the United States government guaranteed 380 million dollars. He also understood that the Allende administration would likely expropriate most of these investments and – as Undersecretary of State for Political Affairs U. Alexis Johnson warned him – that a US–Chilean confrontation could hasten this. Kissinger cut Johnson off: "The President doesn't care about compensation. He will pay his $300 million if Allende can be brought down."[25]

Indeed, some American businessmen exasperated Kissinger. Assistant Secretary of State for Inter-American Affairs Charles Meyer told him that while the US business community in Chile perceived Allende as a nationalist, its members nevertheless found him reasonable enough that they would work with rather than oppose him. Kissinger protested. "The American business community has long been proving that Marx was wrong in thinking that businessmen understand their political interests."[26]

In other cases, American executives asked Nixon and Kissinger's advice. For example, Chairman and CEO of Ford Motor Co. Henry Ford II tried to call Kissinger to discuss Ford's Chilean interests in early December, but he was unable to get through. The company was bidding on an additional production plant in Chile, and Chilean dealers were asking the chairman to travel to Santiago to meet the new president "and express the fact that Ford has been in Chile for some years, that we would like to stay friends." Ed Molina, one of the company's senior vice presidents, finally got through to the national security advisor on 10 December. Ford, he explained, was concerned that Allende might somehow exploit his visit for political or propagandistic purposes, and he worried that this might embarrass the American government, which he did not want to do. Thus, he solicited Nixon and Kissinger's guidance.[27]

Kissinger consulted Nixon and then returned Molina's call nine days later. He told him that "we don't think it is a good idea for the Chairman to go down there. From a political point of view we would like to give them as little opportunity as possible." Perhaps, he suggested, lower-level officers could make a less conspicuous trip and accomplish the same objectives. "They will either make a deal with you on its merits or they won't. We have no opposition for you to continue to operate and, privately, that is your business." Molina thanked Kissinger. "That is the kind of information the Chairman wanted because he will not go if it is contrary to our government."[28]

If those who have argued for the primacy of American business and economic interests when explaining the formulation and implementation of US foreign policy were correct, not only should Kissinger and Molina's conversations have gone the other way around, with Kissinger calling Molina to solicit policy advice based on Ford's interests, but Molina should have cared only, or mostly, about Ford's narrow perceptions and needs and not the American government's wider security strategy – and he should have pressed Kissinger to act on behalf of those perceptions and needs in these telephone calls. It did not go the other way around because Nixon and Kissinger barely gave a thought to Wall Street when they wrote NSDM 93 and its covert annex.

Through this annex, Nixon, Kissinger, and the 40 Committee tasked the CIA to advance NSDM 93's objectives through several supplemental covert operations. The Agency was to back Allende's opposition in order to harass him, undermine his coalition's cohesion, and influence international, regional, and national public opinion against him. Nixon and Kissinger expected this to entail the CIA's supporting the opposition's attempts to recapture political power through presidential, congressional, and municipal elections, especially in March 1973 and September 1976. Although the Agency would not seek to overthrow Allende itself, it would back the opposition if it moved to do so. Thus, Nixon and Kissinger played for the breaks.[29]

The 40 Committee approved this on 19 November. Monthly status reports followed. The CIA contributed about 4 million dollars to the National Party (PN), the PDC, and Radicals over the next three years, and spent an additional 3 million dollars on anti-Allende operations.[30]

Kissinger presided over much of this from the White House. The Department of State's Bureau of Inter-American Affairs tasked its director of the Andean region to stay on top of Chilean politics while ignoring other nations in the area. The Agency's director of Latin American operations – Ted Shackley relieved William Broe in May 1972 and David Atlee Phillips succeeded Shackley in late June 1973 – managed the CIA's covert operations and reporting from Langley. Kissinger's Senior Review Group decided early to leave the Pentagon's army, navy, and air force missions in place, and Allende never asked them to leave. As Deputy Secretary of Defense David Packard understood, this "gives us an opportunity to get across to the [Chilean] military the impression that we might support them if they moved against Allende."[31]

The KGB's Perspective

The KGB's active measures mirrored the Agency's covert operations – and were about as effective. The real difference came down not to disparities in spending, which remained substantial, but rather to the fact – which was not apparent until the end – that Nixon and Kissinger had wagered on a better horse than the Politburo had. Meanwhile, Kuznetsov returned to Santiago to liaise with Allende after his inauguration, at which time Soviets passed him another 30,000 dollars "in order to solidify the trusted relations" with him. KGB officers worked to consolidate Allende's position, to strengthen his coalition's unity, and to impress upon the president "the necessity of reorganizing Chile's army and intelligence services, and of setting up a relationship between Chile's and the USSR's intelligence services."[32]

Neither the Agency nor the KGB were very optimistic about their mission. On the one hand, the Agency could not identify any coherent opposition to support, at least not initially. Nationalists and Christian Democrats had grown apart in the late 1960s, particularly after the *Tacnazo* in October 1969. Many within the PDC still suspected that the conservative establishment had somehow been responsible for it. Nationalists, for their part, thought that Christian Democrats had robbed them of the presidency in the election. The PDC itself remained divided into left, right, and center factions, with many Christian Democrats hoping that some sort of compromise-based cooperation with Allende would materialize.

On the other hand, the KGB worried that Allende was failing "to consolidate his position by bringing the armed forces and security system under his control," while acknowledging that any attempt to do so might paradoxically create military opposition that did not yet exist. This nuanced understanding notwithstanding, Soviets still became increasingly frustrated that the president was apparently not even willing to try. Thus, in the Politburo and KGB's view, Allende seemed incapable of resolving the fundamental problem of power in Chilean politics, and so long as he did not do this, whatever gains he may make in the meantime were susceptible to reversal, even violent reaction. Soviet observers grew more certain of this as time went on.[33]

Thus, Allende remained an idealistic internationalist, friendly to the Soviet Union, Cuba, and likeminded governments and actors throughout the Global South. He was not openly confrontational with the United States. But he was rhetorically hostile to the American Cold War position, particularly to the US-led transatlantic and inter-American communities and their institutions.

Nixon and Kissinger reciprocated this passive hostility. Ideally, they wanted to bring Allende down or perhaps even see the Chilean armed forces overthrow him. Until that happened – and they conceded that it probably would not – they would appear cool and correct while ensuring that Allende and others still got the message. That message, as Nixon rephrased it in conversations with Kissinger, was that the United States opposed Allende. "I feel strongly this line is important regarding its effect on the people of the world. If he can prove he can set up a Marxist anti-American policy others will do the same." Kissinger concurred, adding that it would also affect Europe, "Not only Latin America."[34]

Allende and Nixon began sending each other passive-aggressive but cool and correct messages even as Allende was assuming office in November 1970. Allende's partisans and other Chileans with leftist inclinations, including Chile's *Chargé d'affaires* Armando Uribe in Washington, had long feared that US–Chilean cooperation for conventional hemispheric defense and military assistance was merely a cover for some darker purpose that somehow benefited the United States while undermining Chilean sovereignty. This had come into the open again that September and October, when the joint US–Chilean Air Force Technical Applications Command's (AFTAC) stations in Chile – "Americans' so-called meteorological stations and satellite [tracking] stations" – suddenly became controversial.[35]

The Johnson (1963–9) and Frei (1964–70) administrations had reached an informal agreement to work together to monitor French nuclear testing in the South Pacific more than four years earlier, in March 1966. They established a series of monitoring stations from Easter Island to Quintero and Punta Arenas. These stations served scientific and military purposes, such as assessing the effectiveness of French nuclear weapons and the measuring of radiation in the region. But Uribe remained certain that "the type of equipment set up at the station, as well as the large number and quality of its personnel, implied other objectives." He could only guess about these other objectives, but he cited the Cuban government's denunciation of it as "a North American military base" in the United Nations (UN).[36]

Uribe started querying Meyer and Johnson at the Department of State for additional information on what seemed like every single visa request for US military personnel that crossed his desk while Allende brought these concerns to outgoing President Eduardo Frei. He complained about "an extraordinary influx" of Americans in Chile and demanded the president do something about it. As the CIA noted, "U.S. Government intentions were highly suspect, particularly in Allende and certain government sectors," in September and October 1970. "Suspicions extended to all Americans in Chile for whatever declared purpose." Allende reconfirmed this when he told Meyer, who had traveled to Santiago for his inauguration, that "Chile has never allowed, nor will it allow, any country to set up within its boundaries military or any other kind of bases that would interfere with the country's sovereignty. Never."[37]

No one in Washington or in the US embassy in Santiago understood why this was so or why it had appeared so suddenly. Some speculated that either the Frei administration or the Allende campaign were stoking anti-American perceptions for one purpose or another. Whatever explained it, Nixon and Kissinger recognized it as an opportunity to snub Allende, and did so.

Kissinger and Packard started looking into these stations' legal status and vulnerability at the end of September. Once they confirmed that the only thing keeping them there was a four-year-old executive agreement between Johnson and Frei, they recommended that Nixon authorize them to pull out, which the president did about a month later. They did this a couple of weeks before Allende's inauguration in order to deny that it had had anything to do with him. They did it quite abruptly, taking every piece of equipment, down to the bulldozers, with them. And they declined to offer Chileans an opportunity to buy as much as a single hammer or nail, as was customary in such cases.[38]

This annoyed Allende, as intended. Indeed, Uribe characterized it as "an insult to Chile." In Santiago, Korry, Allende, and Allende's representatives bickered over this several times during the transition. Korry explained, as instructed, that this was merely a budgetary matter, and that the Department of Defense had decided to execute this pullout "some time ago." He added, almost as an afterthought, that Allende should prefer this outcome, since it "would eliminate the whole subject of military bases and there would be no reason therefore in the future to have any problems about or basis for any foreign military installations."[39]

Then it was Allende's turn. Allende's coalition had pledged "meaningful solidarity with the Cuban Revolution, which is the vanguard of revolution and construction of socialism in Latin America." The president followed through and recognized the Castro regime (1959–present) just days after assuming office. This was his sovereign prerogative, but it also snubbed the United States and every nation but Mexico in the inter-American community who had been working to isolate the regime since 1963. Thus, both Allende and Nixon knew precisely where they stood with each other as the former entered *la Moneda*, the presidential palace.[40]

Notes

1. Lubna Qureshi, *Nixon, Kissinger, and Allende: U.S. Involvement in the 1973 Coup in Chile* [2009] (Lanham: Lexington, 2010), xiii. Also see Stephen Rabe, *The Killing Zone: The United States Wages Cold War in Latin America* [2012], 2nd edn (New York: Oxford University Press, 2016); and Lars Schoultz, *Beneath the United States: A History of U.S. Policy toward Latin America* (Cambridge, MA: Harvard University Press, 1998). For US business interests, see Margaret Power, *Right-Wing Women in Chile: Feminine Power and the Struggle against Allende, 1964–1973* (University Park: Pennsylvania State University Press, 2002); and Seymour Hersh, *The Price of Power: Kissinger in the Nixon White House* (New York: Summit Books, 1983).
2. Tanya Harmer, *Allende's Chile and the Inter-American Cold War* (Chapel Hill: University of North Carolina Press, 2011), 76.
3. Régis Debray, *The Chilean Revolution: Conversations with Allende* (New York: Pantheon Books, 1971), 69–70.
4. Augusto Olivares Becerra, "Interview with Salvador Allende and Fidel Castro," November 1971. James Cockcroft, ed., *Salvador Allende Reader: Chile's Voice of Democracy* (Melbourne and New York: Ocean Press, 2000), 134.
5. Popular Unity, Basic Program, 17 December 1969. Cockcroft, *Allende Reader*, 276–7. For the original Spanish, see "El programa básico de gobierno de la Unidad Popular," 17 December 1969. Luis Corvalán, *El gobierno de Salvador Allende* (Santiago de Chile: LOM Ediciones, 2003), 275–302.
6. Debray, *Conversations with Allende*, 96, 126. Also see Salvador Allende, "Address to the Third United Nations Conference on Trade and Development (UNCTAD)," April 1972. Cockcroft, *Allende*

Reader, 156–75; and Carlos Prats, *Memorias: testimonio de un soldado* (Santiago de Chile: Pehuén Editores, 1985), 339.

7. Popular Unity, Basic Program, 276. For the ENU plan and its advocates and critics, see José Díaz Nieva, *Patria y Libertad: el nacionalismo frente a la Unidad Popular* (Santiago de Chile: Ediciones Centro de Estudios Bicentenario, 2015), 206–16.

8. Nikita Khrushchev, "Report of the Central Committee to the Twentieth Party Congress," February 1956; and "Declaration of the Conference of Representatives of Communist and Workers' Parties of Socialist Countries," November 1957. Robert Daniels, ed., *A Documentary History of Communism and the World: From Revolution to Collapse* (Hanover: University Press of New England, 1994), 160–3, 179–80.

9. Carmelo Furci, *The Chilean Communist Party and the Road to Socialism* (London: Zed Books, 1984), 56.

10. Luis Corvalán, *De lo vivido y lo peleado: memorias* (Santiago de Chile: LOM Ediciones, 1997), 59. For a discussion on the connection between Khrushchev's speech and the *Unidad Popular* coalition's strategy of the peaceful road, see Olga Ulianova, "La Unidad Popular y el golpe militar en Chile: percepciones y análisis soviéticos," *Estudios Públicos* 79 (2000): 83–171; and Furci, *Chilean Communist Party*, 56–114.

11. Christopher Andrew and Vasili Mitrokhin, *The World Was Going Our Way: The KGB and the Battle for the Third World* (New York: Basic Books, 2005), 69–88. According to Mitrokhin, the KGB's files on Allende, codenamed LEADER, fill three volumes from the 1950s to 1970.

12. Nikolai Leonov, "La inteligencia soviética en América Latina durante la guerra fría," *Estudios Públicos* 73 (1999): 31–63; and Nikolai Leonov, Eugenia Fediakova, Joaquín Fermandois, et al., "El General Nikolai Leonov en el CEP," *Estudios Públicos* 73 (1999): 65–102. To cite two high-profile cases, the KGB conducted meetings to exchange information and money with Christopher Boyce, Andrew Daulton Lee, and Aldrich Ames in Mexico City and Bogotá. See Sandra Grimes and Jeanne Vertefeuille, *Circle of Treason: A CIA Account of Traitor Aldrich Ames and the Men He Betrayed* (Annapolis: Naval Institute Press, 2012); Tim Weiner, David Johnson, and Neil Lewis, *Betrayal: The Story of Aldrich Ames, an American Spy* (New York: Random House, 1995); and Robert Lindsey, *The Falcon and the Snowman: A True Story of Friendship and Espionage* (New York: Simon & Schuster, 1979).

13. Leonov, "La inteligencia soviética en América Latina," 61–3. The American government later brokered Corvalán's exchange for Soviet dissident Vladimir Bukovsky. See Olga Ulianova, "Corvalán for Bukovsky: A Real Exchange of Prisoners during an Imaginary War: The Chilean Dictatorship, the Soviet Union, and U.S. Mediation, 1973–1976," *Cold War History* 14 (2014): 315–36.

14. Olga Ulianova and Eugenia Fediakova, "Algunos aspectos de la ayuda financiera del partido comunista de la URSS al comunismo chileno durante la guerra fría," *Estudios Públicos* 72 (1998): 113–48; and Corvalán, *De lo vivido y lo peleado*, 108.

15. Andrew and Mitrokhin, *World Was Going Our Way*, 72.

16. Díaz, *Patria y Libertad*, 22; and Julio Faúndez, *Marxism and Democracy in Chile: From 1932 to the Fall of Allende* (New Haven: Yale University Press, 1988), 164–71.

17. Debray, *Conversations with Allende*, 80.

18. Special Review Group, "Chile (NSSM 97)," 19 August 1970; Charles Meyer to U. Alexis Johnson, "NSSM 97 – Chile: Recommendation of Option," 18 August 1970; and Henry Kissinger to William Rogers, Melvin Laird, Richard Helms, and Moorer, "Chile," 24 July 1970. Department of State, *Foreign Relations of the United States, 1969–1976* XXI: *Chile, 1969–1973* (Washington, DC: Government Printing Office, 2014), documents 53, 52, and 46. For the committee's arguments, see Meyer to Kissinger, "Chile – Response to NSSM 97," 18 August 1970; and "Annex NSSM-97," 18 August 1970. Department of State, *Foreign Relations of the United States, 1969–1976* E-16: *Documents on Chile, 1969–1973* (Washington, DC: Government Printing Office, 2015), documents 13 and 14.

19. Frank Chapin, "Minutes of the Meeting of the 40 Committee, 14 October 1970," 14 October 1970. Department of State, *FRUS, 1969–1976* XXI: *Chile, 1969–1973*, document 149.

20. John McCone to Kissinger, 14 September 1970; and Kenneth Millian, "Discussion of Chilean Political Situation," 14 September 1970. Ibid., documents 90 and 89. The CIA facilitated ITT's contributing at least 350,000 dollars to Alessandri's campaign in the months leading up to the election. See "Resume of Contacts with ITT Officials Regarding Chile," 19 March 1972. CDP.

21. Walters to Nixon, "Courses in Latin America," 3 November 1970. Department of State, *FRUS, 1969–1976* XXI: *Chile, 1969–1973*, document 170. Nixon's emphasis.

22. Kissinger to Nixon, "NSC Meeting, November 6 – Chile," 5 November 1970. Ibid., document 172.

23   Minutes of the National Security Council, 6 November 1970. Ibid., document 173.

24. National Security Decision Memorandum 93, 9 November 1970; Minutes of the National Security Council, 6 November 1970; and Minutes of the Senior Review Group, 14 October 1970. Ibid., documents 175, 173, and 150.

25. Minutes of the Senior Review Group, 17 October 1970. Department of State, *FRUS, 1969–1976* XXI: *Chile, 1969–1973*, document 158.

26. Minutes of the Senior Review Group, 29 October 1970. Ibid., document 169.

27. Ed Molina and Kissinger, Telcon, 10 December 1970, 5:40 p.m. Henry Kissinger telephone conversation transcripts (TELCONS), Box 7, "8–12 December 1970." Richard Nixon Library, Yorba Linda, California (RN).

28. Kissinger and Molina, Telcon, 19 December 1970, 3:45 p.m. Henry Kissinger, telephone conversation transcripts (TELCONS), Box 8, "16–21 December 1970." RN.

29. Chapin, "Minutes of the Meeting of the 40 Committee, 13 November 1970; "Covert Annex," 27 October 1970. Department of State, *FRUS, 1969–1976* XXI: *Chile, 1969–1973*, documents 179 and 166.

30. Chapin, "Minutes of the Meeting of the 40 Committee, 19 November 1970," 19 November 1970. Ibid., document 184. For these figures, see CIA, "CIA Activities in Chile," 18 September 2000, at <https://cia.gov>; and United States Senate, *Covert Action in Chile, 1963–1973* (Washington, DC: Government Printing Office, 1975).

31. Minutes of the Senior Review Group, 19 November 1970. Department of State, *FRUS, 1969–1976* XXI: *Chile, 1969–1973*, document 183. Also see Ted Shackley, *Spymaster: My Life in the CIA* [2005] (Dulles: Potomac Books, 2006), 265–72; and David Atlee Phillips, *The Night Watch: 25 Years of Peculiar Service* (New York: Atheneum, 1977), 236–63.

32. Andrew and Mitrokhin, *World Was Going Our Way*, 73, 75.

33. Ibid., 78.

34. Nixon and Kissinger, Telcon, 11 November 1970, 3:40 p.m. Henry Kissinger, telephone conversation transcripts (TELCONS), Box 7, "2–9 November 1970." RN.

35. Armando Uribe, *The Black Book of American Intervention in Chile* [1974], trans. Jonathan Casart (Boston: Beacon, 1975), 65.

36. Ibid., 67.

37. Ibid., 77; CIA, "Report on CIA Chilean Task Force Activities, 15 September to 3 November 1970," 18 November 1970; and Santiago

Station to CIA, 5 September 1970. CDP. For a sample of Uribe's queries, which also came to the Department of State via Ambassador Edward Korry, see the cables and correspondence in RG 84 Foreign Service Posts of the Department of State: Chile/U.S. Embassy, Santiago, Entry P161: Classified Central Subject Files; 1964–1975, Box 34, "Def-6-2 Navy 1970." NA.

38. Kissinger to Rogers and Laird, "Chile," 21 October 1970; Vaky to Kissinger, "Chile – Immediate Operational Issues," *circa* 18 October 1970; and Peter Jessup, "Minutes of the Meeting of the 40 Committee, 29 September 1970," 29 September 1970. Department of State, *FRUS, 1969–1976* XXI: *Chile, 1969–1973*, documents 160, 159, and 127.

39. Uribe, *Black Book*, 65; and Korry to Department of State, "Talk with Allende Emissary," 27 October 1970. Department of State, *FRUS, 1969–1976* XXI: *Chile, 1969–1973*, document 165.

40. Popular Unity, Basic Program, 277.

9   *Jefe de la Plaza*: The Rise of
Augusto Pinochet

The CIA's Santiago Station profiled the politics and views of Brig. Gen. Augusto Pinochet (1973–90), commander of the garrison in Santiago, in a cable it sent to Langley on 6 August 1971. Pinochet assumed this position after his predecessor, Brig. Gen. Camilo Valenzuela, had been convicted for his involvement in *Plan Alfa*, an abortive coup that was meant to preempt President Salvador Allende's (1970–3) election but instead resulted in the death of Chief of Staff of the Army Gen. René Schneider. This was a key post. The commander of the garrison became *jefe de la plaza* and controlled all government forces in the capital during states of emergency.

Santiago Station did not regard Pinochet as a coup plotter, but rather as an officer whose interference opposition plotters might be able to neutralize if the situation required it. One of the station's informants had observed Pinochet at a dinner party on Thursday evening, 5 August 1971. He had arrived late, explaining that he was discussing security with the president. He excused himself from the table half a dozen times to take situation reports. "It was quite clear," the station advised Langley, "that as jefe de la plaza he is not ceremonial figure. Pinochet appeared . . . totally immersed in new field of security, public order and political events," and he "enjoyed feeling of being important."[1]

Santiago Station commented that this report was "completely consistent with his known pattern." In other words, the Agency saw Pinochet as an apolitical career officer. It could not quite ascertain his politics or even grasp whether he had any. It seemed clear, however, that he was not interested in joining any move against Allende that August.[2]

Of course, Pinochet's attitude changed after he became chief of staff of the army two years later, in August 1973. This chapter argues that Allende's national and international politics and indecisive leadership style cultivated a broad, foreign-backed opposition against his government while alienating the professional officer corps to such a degree that he drew a reluctant Pinochet into the plotting, transforming him into the coup's leader by early September 1973. It reconstructs the rise of Pinochet's dictatorship as the climax of Chile's century-long Cold War experience. Chile remained just one of many countries where conflicts relating to the forces industrialization and globalization had unleashed in the late nineteenth century continued to unfold until they were resolved in the late twentieth.

The chapter emphasizes the national, inter-American, and especially the transatlantic nature of Allende and Pinochet's thinking and actions. It highlights Allende's strategy to use Soviet military sales to replace American influence over the Chilean armed forces while reorienting their doctrine, training, and even spare parts requirements toward the Red Army and, through it, Moscow. He thereby hoped to subordinate, obliquely, the armed services to his government's foreign and domestic political program while resolving Chile's Cold War crisis. This helps to account not only for the coup's occurrence but for its timing and the virulent nature of its perpetrators' anticommunism as well.

It offers five insights on the coup and subsequent dictatorship. First, Allende never achieved the parliamentary majority he needed to implement the peaceful road to revolution. Yet he remained uncompromising while acting indecisively and failing to bring the power of the presidency to bear against the mounting problems his administration faced, particularly in security and intelligence. He lost Soviets' confidence, he lost the initiative, and then he lost power.

Second, the momentum that led to the coup came from below, from commanders, lieutenants, and ensigns stationed in the *Primera Zona Naval* (PRIZONA), fleet headquarters at Valparaíso, and not from flag officers or their senior staffs at the Ministry of Defense or in the army in Santiago. This was uncoordinated, featuring spontaneous outbursts at the unit and even individual level until service commanders brought it under their control and only then, lacking alternatives, decided to support it. These mid-career and junior officers were frightened and angry about the pending Soviet arms deal, several other of Allende's policies, particularly in national education, and the general sense of anarchy and imminent civil war that pervaded Chilean politics and society after the congressional elections in March 1973.

Third, service commanders, including Pinochet, acquiesced to but did not create or direct this process. Fourth, Pinochet was the last one to commit to the coup, about forty-eight hours before it was launched, and he seemed to do so warily. But when he did sign on to it, he did not hesitate. He did so as a transatlantic-oriented internationalist who, citing the larger, Cold War struggle that was under way, compared Chile's difficulties to the Spanish Civil War while moving to find a solution similar to the one *Generalísimo* Francisco Franco (1936–75) had imposed in Spain more than thirty years before.

Fifth, foreign military and intelligence services (particularly American, Soviet, Cuban, and Brazilian officers) were well informed and involved in these processes – in some cases, intimately so; in others, in ways that remain unclear, given the limitations and provisional nature of the evidence available today – as the above CIA report suggests. This notwithstanding, these services did not decide this history. They certainly did not act as the architects, engineers, or directors of Chilean history. No one in the Chilean armed forces needed their complicity, encouragement, or expertise.

Storm Clouds on the Horizon: November 1971 to March 1973

More than anything else, Allende and the *Unidad Popular*'s (UP) authoritarian unilateralism and some UP officials' intransigence toward the Christian Democratic Party (PDC) broadened, deepened, and united the opposition throughout 1971 and 1972. This polarized Chilean politics in 1972 and 1973. It agitated the professional officer corps, leaving servicemen and their wives increasingly discontented. Indeed, it politicized them.[3]

Minister of Economy Pedro Vuskovic's mismanagement of the economy exacerbated this already bad situation. The UP's disastrous economic program remained more emotionally satisfying to Socialists than economically sound – as some Communists, leading voices from the opposition, and, later, historians have pointed out. For example, historian Jonathan Haslam has characterized Vuskovic's policies as "a triumph for voluntarism over an understanding of the market."[4]

The administration's nationalization of American-owned copper production met with widespread approval in Chile in mid-1971. But the scope and pace of subsequent seizures deprived the economy of much capital, and no one in government had thought about where new investments might come from. Further, the administration drastically increased public spending, relying on credit and inflationary measures to pay for it. Workers demanded large increases in salary and benefits while they spent their working hours attending a growing number of protests, strikes, and other political events. This, too, slowed production and undermined the economy.[5]

An early form of organized resistance appeared in October 1972. Chilean truck drivers – backed by professional associations, or *gremios*, and National Party (PN) and PDC leaders – launched a stoppage in opposition to the government's plan to force them into a centrally controlled trucking company that month. The Christian Democrats' Secretary General Renán Fuentealba accused the administration of "acting openly in defiance of the constitution and the laws, as well as of fundamental human rights." *El Mercurio* alleged that the government had become illegitimate. From the Nixon administration, 40 Committee money, distributed by the Agency, certainly amplified this strike's effectiveness. But Allende had created the conditions that made it possible when he tried to impose a state-run collective, while truckers and others at the grassroots level remained the ones who responded to it.[6]

This threw Allende onto the defensive. He declared a state of emergency and invited Chief of Staff Gen. Carlos Prats and the other service commanders into the cabinet to help bolster his government's legitimacy, restore order, and assuage fears. Allende appointed Prats minister of interior. This calmed some within the opposition, for the moment, but the underlying tensions remained unresolved – and, as Soviets noted, Allende had encouraged the armed forces, who remained outside PCCh and Socialist discipline, to deliberate political matters again.

Soviet leaders, initially optimistic about Allende's presidency, now entertained serious doubts about his administration's viability. Moscow's optimism had derived from its close, fifty-year partnership with the PCCh and its continuing confidence in the peaceful road. Chile had always seemed more European than Latin American to many in the Kremlin. For example, Chileans had produced a well-organized labor movement that participated in national politics. Allende, moreover, remained friendly to the Soviet Union, sharing its perceptions and politics. Thus, Soviet leaders, responding to Allende's requests, offered some assistance. They even dispatched a Committee for State Planning (GOSPLAN) mission to Chile, which arrived in Santiago around July 1973.[7]

Soviet views changed in mid- to late 1972, however. Allende traveled to Moscow to seek additional support that December. The Kremlin consulted its departments, agencies, and Latin Americanists when preparing for his visit. Soviet leaders worried that Allende was failing to deal with the fundamental question of power. He had accepted the PDC's constitutional guarantees in September and October 1970, which included his promise to refrain from intervening in military promotions and from politicizing the professional officer corps. Then he had bragged to journalist Régis Debray that this merely represented "a tactical necessity," something that he had never taken seriously. "At the time, the important thing was to take control of the government." Allende had not only left the armed services alone, but he had also invited them into the cabinet. All of this worried the USSR.[8]

Further, Allende seemed to have unrealistic expectations about what the Soviet Union could do for Chile and this, too, undermined Moscow's confidence in him. His administration wanted Moscow to sell it critical products such as wheat, beef, and butter at low prices, through favorable, long-term credits, while the Kremlin would buy Chilean products it did not need and pay for them with hard currency. Soviet leaders complained that no other nation in the Global South, save Cuba, enjoyed such unbalanced trade relations with the USSR.[9]

Still, Soviets offered Allende a 100 million-dollar loan to purchase Soviet tanks, artillery, and other conventional arms that December. This was the kind of modern equipment that Chilean army commanders had been asking for since the late 1960s. But it was not from the suppliers that they had in mind. Further, all knew that such an infusion of Red Army doctrine, training, and spare parts regimes would reorient the army, moving it away from American-led hemispheric defense and interoperability, and toward Soviet politics, which the army and other services clarified that they did not want. Allende pressed forward as if he had not heard their objections.[10]

The Center Does Not Hold: March to June 1973

Chile's hyperpoliticization and seemingly never-ending campaign seasons contributed to the further destabilization of civilian-dominated civil–military relations that had been undermining military discipline since the late 1960s. Allende, the UP, and the increasingly united opposition – which called itself the *Confederación Democrática* (CODE), primarily consisting of PN and PDC candidates – approached the congressional elections of March 1973 as an opportunity to get the upper hand and then use it to resolve the situation in their favor. If the UP achieved a majority, this would bolster its legitimacy and reinvigorate its program. If CODE increased its majority to two-thirds, it would have the strength it required to impeach Allende or at least to stop – rather than merely obstruct – his program.

The Nixon administration and the Soviet leadership understood the stakes in this election, too, and they backed each side as best they could. Washington outspent Moscow more than ten to one, with the 40 Committee investing about 1.6 million dollars in CODE's campaign to the Politburo's 100,000 dollars to the UP. Both the CIA and KGB's covert operations attempted to consolidate and improve their side's position while dividing and weakening the other. Both endeavored to influence public opinion both inside and outside of Chile. Both seemed moderately successful. For example, the Agency's post-election report stated that PN and PDC leaders regarded the financial assistance they received as "essential in enabling them to campaign effectively."[11]

These attempts to influence Chilean politics did not change Chilean ground conditions very much, however. CODE won approximately 55 percent of the vote while the UP took around 43 percent. This roughly corresponded to the results of the last two-way race that had occurred, where President Eduardo Frei (1964–70) had defeated Allende 55 percent to 38 percent. It reconfirmed the anticommunist majority that had existed in Chile since the 1920s. But it left CODE without the votes it needed to impeach Allende while the UP still lacked the parliamentary majority it required to implement the peaceful road to revolution – an outcome that frustrated both sides.[12]

Prats, still serving as Allende's minister of interior, outlined the two remaining courses the president could take, given the election's results. He might reconcile his differences with CODE, or at least the PDC, while slowing an inflationary trend that was spiraling out of control, or he could choose to continue taking an extremist, unilateral route. If Allende chose the former, the armed forces might be able to remain in the cabinet to help broker a truce between the UP and PDC, but they would have to withdraw should the president choose the latter. Prats also informed Allende that the armed services were reiterating that "Chile remained outside of the Soviet sphere of influence" in world affairs, and that their officers would not accept a relationship of economic or military dependency with the Moscow.[13]

Allende, characteristically, declined to choose. This created a wedge that eventually drove Prats and his colleagues in the army apart. As if on cue, Socialist Party (PS) Senator Carlos Altamirano, a particularly combative politician, declared in a public speech that the administration should reject all negotiation and compromise with the opposition. Prats cited this speech when following up with Allende a couple of days later. All the president could do was promise to consider the matter.[14]

Both Allende, and more worrisome, Prats, began to lose influence over the armed forces that March. The Chilean air force's

(FACH) commander, Gen. César Ruiz, expressed his intention to leave the cabinet. FACH's officers preferred that Ruiz do this in concert with his colleagues, while forming a united army, navy, air force, and *Carabineros* front that would check and possibly moderate the government's behavior, but they would ask him to leave on his own, if necessary.[15]

Prats's colleagues in the high command urged him to resign from the cabinet as well. These officers argued that the chief of staff and the other service commanders had accomplished the objectives they had identified when they joined the administration the previous November, that Chilean politics had entered a new stage, and that further military involvement was unwarranted. Thus, Prats and the others formally quit the cabinet on 27 March. Allende never responded to Prats's suggestions.[16]

Prats's upcoming transatlantic trip, which included several days in the Soviet Union as well as the United States, Britain, France, Spain, and Yugoslavia, deepened the wedge that was driving him and his subordinates apart. The US defense attaché reported on Prats's efforts to calm his subordinates that April. The general restated his ongoing policy of restoring respect for the chain of command and military discipline, and he explicitly asked officers to stay out of the government's arguments with the opposition about the controversial *Escuela Nacional Unificada* (ENU) plan, which was angering many of them and their families, to no avail.[17]

Officers' grumblings increased when Prats left the country on 2 May. Ruiz and his colleagues in FACH were particularly unhappy with the general's agenda in Moscow. Field and company grade officers in FACH, the army, and the navy were end-running their commanders and reaching out to each other across the services, asking what they could do. Hundreds of them considered resigning *en masse* or taking some other dramatic action to illustrate the gravity of the situation. Ruiz felt sufficient pressure that he called a press conference to clarify that he alone spoke for the air force and determined the arms and equipment that it would purchase. And he insisted that FACH did not want Soviet matériel.[18]

Meanwhile, Prats met Soviet Minister of Defense Marshal Andrei Grechko. Prats learned that, following Allende's request and the Politburo's deliberations, the Soviet Union had approved its offer to supply arms to the Chilean government on "extraordinarily favorable terms." The marshal spoke of Moscow's hope that the Chilean and Peruvian governments – Peru was also receiving Soviet military aid – would cultivate friendly, cooperative relations in the future, and he showed the general a demonstration of Soviet combined-arms, where tanks, artillery, and rockets supported a motorized infantry assault in a well-choreographed exercise. Prats commented that he doubted these weapons would ever arrive in Chile, explaining that the Chilean army might revolt against such a thing. Soviets still put them in the pipeline that June.[19]

The Collapse of Military Discipline: June and July 1973

Prats returned to a Chile seething in rage in early June 1973. The Allende administration continued to press its policies, including price controls and the ENU plan; it alienated the opposition and the armed forces even further; and black markets, strikes, street fighting, and states of emergency were the order of the day. This had been building up for several months, but it still did not seem as though anyone had crossed the point of no return yet. Then, without warning, a rapid series of events drove the wedge that was forcing Prats and his subordinates apart so deep that they lost respect for each other as fellow officers. These events unleashed the energy that led to the coup and, ultimately, to the assassination of Prats and his wife, Sofía, in Buenos Aires by car bomb in September 1974.

On 27 June, Brig. Gen. Mario Sepúlveda, who had replaced Pinochet as commander of the Santiago garrison (Pinochet, as the second ranking general in the army, had been promoted to deputy chief of staff), informed Prats that the army had arrested Capt. Sergio Rocha of the 2nd Armored Battalion the previous night. Rocha and several noncoms were collaborating with the *Frente Nacionalista Patria y Libertad*, a right-wing paramilitary organization that was pressing the armed services to overthrow Allende. They planned to detain the president in his residence before seizing power. They had already taken weapons from an armory.[20]

Prats received briefings on this before meeting with others on more routine matters that morning. Then he returned to his residence in Las Condes for lunch with Sofía. He got back into his official car to return to his office via the *Costanera*, a thoroughfare that took him back to the Ministry of Defense, just after this.

About two or three cars caught Prats's attention on the *Costanera* that afternoon. They seemed to be maneuvering to harass or possibly to obstruct him. Their drivers were making obscene gestures and shouting insults at him. He was concerned that these were no mere hecklers. He had been carrying a submachine gun in his lap ever since the attack against the former chief of staff, Schneider. He believed that these cars' movements were somehow similar to the ones that had preceded his predecessor and friend's death, and he was determined to avoid that fate. Finally, one driver stuck his tongue out at him near a light and said something offensive enough that he lost his temper, got out of his vehicle with his service revolver in his hand, approached the car, fired into it, and demanded that the driver get out and explain himself.

Prats was mortified to discover that he had not fired on a man but rather a woman named Alejandrina Cox, who has insisted that she acted spontaneously and alone that day ever since. When he realized this, he apologized to her immediately. Meanwhile, a hostile crowd gathered around the general. He found a taxi, fled the scene, and went to explain what had happened, first to the police, then to Allende, and finally to his colleagues in the Ministry of Defense. He offered his resignation to the president, who refused to accept it. Cox did not press charges, either, but as historian Margaret Power understood, this "wounded Prats and weakened his standing within the military."[21]

Two days later, Lt. Col. Roberto Souper, who commanded the 2nd Armored Battalion, had ties to *Patria y Libertad*, and was offended that the Ministry of Defense rather than he would court-martial Rocha, who reported to him, launched an attempted coup. Souper mobilized four to six Second World War-era tanks – thus, Chileans called it the *tancazo*, or, alternatively, the *tanquetazo* – and two trucks carrying about eighty riflemen. He moved them into position to assault *la Moneda*, the presidential palace, and the

Ministry of Defense, and to liberate Rocha while trying to spark a larger uprising.[22]

Prats, Pinochet, and Sepúlveda assumed personal command of the Santiago garrison and suppressed the *tancazo*. They accomplished this by containing Souper's forces and instructing them to stand down, which some of them did immediately. Others, led by Rocha, returned to the 2nd Armored Battalion's headquarters and prepared to fight. Prats ordered Col. Luis Ramírez, who commanded the Tacna Artillery Regiment, to surround Rocha's unit and *"la haga desaparecer"* – make it disappear. Ramírez complied, shooting Rocha dead while shelling the battalion's headquarters. He killed more than twenty uniformed soldiers and two civilian journalists, wounded another thirty soldiers, and seized about fifty soldiers and civilians that day.[23]

Allende, who had earlier called his supporters to the streets but asked them to remain peaceful, brought Prats, Chief of Naval Operations Adm. Raúl Montero, and Ruiz onto the balcony at *la Moneda* to present them as the government's champions that afternoon. Prats interpreted this as Allende's way of ensuring that UP partisans saw that the president remained on good terms with the armed forces, whose commanders remained loyal. But these three officers, concerned about their subordinates' perceptions and loyalties, experienced it as the kiss of death.[24]

Several developments followed, starting with the professional officer corps' nearly unanimous rejection of Prats, Montero, and Ruiz that weekend. These commanders and their peers at the command and staff level met several times to discuss the situation and what, if anything, they should do. In one meeting, on Saturday, 30 June, an admiral informed Prats that "junior officers in the navy sympathized with the cause of the 2nd Armored Battalion."[25]

Prats forwarded this report to Allende, Altamirano, and other Socialist leaders several days later. He beseeched them to come to terms with the situation. He implored them to interpret the *tancazo* as an illustration of how the armed services as institutions, and not merely the flag officers who dealt with the administration on a daily basis, regarded the Allende government. They responded with indignation, complaining about the army's *golpismo*.[26]

Prats called new consultations with the other service commanders and with his colleagues in the army. He repeated what had been his position on this problem since Frei had appointed Schneider and him to their positions in 1969. This problem remained a political and not a military one. Politicians, working through the three branches of government, had to solve it on their own. This was the only way to avoid civil war. The best the armed forces could do was to keep out of this and maintain the peace. Prats, Montero, and Ruiz all concurred. But they seemed to fail to understand that they were no longer actually in command.[27]

Allende tried to attract these three officers back into the cabinet on 2 July, which left them incredulous. Prats explained that he could not answer until he had spoken with his colleagues in the army. When he did, they advised him, after a tense exchange, to retire from the service and join the UP government as a civilian. He declined to do this. They told him that junior officers in the army had no confidence in his leadership, that their image of him was entirely negative. He retorted that if this was so, it was because his fellow generals had acted in bad faith and failed to represent his position fairly and accurately. Prats returned to Allende and told him that he could not accept any cabinet position, and that his only concern was to restore the chain of command and military discipline within the army, which the *tancazo* had shattered.[28]

Things Fall Apart: August and September 1973

Meanwhile, at PRIZONA in Valparaíso, Vice Adm. José Toribio Merino, the second ranking admiral in the navy, made plans to seize power. He and his colleagues at PRIZONA admitted to themselves that they did not have confidence in Allende while acknowledging that the president, in turn, did not trust them or the other services, either. Allende had confessed to Debray that he had lied about the constitutional guarantees he had signed, and he was openly employing a private, Cuban-trained protection detail rather than one from the Chilean security services. He had done this "because I had no confidence in the Political Police of the bourgeoisie ... top police officials were political puppets."

Merino and the admiralty found this situation intolerable after the *tancazo*, and they decided to put an end to it.[29]

Merino and his colleagues were not alone. As the CIA reported after the *tancazo*, coup plotting was becoming widespread throughout the armed forces, and "flag rank officers of all three services are meeting regularly for this purpose." A consensus quickly emerged that Prats and Sepúlveda were standing in the way. They represented "a vertical command impediment" that the army and the other armed forces would need to overcome. According to the Agency, plotters preferred Brig. Gen. Manuel Torres, who commanded the Fifth Division in Punta Arenas, to Pinochet, whom they still regarded as a potential obstacle. But Torres was too far away to be very effective.[30]

Naval officers' attitudes further hardened at the end of July, after a crowd had gathered to jeer Capt. Arturo Araya, Allende's naval aide, at his home late one night. Araya came out onto his balcony brandishing a submachine gun. Someone from the crowd shot him dead. Whether the far left or far right had perpetrated this, naval officers held Allende responsible for it. The president had cultivated a climate of revolution and uncertainty, and he had allowed the proliferation of armed groups all over Chile. Vice Adm. Ismael Huerta, who reported to Merino and had become a coup plotter after the *tancazo*, mentioned to a CIA informant that "Araya's death was one more proof of the need to remedy the various ills affecting Chile." Naval officers expressed their feelings by treating Allende quite coldly at Araya's funeral.[31]

Director of the KGB Yuri Andropov, Nikolai Leonov, and their staff at the First Chief Directorate (FCD) took a final look at Allende that month, after Araya's murder. Soviets' 100 million-dollar arms shipment was *en route* to Chile, but the Soviet Union could still recall its ships. There was another 30 million-dollar loan in the pipeline as well. Should Moscow follow through with these measures? Was the Allende administration viable? Could the UP government still prevail, or was it too late? Leonov, the FCD, and its *rezidenturas* in New York, Washington, and Havana were unanimous in advising Andropov and the Politburo that the correlation of forces was decidedly against the Allende administration's survival. Allende was indecisive about the power issue, and not only was he vulnerable to a coup, but such an outcome seemed imminent. Thus, Soviets washed their hands of it, turned their ships around, canceled the loan, and advised nonessential diplomatic personnel and dependents to leave Santiago in August.[32]

Within days of this decision, Merino's command arrested a marine sergeant and approximately sixty sailors for attempting to incite mutiny aboard several Chilean warships in Valparaíso. PRIZONA had jurisdiction, and Merino, who presided over the court-martial, held Altamirano, Socialist Deputy Oscar Guillermo Garretón, and the Movement of the Revolutionary Left's (MIR) Secretary General Miguel Enriquez responsible, and he sought them for questioning. The *Policía de Investigaciones* (PDI) claimed that they could not locate them. Merino and his colleagues did not believe them.[33]

Back in Santiago, Prats, Sepúlveda, Montero, and Ruiz's subordinates pressed them to retire while taking the extraordinary step of relieving them themselves days later, in mid-August. These three service commanders had rejoined Allende's cabinet, on their own, to help the president deal with the resumption of the truckers' strike, which was clearly designed to cripple the government and provoke military intervention that month. Ruiz intended to use this as an opportunity to bring the administration under control, but this was frustrated immediately. Prats and Montero seemed carried along by events that they could no longer influence or even understand. For field and company grade officers in the army, navy, and air force, this was the straw that broke the camel's back.

Ruiz, whose relationship with Allende had become very tense, resigned from the cabinet and from FACH on 17 August. Gen. Gustavo Leigh was next in line and now acting commander of the air force, and he turned Allende down – both to join the cabinet and to accept official appointment as commanding officer, indignantly telling the president that he was not an ambitious man. Leigh informed Prats that no other general would accept the appointment, either. Meanwhile, Leigh mobilized FACH on his own authority, redeploying the air force's Hawker Hunter attack squadrons from Santiago to Talcahuano to better control their movements and protect them from possible sabotage.[34]

Prats was next. Approximately 300 army wives came to his house to present a formal complaint to Sofía on 21 August. They appealed to her as patriotic mothers and complained that their husbands were being insulted, ridiculed, and threatened because of Prats's association with Allende and his refusal to overthrow him or to stand aside and make way for someone to do it. Prats estimated that their numbers grew to approximately 1,500 men and women that evening, many of them fellow officers and, humiliatingly, even friends of the family. Finally, a uniformed captain stood up and called for silence. When he had the crowd's attention, he denounced Prats as a traitor.[35]

The following day, Prats asked Pinochet and the other remaining generals – Sepúlveda and other Prats loyalists had already stepped down – to express their solidarity with him and secure an apology from the officer corps and their wives. He chastised them for failing to support him but promised to let it go if they backed him now. Pinochet, still noncommittal but clearly distancing himself from the besieged chief of staff, suggested that he talk with the officers himself. Prats submitted his resignation to Allende the next day, on 23 August.[36]

Pinochet succeeded Prats as chief of staff that day, but he kept well clear of Allende and the cabinet. About two weeks later, in the first week of September, an Agency informant reported that he had become "resigned to an eventual overthrow of the Chilean government." But he hoped politicians would explore all other avenues first. He seemed "frightened by the specter of civil bloodshed." And he clarified that the army would not seize power "until the overwhelming majority of the people call for such an action . . . the political parties must ask the military to intervene before he personally would consent to move." He had already convened a council of generals, on 28–9 August, and formed a solid consensus with them. The army's most pressing problem remained "to strengthen its own internal unity and, at the same time, join forces with the air force, navy, and Carabineros to maintain a common position." Pinochet predicted that September would see the resolution of "the conflict to rid Chile of Marxist control."[37]

Merino, who remained in Valparaíso, had a much more difficult time getting Montero, who was still a cabinet member and in

Santiago, to resign. Merino and commandant of marines Vice Adm. Sergio Huidobro traveled to the capital to meet with Montero on 5 September. They told him that the Naval Council and the entire officer corps had expressed no confidence in his leadership and were asking him to resign. "His retirement was necessary if the navy and marines were to calm their captains, lieutenants, ensigns, sergeants, and other personnel," they reasoned. Montero, Merino pointed out, was serving Allende, "an internal enemy."[38]

Montero called Allende, who invited Merino and Huidobro to discuss this at the presidential residence on Tomás Moro that evening. When they arrived late that night, all present angrily confronted each other for two or three hours, finding no common ground. Finally, Allende asked Merino whether the navy was at war with him. "Yes, sir," the admiral replied. "We are at war with you. The navy is at war because it is not and never will be communist – not the admirals, not the Naval Council, not a single sailor."[39]

Allende invited Merino to continue this discussion at lunch in Santiago on 7 September. As the US naval attaché reported that day, the Chilean navy was suffering "serious internal conflicts . . . essentially a power play," and Merino was struggling to gain legal status as chief of naval operations and control over his unruly subordinates before the institution's discipline broke down entirely. Not only were officers already addressing him as commander of the navy in correspondence, but the captains and crews of those ships detailed to the annual UNITAS maneuvers were refusing Allende and Minister of Defense Orlando Letelier's increasingly frantic orders that they put to sea.[40]

Merino still hoped to resolve all of this, but matters only worsened that day. After lunch, Allende dismissed Letelier and then took Merino by the arm, bizarrely confiding to him that "if you want to effect a personnel change, see [Senator Volodia] Teitelboim, Shorty [Luis Corvalán], or Altamirano. They are the ones in charge. I'm not in charge of anything." This left Merino speechless, who recalled in his memoirs that he fully committed himself to leading a coup against Allende, unilaterally if necessary, just after this meeting.[41]

In the realm of foreign intelligence services, the CIA and KGB both picked up each other's signals confirming that they had concluded that a coup was forming up around the navy the following day, 8 September. They understood that the air force and *Carabineros* would support it. Pinochet and the army would "not oppose the navy's action."[42]

In the last two or three days before Merino launched the coup, Prats, now an informal civilian advisor to Allende, pled with the president to leave the country for a year. Perhaps, the retired general reasoned, if he permitted someone else to govern for a time, this would settle the situation down. But Allende, probably recognizing it as a resignation cloaked as a foreign trip, refused to hear him out. He explained that he was attempting to cashier Merino while soothing some of his opponents with talk of a possible plebiscite in the next month or so. No one was taking his calls. He was going to get on top of the situation, however. Prats warned him that he was "swimming in a sea of illusions." It was all good advice. But he may as well have been talking to himself.[43]

Resolutions: September 1973 to October 1988

Merino had finalized *Plan Cochayuyo* [Seaweed], a counterinsurgency operation that would enable the navy, acting on behalf of the government, to secure Valparaíso and other cities under PRIZONA's jurisdiction, that July. He had forwarded it to Montero, who authorized naval commands from Iquique to Talcahuano and Punta Arenas to copy and file it for future reference. Each command created seven task forces that would seize the coastal area under its responsibility, suppress any insurgents who were fighting there, and ensure the continuance of essential services such as communications, electricity, and water.[44]

After Merino's encounter with Allende on 7 September, the admiral revised *Plan Cochayuyo*, giving it an offensive, anti-government capability. He preferred to initiate it himself, using surprise to achieve quick, decisive results. But he also anticipated the possibility that a pro-government insurgency might arise or that one of his units might move on its own before he was ready. He planned for these problems, too. PRIZONA's intelligence group estimated that UP forces, including a small, well-trained collection of Socialist and MIR militants and a larger group of armed but untrained workers, could number as high as 30,000 in the Valparaíso area alone. Merino counted on his 6,000 marines and sailors, backed by warships, helicopters, and hundreds of anti-government civilian trucks parked in nearby Reñaca, to rout these forces. He was aware that both Congress and the Supreme Court had passed resolutions against Allende and were calling on the armed services to overthrow him, and this increased his confidence.[45]

Merino's warships finally put to sea, ostensibly to join UNITAS, on the evening of 9 September. But the admiral was actually using UNITAS as cover to deploy his ships in support of *Plan Cochayuyo*. He also sent Huidobro and another marine to Santiago carrying a note to Leigh and Pinochet. It read:

Gustavo and Augusto,

On my word of honor, D-Day will be 11 September and H-Hour 0600.
If you cannot back this with all of the forces under your command in Santiago, please explain so on the other side.
Adm. Huidobro is authorized to discuss any issue with you. I hope we will reach an understanding.
J.T. Merino

Gustavo: This is the last opportunity to act. J.T.
Augusto: If you do not join us with all of your forces in Santiago, we will not live to see the future. Pepe

Both Leigh and Pinochet wrote "*conforme*" – agreed – before signing their names to this note and becoming part of the coup that day.[46]

Merino sent two fleet-wide messages about thirty-six hours later, on 11 September at 6:00 a.m. The first explained that he was assuming the office of chief of naval operations and personally taking control of the entire Chilean fleet. The second instructed all commands to execute *Plan Cochayuyo*. The UP government did not resist, although Allende, whom Leigh and Pinochet's forces assaulted in *la Moneda*, remained defiant until the moment that he took his own life with an AK-47 later that day. As the president had admitted about a week before the coup, "popular power was a good term for speeches, but, realistically, the people who support him are without weapons, and they could not face the armed forces' firepower."[47]

By 9:00 a.m., Merino controlled the Chilean coast and the navy was "detaining everyone responsible for the disaster." That is, naval officers, like their counterparts in the army, air force, and *Carabineros*, were seizing UP partisans and foreign sympathizers, real and suspected. Around 8:30 p.m., Merino flew to Santiago to create a *junta*, or military government, in partnership with Leigh, Pinochet, and the *Carabineros*' director general at the *Escuela Militar*.

The *junta*'s earliest acts were to announce that Pinochet would preside over the new government and to confirm that Chile would remain aligned with the liberal international community, whose worldviews and politics these flag officers shared. According to the *junta*'s first press release, Chile found itself within in a dangerous state of crisis where only two alternatives existed – a Western-led, liberal alternative, and a Marxist-Leninist one. The *junta* chose the former, explaining that "our Fatherland has decided to directly confront international communism and the Marxist ideology that sustains it, inflicting it with the most serious defeat it has suffered over the last thirty years."[48]

The *junta*'s subsequent behavior shocked many Chileans and most foreign observers – even some within the armed forces. The Pinochet dictatorship sincerely intended to defend liberal internationalism, cement Chile's place within it, and put an end to the Marxist-Leninist threat that had challenged it since the 1920s. But the dictatorship's achievements with respect to the first two of these objectives, which included a new constitutional order, economic reinvigoration, and an eventual return to democratic, civilian rule, will remain forever marred by the brutal way it approached the third.

The dictatorship closed Congress and suspended political parties, banning Marxist-Leninist ones. It declared an internal war against the left and established improvised detention, torture, and execution centers in Chilean stadia and other locations. It kidnapped some and made them disappear. It enforced martial law and imposed a curfew, subjected civilians to military courts, and burned books. Chileans later established, conservatively, that the dictatorship was responsible for more than 3,000 extra-judicial killings. Thousands fled into exile, primarily in the Americas,

Europe, and the Soviet Union, while a few found refuge in developing nations like Mozambique and others in sub-Saharan Africa.[49]

Voices from the United Nations (UN), the Organization of American States (OAS), and elsewhere within the international community – including US President Jimmy Carter (1977–81) and Democrats such as Senator Edward Kennedy – repeatedly condemned the dictatorship's systematic human rights violations in the 1970s and 1980s. The dictatorship partly represented the conservative Chilean establishment's continuing reliance on Portalian autocracy. It was merely one of several expressions of the Chilean army's antipolitics, or contempt for civilian rule, partisanship, and general political dealings, in the twentieth century. Several of Pinochet's predecessors had resorted to similar repressive devices – such as military rule, *relegación*, or internal exile, and internment in locations such as Pisagua, Más Afuera, and Punta Arenas. But the sustained nature of Pinochet's heavy-handed savagery exceeded all of this.

The Pinochet dictatorship joined a collection of like-minded military governments that arose in southern South America in the 1960s and 1970s. These governments essentially settled the Cold War in that region. Pinochet's intelligence service, the *Dirección Nacional de Inteligencia* (DINA), backed these governments' aggressive surveillance and continuing suppression of leftist exiles in each other's national territory in the 1970s and into the 1980s, when all of this started to recede.

Meanwhile, these military governments reached beyond southern South America. For example, DINA assassinated Prats and his wife by car bomb in Buenos Aires in 1974. Pinochet believed that Prats had attempted to organize a resistance against the *junta* in the Chilean south during the coup, and the general had criticized the dictatorship from Argentina thereafter. DINA's attempt to shoot and kill Bernardo Leighton, Frei's former minister of interior, in Rome failed in 1975. But it succeeded in murdering Letelier and US citizen Ronni Moffit in Washington in 1976, also by detonating an explosive in a vehicle.[50]

By the late 1980s, a consensus against the dictatorship emerged in international opinion, including the Reagan administration (1981–9) in the United States. This unfolded within a larger wave of democratization and calls to enforce human rights that followed the Conference on Security and Cooperation in Europe, held in Helsinki in the 1970s, and which helped bring an end to the Cold War. A frustrated Pinochet, who could do little else about this, complained to a visiting US Congressman in 1987, "What kind of allies are you?"

> Why should I believe anything the U.S. says or stands for? The U.S. won World War II but lost half of Europe. They lost half of Korea. You lost Cuba. You lost Nicaragua and you will lose El Salvador if you are not careful.[51]

Pinochet nevertheless succeeded in creating a new constitutional order in 1980, a protected liberal democracy that, he hoped, would exclude Marxist-Leninists from Chilean politics, labor relations, education, and even daily life for all time. He also committed himself to holding a plebiscite in 1988, where Chileans would decide whether to continue under military government or return to civilian rule. This attracted global commentary. For example, voices like Sting, a British songwriter, had dramatically interpreted Chilean women's performance of a folk dance called *la cueca* while protesting the disappearance of their loved ones in a tune called "They Dance Alone (Cueca Solo)" in fall 1987. This plebiscite generated much excitement within Chile, where a center-left coalition, *la Concertación*, campaigned against Pinochet, who lost the vote, 55 percent to 43 percent, that October. This occurred at roughly the same time Poles and Hungarians were peacefully throwing communists out of power, and it preceded the fall of Erich Honecker in East Germany, Nicolae Ceaușescu in Romania, and the Berlin Wall by about a year.[52]

Notes

1. Santiago Station to CIA, 6 August 1971. Chile Declassification Project (CDP), at <http://www.state.gov>.
2. Ibid.

3. For the latter point, see Margaret Power, *Right-Wing Women in Chile: Feminine Power and the Struggle against Allende, 1964–1973* (University Park: Pennsylvania State University Press, 2002), 126–58.

4. Jonathan Haslam, *The Nixon Administration and the Death of Allende's Chile: A Case of Assisted Suicide* (London: Verso, 2005), 103.

5. For a fuller critique of Vuskovic's mismanagement of the Chilean economy, see ibid., 98–233.

6. Ted Shackley, *Spymaster: My Life in the CIA* [2005] (Dulles: Potomac Books, 2006), 269–70; Haslam, *Death of Allende's Chile*, 141; and Brian Loveman, *Chile: The Legacy of Hispanic Capitalism* [1979], 3rd edn (New York: Oxford University Press, 2001), 253. The 40 Committee was the Nixon administration NSC's sub-committee that authorized and oversaw covert operations.

7. Olga Ulianova, "La Unidad Popular y el golpe militar en Chile: percepciones y análisis soviéticos," *Estudios Públicos* 79 (2000), 86–90.

8. Régis Debray, *The Chilean Revolution: Conversations with Allende* (New York: Pantheon Books, 1971), 119–20. For Soviet worries, see Ulianova, "La Unidad Popular y el golpe militar en Chile," 95–103.

9. Ulianova, "La Unidad Popular y el golpe militar en Chile," 95–103.

10. Ibid., 108–10; Nikolai Leonov, "La inteligencia soviética en América Latina durante la guerra fría," *Estudios Públicos* 73 (1999), 55–7; and Nikolai Leonov, Eugenia Fediakova, Joaquín Fermandois, et al., "El General Nikolai Leonov en el CEP," *Estudios Públicos* 73 (1999), 72–4.

11. CIA to 40 Committee, "Outcome of 4 March 1973 Chilean Congressional Elections," 6 April 1973. CDP. For Soviet intervention in this election, see Christopher Andrew and Vasili Mitrokhin, *The World Was Going Our Way: The KGB and the Battle for the Third World* (New York: Basic Books, 2005), 79–84.

12. Ibid. For additional analysis and discussion of the congressional elections in March 1973, see José Díaz Nieva, *Patria y Libertad: el nacionalismo frente a la Unidad Popular* (Santiago de Chile: Ediciones Centro de Estudios Bicentenario, 2015), 196–206. For the results of the presidential election in 1964, refer back to Ricardo Cruz-Coke, *Historia electoral de Chile, 1925–1973* (Santiago de Chile: Editorial Jurídica de Chile, 1984), 107–10.

13. Carlos Prats, *Memorias: testimonio de un soldado* (Santiago de Chile: Pehuén Editores, 1985), 369; and DIA Intelligence Summary, Chile, 16 March 1973. CDP.

14. Prats, *Memorias*, 369–70.
15. DIA Intelligence Summary, Chile, 14 March 1973. CDP.
16. Prats, *Memorias*, 368–75.
17. US Defense Attaché to Pentagon, "General Prats' 13 Apr. Meeting with Santiago Officer Corps," 23 April 1973. CDP.
18. US Defense Attaché to Pentagon, "Military Grumblings," 18 May 1973. CDP.
19. Ulianova, "La Unidad Popular y el golpe militar en Chile," 108–10; Leonov, "La inteligencia soviética en América Latina," 55–7; Leonov et al., "El General Nikolai Leonov en el CEP," 72–4; and Prats, *Memorias*, 380–1, 385–94. For an introduction to Gen. Juan Velasco's dictatorship (1968–75) in Peru, see Thomas Wright, *Latin America in the Era of the Cuban Revolution and Beyond* [1991], 3rd edn (Santa Barbara: ABC-CLIO/Praeger, 2018), 121–39.
20. Díaz, *Patria y Libertad*, 253–6; Mario Valdés Urrutia and Danny Monsálvez Araneda, "Recogiendo los pasos: los movimientos deliberativos al interior de las filas del Ejército (1969–1973)," *Notas Históricas y Geográficas* 13–14 (2002–3), 209–13; Power, *Right-Wing Women in Chile*, 222–6; and Prats, *Memorias*, 413–17.
21. Power, *Right-Wing Women in Chile*, 226. Power interviewed Cox when researching her book. She seems to believe Cox's sincerity, but remains uncertain whether she had truly acted alone that day. Cox's regret about her role in Prats's resignation and her knowledge of his and his wife's subsequent assassination may have influenced her memory and recollections later in life.
22. Valdés and Monsálvez, "Recogiendo los pasos," 210.
23. Ibid., 210–13; Kissinger to Nixon, "Attempted Chilean Rebellion Ends," 29 June 1973; and Kissinger to Nixon, "Attempted Coup in Chile," 29 June 1973. CDP.
24. Prats, *Memorias*, 422–3; CIA report, 9 July 1973; CIA report, 7 July 1973. CDP.
25. Prats, *Memorias*, 423.
26. Ibid., 424.
27. Ibid., 423.
28. Ibid., 424–5, 478; and CIA report, 9 July 1973.
29. Cristián Pérez, "Salvador Allende, Apuntes sobre su dispositivo de seguridad: el grupo de amigos personales (GAP)," *Estudios Públicos* 79 (2000): 31–81; José Toribio Merino, *Bitácora de un almirante: memorias* (Santiago de Chile: Editorial Andrés Bello, 1998), 204–5; and Debray, *Conversations with Allende*, 91.
30. CIA report, 9 July 1973; and CIA report, 7 July 1973.

31. Directorate of Operations report, 30 July 1973. CDP.
32. Leonov, "La inteligencia soviética en América Latina," 54. Also see Andrew and Mitrokhin, *World Was Going Our Way*, 83–5; and Leonov et al., "El General Nikolai Leonov en el CEP," 72–4.
33. Merino, *Bitácora de un almirante*, 210–14; Prats, *Memorias*, 459.
34. Prats, *Memorias*, 469–71.
35. Ibid., 478. Also see Power, *Right-Wing Women in Chile*, 227–8.
36. Prats to Allende, 23 August 1973. Prats, *Memorias*, 487–9.
37. Directorate of Operations report, 7 September 1973; and Santiago Station to CIA, 6 September 1973. CDP.
38. Merino, *Bitácora de un almirante*, 216.
39. Ibid., 218.
40. US Naval Attaché to Pentagon, 7 September 1973. CDP.
41. Merino, *Bitácora de un almirante*, 223.
42. Ulianova, "La Unidad Popular y el golpe militar en Chile," 106–7; Directorate of Operations report, 8 September 1973; DIA Intelligence Summary, Chile, 8 September 1973; US Embassy Santiago to Department of State, 8 September 1973; and Santiago Station to CIA, 6 September 1973. CDP.
43. Prats, *Memorias*, 510.
44. Merino, *Bitácora de un almirante*, 206–8, 238–45.
45. Ibid., 216.
46. Merino to Gustavo Leigh and Pinochet, 9 September 1973. Ibid., 230–1.
47. Ibid., 250; and Directorate of Operations report, 6 September 1973. CDP. For Allende's suicide, see "Allende: director del SML dice que informe ratifica autopsia de 1973," *La Nación*, 19 Julio 2011, at <http://www.lanacion.cl>. This was accompanied by a photograph of Allende's skull and links to all expert reports, including a Scotland Yard ballistic expert's findings, in pdf. Also see "Chile: Court Closes Probe into Ex-President Allende's Death," BBC, 7 January 2014, at <http://www.bbc.com>. Allende had been contemplating suicide for about two years. See "Socialist Says Allende Once Spoke of Suicide," *New York Times*, 12 September 1973.
48. Junta Militar de Gobierno, "Chile en el contexto mundial: base para una definición," 11 September 1973. Merino, *Bitácora de un almirante*, 476.
49. Wright, *Latin America in the Era of the Cuban Revolution*, 196–201; and Thomas Wright and Rode Oñate, *Flight from Chile: Voices of Exile* (Albuquerque: University of New Mexico Press, 1998). Also see Carlos Cerda, *To Die in Berlin* (Pittsburgh: Latin American Literary Review Press, 1999).

50. Thomas Wright, *State Terrorism in Latin America: Chile, Argentina, and International Human Rights* (Lanham: Rowman & Littlefield, 2007); and John Dinges, *The Condor Years: How Pinochet and His Allies Brought Terrorism to Three Continents* [2004] (New York: The New Press, 2005).

51. Paul Sigmund, *The United States and Democracy in Chile* (Baltimore: Johns Hopkins University Press, 1993), 149. For this larger wave of democratization and human rights, see Samuel Huntington, *The Third Wave: Democratization in the Late Twentieth Century* (Norman: University of Oklahoma Press, 1991).

52. Loveman, *Chile*, 302–4; and Sting, "They Dance Alone (Cueca Solo)," *Nothing Like the Sun* (Santa Monica: A&M Records, 1987).

Conclusion

When President Barack Obama (2009–17) visited Chile in March 2011, President Sebastián Piñera (2010–14) asked him to declassify additional American documents on the coup and the Pinochet dictatorship (1973–90), especially concerning its human rights violations. Other Chileans asked him to accept responsibility and apologize for these events. Obama acknowledged that US–Latin American relations had been rocky in the past and agreed to give any request for information due consideration. But he would not accept responsibility for previous administrations' behavior, and he declined to apologize. He suggested that "It is important for us to learn from our history, to understand our history, but not be trapped by it."[1]

Obama correctly assented to Piñera's request. The American government should continue to declassify any information it possesses that pertains to Chile's Cold War experience. Too much within the existing declassified record remains redacted. There must be not only additional papers but also undisclosed lines of text that better illuminate the relationship between the Kennedy (1961–3), Johnson (1963–9) and Nixon administrations (1969–74), on the one hand, and the Frei administration (1964–70), on the other. This might show the CIA and Frei's private communications and possible collaboration in preempting President Salvador Allende's (1970–3) election in 1970. But this well-traveled, US-centered line of inquiry, having produced much of value since the 1970s, has become insufficient in the increasingly international historiography of the twenty-first century, particularly as we continue to explore Chile's Cold War history from Chilean, inter-American and transatlantic perspectives. American decision making, policies, directives, and implementation, no matter how thoroughly declassified, will never fully explain the totality of this experience.

Obama also rightly refrained from apologizing – and for more reasons than he may have had in mind at the time. Not only must we learn from our history while avoiding being trapped by it, but we should not allow ourselves to be seduced by any one perspective or become wedded to any single narrative, either. From the point of view of international history, continuing investigation into the inter-American and transatlantic Cold War will likely make these and other reasons more apparent. This should include new research into the history of Cuban foreign relations, the Condor alliance (which entails closer looks at Chilean, Brazilian, Paraguayan, Uruguayan, and Argentine cooperation in security and intelligence matters from southern South America to the United States and Europe), Argentine intervention in Sandinista Nicaragua, Argentine–Chilean relations, particularly the Beagle Channel dispute and the Pinochet dictatorship's decision to covertly back British forces against Buenos Aires during the Falklands War, and the history of the dictatorship's decline and fall to the general's detention in London in the late 1990s. Inquiries into the history of Brazilian foreign relations from the Second World War to the present should yield much of interest with respect to Chile's Cold War experience and other issues in southern South America, given the Brazilian government's longstanding interest in playing a more meaningful role in world affairs and its determination to showcase its ability to lead in the region. Sources may remain scarce or unavailable (and, in some cases, destroyed and irrecoverable). But these remain the issues we must address if we hope to appreciate and explain anything approximating a comprehensive understanding of Chile and Latin America's Cold War history in the future.[2]

Further research into American intervention in Chile, then, while still relevant, remains only one part of a larger and far more complex story that finds Chileans, above all others, in the center of their own politics and history. Our earlier focus on the United States and its intelligence services has tended to obscure this – which partly accounts for the perceptions of those Chileans who asked Obama to apologize. I have attempted to redress much of this via three interrelated arguments. First, Chileans made their own history, and ultimately, they remain the ones responsible for it. Second, they did this as highly engaged internationalists who operated within local, national, inter-American and transatlantic contexts. Third, although foreign and domestic intelligence operations, surveillance and secret warfare pervaded Chile and the rest of Latin America's Cold War experience, the foreign elements of these operations did not decide it. Ground conditions in Chile, southern South America and elsewhere in the region were far more significant. Of course, much remains to be uncovered, interpreted, and discussed, and these findings remain provisional, part of a still unfolding process that may take unexpected turns in the future as more information becomes available and our perspectives evolve.

These arguments, and the evidence and discussions supporting them, have also revealed Chileans' involvement in the long Cold War that historian Odd Arne Westad has sketched out, which began in the late nineteenth century and ended in the late twentieth. Chileans' struggles – including Allende's – represented but part of this larger struggle over a series of problems and crises that industrialization and globalization unleashed. Much of the literature still ignores Chile's part in the earliest decades of this struggle, the years before the Cuban Revolution in 1959 – even, in many cases, before President Eduardo Frei's election in 1964 – while failing to connect these decades to the 1960s and 1970s. If this book makes the kind of contribution that I hope it might, it should be clear that there remains more to know about Chile's Cold War experience than this literature has shown us, and that we should continue to integrate Latin America's Cold War history into transatlantic and even larger world-historical patterns to compensate for this while moving forward in a more balanced, equitable and inclusive manner.[3]

Notes

1. "Chile President [Sebastián Piñera] to Ask Obama for Pinochet Files," BBC, 23 March 2011, at <http://www.bbc.com>.
2. Many have already moved in this direction. For example, Jonathan Brown, *Cuba's Revolutionary World* (Cambridge, MA: Harvard University Press, 2017); Piero Gleijeses, *Visions of Freedom: Havana,*

Washington, Pretoria, and the Struggle for Southern Africa, 1976–1991 (Chapel Hill: University of North Carolina Press, 2013); Tanya Harmer, "Brazil's Cold War in the Southern Cone, 1970–1975," *Cold War History* 12 (2012): 659–81; Tanya Harmer, *Allende's Chile and the Inter-American Cold War* (Chapel Hill: University of North Carolina Press, 2011); John Dinges, *The Condor Years: How Pinochet and His Allies Brought Terrorism to Three Continents* [2004] (New York: The New Press, 2005); Piero Gleijeses, *Conflicting Missions: Havana, Washington, and Africa, 1959–1976* (Chapel Hill: University of North Carolina Press, 2002); and Ariel Armony, *Argentina, the United States, and the Anti-Communist Crusade in Central America, 1977–1984* (Athens: Ohio University Press, 1997).

3. Odd Arne Westad, *The Cold War: A World History* (New York: Basic Books, 2017). For those who have begun to connect these decades to the 1960s and 1970s, see Kirsten Weld, "The Spanish Civil War and the Construction of a Reactionary Historical Consciousness in Augusto Pinochet's Chile," *Hispanic American Historical Review* 98 (2018): 77–115; Jody Pavilack, *Mining for the Nation: The Politics of Chile's Coal Communities from the Popular Front to the Cold War* (University Park: Pennsylvania State University Press, 2011); and Carlos Huneeus, *La guerra fría chilena: Gabriel González Videla y la ley maldita* (Santiago de Chile: Random House Mondadori, 2008).

Select Bibliography

Archives

Archivo Nacional, Archivo del Ministerio de Relaciones Exteriores (AMRREE Chile), Santiago de Chile
  Fondo Organismos Internacionales
British National Archives, Kew Gardens, London
  Foreign and Commonwealth Office papers (after 1968)
  Foreign Office papers (to 1968)
Comisión Chilena de Energía Nuclear (CChEN), Centro Nacional de Estudios Nucleares (CNEN), La Reina, Chile
  CChEN, "Cronología Nuclear Chilena, 1945–98"
  "Comisión Chilena de Energía Nuclear, 1964–1989." Santiago: CChEN, 1989
  Memorias anuales, 1966–70
Dirección de Bibliotecas, Archivos y Museos (DIBAM), at <http://www.memoriachilena.cl>
Harry Truman Library, Independence, Missouri
  National Security Files
  Papers of Harry Truman
  President's Secretary's Files
John Kennedy Library, Boston, Massachusetts
  Craig Van Grasstek, interviewer and editor, "Lincoln Gordon and the Alliance for Progress: An Annotated Oral History"
  National Security Files
  Papers of President Kennedy
Museo de la Memoria y los Derechos Humanos, Santiago de Chile
National Archives, College Park, Maryland
  CIA Records Search Tool (CREST)
  Record Group 84, Foreign Service Posts of the Department of State: Chile/U.S. Embassy Santiago

262

Lyndon Johnson Library, Austin, Texas
    Department of State, "The Department of State during the Admin-
    istration of President Lyndon B. Johnson, November 1963–January
    1969"
    Lincoln Gordon, oral history, 10 July 1969
    National Security Files
    Oliver Covey, oral history I, 2 December 1968
    Oliver Covey, oral history II, 12 December 1968
    Papers of Lyndon Johnson
    Thomas Mann, oral history, 4 November 1968
Richard Nixon Library, Yorba Linda, California
    Henry Kissinger telephone conversation transcripts (TELCONS)

Newspapers and Periodicals

El Clarín (Chile)
El Mercurio (Chile)
El Siglo (Chile)
Foreign Affairs
La Nación (Chile)
Los Angeles Times
New York Times
Washington Post

Published Primary Sources

Central Intelligence Agency. "CIA Activities in Chile." 18 September
    2000, at <https://cia.gov>.
Department of State, Bureau of Intelligence and Research, Office of
    the Geographer. "International Boundary Study No. 65: Chile-Peru
    Boundary." 28 February 1966, at <http://www.law.fsu.edu>.
Department of State. Chile Declassification Project (CDP), at <http://
    www.state.gov>.
Department of State. *Department of State Bulletin.*
Department of State. *Foreign Relations of the United States* (FRUS).
    Washington, DC: Government Printing Office, 1861–.
Pavlov, Yuri. CNN interview, roll 10842. Transcript courtesy of the
    National Security Archive, at <http://www.nsarchive.gwu.edu>.

Ulianova, Olga and Alfredo Riquelme Segovia, eds. *Chile en los archivos soviéticos, 1922–1991* I: *Komintern y Chile, 1922–1931*. Santiago de Chile: Dirección de Bibliotecas, Archivos y Museos/LOM Ediciones, 2005.

Ulianova, Olga and Alfredo Riquelme Segovia, eds. *Chile en los archivos soviéticos, 1922–1991* II: *Komintern en Chile, 1931–1935: crisis e ilusión revolucionaria*. Santiago de Chile: Dirección de Bibliotecas, Archivos y Museos/LOM Ediciones, 2009.

United States Senate. Committee on Foreign Relations. Staff Report of the Select Committee to Study Governmental Operations with Respect to Intelligence Activities. *Alleged Assassination Plots Involving Foreign Leaders*. Washington, DC: Government Printing Office, 1975.

United States Senate. Staff Report of the Select Committee to Study Governmental Operations with Respect to Intelligence Activities. *Covert Action in Chile, 1963–1973*. Washington, DC: Government Printing Office, 1975.

Memoirs

Bowers, Claude. *Chile through Embassy Windows, 1939–1953* [1958]. Westport: Greenwood Press, 1977.

Chalfont, Alun. *The Shadow of My Hand: A Memoir*. London: Weidenfeld & Nicolson, 2000.

Colby, William. *Honorable Men: My Life in the CIA*. New York: Simon & Schuster, 1978.

Corvalán, Luis. *Algo de mi vida: memorias clandestinas del secretario general del Partido Comunista de Chile*. Barcelona: Grupo Editorial Grijalbo, Editorial Crítica, 1978.

Corvalán, Luis. *De lo vivido y lo peleado: memorias*. Santiago de Chile: LOM Ediciones, 1997.

Fuentes W., Manuel. *Memorias secretas de Patria y Libertad y algunas confesiones sobre la guerra fría en Chile*. Santiago de Chile: Editorial Grijalbo, 1999.

González Videla, Gabriel. *Memorias*. 2 vols. Santiago de Chile: Editora Nacional Gabriela Mistral, 1975.

Helms, Richard. *A Look over My Shoulder: A Life in the Central Intelligence Agency*. New York: Random House, 2003.

Kissinger, Henry. *White House Years*. Boston: Little, Brown, 1979.

Kissinger, Henry. *Years of Renewal*. New York: Simon & Schuster, 1999.

Kissinger, Henry. *Years of Upheaval* [1982]. New York: Simon & Schuster, 2011.

Merino, José Toribio. *Bitácora de un almirante: memorias*. Santiago de Chile: Editorial Andrés Bello, 1998.

Neruda, Pablo. *Memoirs* [1974]. Trans. Hardie St. Martin. New York: Farrar, Straus and Giroux, 1977.

Nixon, Richard. *RN: The Memoirs of Richard Nixon*. New York: Grosset & Dunlap, 1978.

Phillips, David Atlee. *The Night Watch: 25 Years of Peculiar Service*. New York: Atheneum, 1977.

Pinochet, Augusto. *Camino recorrido: biografía de un soldado*. 2 vols. Santiago de Chile: Talleres Gráficos del Instituto Geográfico Militar de Chile, 1990, 1991.

Pinochet, Augusto. *El día decisivo: 11 de Septiembre de 1973*. Santiago de Chile: Editorial Andrés Bello, 1979.

Prats, Carlos. *Memorias: testimonio de un soldado*. Santiago de Chile: Pehuén Editores, 1985.

Rodríguez Grez, Pablo. *Entre la democracia y la tiranía*. Santiago de Chile: Imprenta Printer, 1972.

Shackley, Ted. *Spymaster: My Life in the CIA* [2005]. Dulles: Potomac Books, 2006.

Smith, Russell Jack. *The Unknown CIA: My Three Decades with the Agency*. Washington, DC: Pergamon-Brassey's International Defense Publishers, 1989.

Walters, Vernon. *The Mighty and the Meek: Dispatches from the Front Line of Diplomacy*. London: St Ermin's Press, 2001.

Walters, Vernon. *Silent Missions*. New York: Doubleday, 1978.

Secondary Literature

Alegria, Fernando. "The Fall of Santiago." *Ramparts* 12 (December 1973): 32–7.

Blakemore, Harold. *British Nitrates and Chilean Politics, 1886–1896: Balmaceda and North*. London: Athlone Press for the Institute of Latin American Studies, 1974.

Brands, Hal. *Latin America's Cold War*. Cambridge, MA: Harvard University Press, 2010.

Bravo, Bernardino. *De Portales a Pinochet: gobierno y régimen de gobierno en Chile*. Santiago de Chile: Editorial Jurídica de Chile/Editorial Andrés Bello, 1985.

Brown, Jonathan. *Cuba's Revolutionary World*. Cambridge, MA: Harvard University Press, 2017.

Cockcroft, James, ed. *Salvador Allende Reader: Chile's Voice of Democracy*. Melbourne and New York: Ocean Press, 2000.

Collier, Simon and William Sater. *A History of Chile, 1808–2002* [1996], 2nd edn. Cambridge: Cambridge University Press, 2004.

Corvalán, Luis. *El gobierno de Salvador Allende*. Santiago de Chile: LOM Ediciones, 2003.

Cruz-Coke, Ricardo. *Historia electoral de Chile, 1925–1973*. Santiago de Chile: Editorial Jurídica de Chile, 1984.

Davis, Harold Eugene, John Finan, and F. Taylor Peck. *Latin American Diplomatic History*. Baton Rouge: Louisiana State University Press, 1977.

Davis, Nathaniel. *The Last Two Years of Salvador Allende*. Ithaca: Cornell University Press, 1985.

Debray, Régis. *The Chilean Revolution: Conversations with Allende*. New York: Pantheon Books, 1971.

Díaz Nieva, José. *Patria y Libertad: el nacionalismo frente a la Unidad Popular*. Santiago de Chile: Ediciones Centro de Estudios Bicentenario, 2015.

Dinges, John. *The Condor Years: How Pinochet and His Allies Brought Terrorism to Three Continents* [2004]. New York: The New Press, 2005.

Faúndez, Julio. *Marxism and Democracy in Chile: From 1932 to the Fall of Allende*. New Haven: Yale University Press, 1988.

Fermandois, Joaquín. *Chile y el mundo, 1970–1973: la política exterior del gobierno de la Unidad Popular y el sistema internacional*. Santiago de Chile: Ediciones Universidad Católica, 1985.

Frei Montalva, Eduardo. "The Alliance That Lost Its Way." *Foreign Affairs* 45 (1967): 437–48.

Frei Montalva, Eduardo. *Pensamiento y acción*. Santiago de Chile: Editorial de Pacífico, 1956.

Furci, Carmelo. *The Chilean Communist Party and the Road to Socialism*. London: Zed Books, 1984.

Garay, Cristián. *Genocidio en un país lejano: Chile y la revolución húngara de 1956*. Santiago de Chile: MAGO Editores, 2009.

Garay, Cristián and Ángel Soto. *Gabriel González Videla: "No a los totalitarismos, ya sean rojos, pardos o amarillos . . . ."* Santiago de Chile: Centro de Estudios Bicentenario, 2013.

García Márquez, Gabriel. "The Death of Salvador Allende." Trans. Gregory Rabassa. *Harper's* (March 1974): 46–53.

Gavras, Konstantinos [Costa Gavras]. *Missing*. Hollywood: Universal Pictures, 1982.

Gustafson, Kristian. *Hostile Intent: U.S. Covert Operations in Chile, 1964–1974*. Washington, DC: Potomac Books, 2007.

Gustafson, Kristian and Christopher Andrew. "The Other Hidden Hand: Soviet and Cuban Intelligence in Allende's Chile." *Intelligence and National Security* 33 (2017). Published online on 1 December 2017, at <http://www.tandfonline.com>.

Harmer, Tanya. *Allende's Chile and the Inter-American Cold War*. Chapel Hill: University of North Carolina Press, 2011.

Harmer, Tanya. "Brazil's Cold War in the Southern Cone, 1970–1975." *Cold War History* 12 (2012): 659–81.

Haslam, Jonathan. *The Nixon Administration and the Death of Allende's Chile: A Case of Assisted Suicide*. London: Verso, 2005.

Hauser, Thomas. *The Execution of Charles Horman: An American Sacrifice*. New York: Harcourt Brace Jovanovich, 1978.

Hersh, Seymour. *The Price of Power: Kissinger in the Nixon White House*. New York: Summit Books, 1983.

Hitchens, Christopher. *The Trial of Henry Kissinger*. London: Verso, 2001.

Huneeus, Carlos. *El régimen de Pinochet* [2001], rev. edn. Santiago de Chile: Penguin Random House Grupo Editorial, 2016.

Huneeus, Carlos. *La guerra fría chilena: Gabriel González Videla y la ley maldita*. Santiago de Chile: Random House Mondadori, 2008.

Huneeus, Carlos and Javier Couso, eds. *Eduardo Frei Montalva: un gobierno reformista*. Santiago de Chile: Editorial Universitaria, 2016.

Kornbluh, Peter. *The Pinochet File: A Declassified Dossier on Atrocity and Accountability* [2003], 2nd edn. New York: The New Press, 2013.

Leonov, Nikolai. "La inteligencia soviética en América Latina durante la guerra fría." *Estudios Públicos* 73 (1999): 31–63.

Leonov, Nikolai, Eugenia Fediakova, Joaquín Fermandois, et al. "El general Nikolai Leonov en el CEP." *Estudios Públicos* 73 (1999): 65–102.

Lira Massi, Eugenio. *¡Ahora le toca al golpe!* Santiago de Chile: Abumohor Impresores, 1969.

Loveman, Brian. *Chile: The Legacy of Hispanic Capitalism* [1979], 3rd edn. New York: Oxford University Press, 2001.

Loveman, Brian. *The Constitution of Tyranny: Regimes of Exception in Spanish America*. Pittsburgh: University of Pittsburgh Press, 1993.

Loveman, Brian. *For* la Patria: *Politics and the Armed Forces in Latin America*. Wilmington: Scholarly Resources, 1999.

Maxwell, Kenneth. "The Other 9/11: The United States and Chile, 1973." *Foreign Affairs* 82 (Nov.–Dec. 2003): 147–51.

Neruda, Pablo. *Canto general* [1950]. Trans. Jack Schmitt. Berkeley and Los Angeles: University of California Press, 2011.

Nunn, Frederick. *Chilean Politics, 1920–1931: The Honorable Mission of the Armed Forces*. Albuquerque: University of New Mexico Press, 1970.

Nunn, Frederick. *The Military in Chilean History: Essays on Civil–Military Relations, 1810–1973*. Albuquerque: University of New Mexico Press, 1976.

Partido Comunista de Chile (PCCh). *Ricardo Fonseca, combatiente ejemplar*. Santiago de Chile: Talleres Gráficos Lautaro, 1952.

Pavilack, Jody. *Mining for the Nation: The Politics of Chile's Coal Communities from the Popular Front to the Cold War*. University Park: Pennsylvania State University Press, 2011.

Pedemonte, Rafael. "La 'diplomacia cultural' soviética en Chile (1964–1973)." *Bicentenario* 9 (2010): 57–100.

Pérez, Cristián. "Salvador Allende, Apuntes sobre su dispositivo de seguridad: el grupo de amigos personales (GAP)." *Estudios Públicos* 79 (2000): 31–81.

Petras, Betty and James F. Petras. "Ballots into Bullets: Epitaph for a Peaceful Revolution." *Ramparts* (November 1973): 20, 26–8, 59–62.

Pieper Mooney, Jadwiga. *The Politics of Motherhood: Maternity and Women's Rights in Twentieth-Century Chile*. Pittsburgh: University of Pittsburgh Press, 2009.

Pike, Frederick. *Chile and the United States, 1880–1962: The Emergence of Chile's Social Crisis and the Challenge to United States Diplomacy*. Notre Dame: University of Notre Dame Press, 1963.

Power, Margaret. *Right-Wing Women in Chile: Feminine Power and the Struggle against Allende, 1964–1973*. University Park: Pennsylvania State University Press, 2002.

Qureshi, Lubna. *Nixon, Kissinger, and Allende: U.S. Involvement in the 1973 Coup in Chile* [2009]. Lanham: Lexington, 2010.

Ramírez Necochea, Hernán. *Balmaceda y la contrarrevolución de 1891*. Santiago de Chile: Editorial Universitaria, 1958.

Ramírez Necochea, Hernán. *Historia del imperialism en Chile*. Santiago de Chile: Austral, 1960.

Ramírez Necochea, Hernán. *Origen y formación del Partido Comunista de Chile*. Santiago de Chile: Editora Austral, 1965.

Rogers, William and Kenneth Maxwell. "Fleeing the Chilean Coup: The Debate over U.S. Complicity." *Foreign Affairs* 83 (2004): 160–5.

Ryan, Patrick. "Allende's Chile: 1000 Bungled Days." New York: American–Chilean Council, 1976.

San Francisco, Alejandro, ed. *La Academia de Guerra del Ejército de Chile, 1886–2006: ciento veinte años de historia.* Santiago de Chile: Ediciones Centro de Estudios Bicentenario, 2006.

San Francisco, Alejandro, ed. *La guerra civil de 1891.* 2 vols. Santiago de Chile: Ediciones Centro de Estudios Bicentenario, 2016.

San Francisco, Alejandro, ed. *La toma de la Universidad Católica de Chile (Agosto de 1967).* Santiago de Chile: Globo Editores, 2007.

Sigmund, Paul. *Multinationals in Latin America: The Politics of Nationalization.* Madison: University of Wisconsin Press, 1980.

Sigmund, Paul. *The Overthrow of Allende and the Politics of Chile, 1964–1976.* Pittsburgh: University of Pittsburgh Press, 1977.

Sigmund, Paul. *The United States and Democracy in Chile.* Baltimore: Johns Hopkins University Press, 1993.

Ulianova, Olga. "Corvalán for Bukovsky: A Real Exchange of Prisoners during an Imaginary War: The Chilean Dictatorship, the Soviet Union, and U.S. Mediation, 1973–1976." *Cold War History* 14 (2014): 315–36.

Ulianova, Olga. "La Unidad Popular y el golpe militar en Chile: percepciones y análisis soviéticos." *Estudios Públicos* 79 (2000): 83–171.

Ulianova, Olga and Eugenia Fediakova. "Algunos aspectos de la ayuda financiera del Partido Comunista de la URSS al comunismo chileno durante la guerra fría." *Estudios Públicos* 72 (1998): 113–48.

Uribe, Armando. *The Black Book of American Intervention in Chile* [1974]. Trans. Jonathan Casart. Boston: Beacon, 1975.

Valdés Urrutia, Mario and Danny Monsálvez Araneda. "Recogiendo los pasos: los movimientos deliberativos al interior de las filas del Ejército (1969–1973)." *Notas Históricas y Geográficas* 13–14 (2002–3): 191–214.

Varas, Augusto, ed. *El partido comunista en Chile: estudio multidisciplinario.* Santiago de Chile: Centro de Estudios Sociales/FLACSO, 1988.

Varas, Florencia. *Conversaciones con Viaux.* Santiago de Chile: Impresiones EIRE, 1972.

Verdugo, Patricia. *Allende: cómo la Casa Blanca provocó su muerte.* Santiago de Chile: Catalonia, 2003.

Weld, Kirsten. "The Spanish Civil War and the Construction of a Reactionary Historical Consciousness in Augusto Pinochet's Chile." *Hispanic American Historical Review* 98 (2018): 77–115.

Westad, Odd Arne. *The Cold War: A World History*. New York: Basic Books, 2017.

Westad, Odd Arne. *The Global Cold War: Third World Interventions and the Making of Our Times* [2005]. Cambridge: Cambridge University Press, 2007.

Wright, Thomas. *Latin America in the Era of the Cuban Revolution and Beyond* [1991], 3rd edn. Santa Barbara: ABC-CLIO/Praeger, 2018.

Wright, Thomas. *State Terrorism in Latin America: Chile, Argentina, and International Human Rights*. Lanham: Rowman & Littlefield, 2007.

Index